Thy Word Is Truth

P 194
p. 176
sin 159
ostensive P. 35

Thy Word Is Truth

BARTH ON SCRIPTURE

Edited by

George Hunsinger

William B. Eerdmans Publishing Company
Grand Rapids, Michigan / Cambridge, U.K.

Published 2012 by

Wm. B. Eerdmans Publishing Co.

2140 Oak Industrial Drive N.E., Grand Rapids, Michigan 49505 /

P.O. Box 163, Cambridge CB3 9PU U.K.

www.eerdmans.com

Printed in the United States of America

18 17 16 15 14 13 12   7 6 5 4 3 2

Library of Congress Cataloging-in-Publication Data

Thy Word is truth: Barth on Scripture / edited by George Hunsinger.
     p.   cm.
    ISBN 978-0-8028-6674-5 (pbk.: alk. paper)
    1. Barth, Karl, 1886-1968.   2. Bible — Criticism, interpretation, etc.
    I. Hunsinger, George.

    BS511.3.T49   2011
    220.6 — dc23
                        2011040631

The editor and publisher gratefully acknowledge permission to reprint materials granted by the individuals and institutions listed on p. ix.

To William B. Eerdmans, Jr.,
with thanks for his inestimable, lifelong
contribution in promoting theological scholarship
as well as for his assistance to Barth studies in particular

Their own dogmas: p9

Contents

II. Exemplification

III. Application

APPENDICES: Examples of Barth on Scripture

Acknowledgments

Robert McAfee Brown, "Scripture and Tradition in the Theology of Karl Barth," in *Scripture and Ecumenism,* ed. Leonard J. Swidler (Pittsburgh: Duquesne University Press, 1965). Reprinted by permission.

Hans W. Frei, "Scripture as Realistic Narrative: Karl Barth as Critic of Historical Criticism." Previously unpublished ms. Used by permission of Geraldine Frei.

John Webster, "Barth's Lectures on the Gospel of John." Previously published in *What Is It That Scripture Says?* ed. Philip McCosker (London: T. & T. Clark, 2006). Reprinted by permission.

Paul D. Molnar, "'Thy Word Is Truth': The Role of Faith in Reading Scripture Theologically with Karl Barth." A different version of this essay was previously published in *Scottish Journal of Theology* 63 (2010): 70-92. Used by permission.

Χ The following excerpts are from Karl Barth, *Church Dogmatics,* 4 vols. (Edinburgh: T. & T. Clark, 1936-1969). Reprinted by kind permission of Continuum International Publishing Group.

On 1 Samuel 25: David and Abigail (IV/2, pp. 424-32)

On the Gospel of John: The Prophetic Work of Christ (IV/3, pp. 231-37)

On the Barmen Declaration: How Scripture Continually Saves the Church (II/1, pp. 172-78)

Abbreviations

References to Karl Barth, *Church Dogmatics,* 4 vols. (Edinburgh: T. & T. Clark, 1936-1969), are listed in the text by volume and part number as follows: II/1, for example, is the abbreviation for vol. II, part 1.

ACW Ancient Christian Writers
ANF Ante-Nicene Fathers
FC Fathers of the Church
KD Karl Barth. *Die Kirchliche Dogmatik.* Zollikon-Zurich: Evangelischer Verlag, 1932-67
NPNF Nicene and Post-Nicene Fathers
NRSV New Revised Standard Version
rev. revised translation
RSV Revised Standard Version

Introduction

It was once suggested by Calvin that the main reason for studying theology is to make us better readers of Holy Scripture. No one took this proposition more seriously than Karl Barth. The 150-page Scripture Index to his massive *Church Dogmatics* testifies impressively to his biblical engagement. Using the Scripture Index can be a good way of gaining access to his theology.

Barth's scriptural interpretation was strongly christocentric. He believed that Jesus Christ is attested, directly or indirectly, by virtually any biblical passage, whether in the Old Testament or the New. He therefore read all of Scripture from a center in Jesus Christ. Scripture was to be interpreted with an eye toward Christ as the one who had become incarnate, was crucified, and was raised again for our sakes. Barth ingeniously discerned parallels in Scripture — both literary and theological — to the narrative of this saving history. Other biblical events and figures could be read as "types" for which Christ served as the "antitype." How could it be otherwise if the entire sweep of God's covenant, as attested in Holy Scripture, was fulfilled in him?

The narrative of Incarnation, Crucifixion, and Resurrection involved a deep structure that might be described as "affirmation," "negation," and "negation of the negation." Since these structural or grammatical elements were essentially formal, their presence could also be discerned in other biblical stories. Insofar as the stories displayed some elements of the same pattern, they could be read as pointing to Christ at the center. They could be taken as attesting the uniqueness of Christ without losing their essential distinction from him.

Jesus Christ — fully God, fully human — was thus the mysterious center, the hidden subject matter, the concealed referent, at stake in biblical passages whose surface content obviously had nothing to do with him. Think, for example, of the stories about Joseph, Moses, David, or Job. With their characters, always imperfect though sometimes honorable, their negative twists in the plot, and their positive or ambiguous outcomes, such stories were susceptible to a typological reading. Each somehow found its ultimate reference in Christ — its deepening or correction or healing. In various ways each displayed elements of the same underlying pattern (though usually partially) of "affirmation," "negation," and "negation of the negation." With Christ in view, think of Joseph, his father's favorite, in the pit, or later in Pharaoh's prison, or still later in his role as the Provider. Think of Moses, as the abandoned and rescued child, as the one-time murderer, as the Liberator from Egypt, or later as the Lawgiver and prophet, who died in exile from the promised land. Think of David, the messianic though notoriously flawed king; or of Job, with his innocence, his languishing in terrible affliction, and finally his unexpected restoration.

Each of these figures in its own way was a pointer or type that was somehow reconfigured, restored, and surpassed in Christ. Their ultimate significance could only emerge when the type was juxtaposed to Christ as the antitype. Interpretation of this kind required a reading that took place on two different levels at the same time: the one straightforward, the other christological, if the type was not simply to be overpowered by the antitype. A similar move could sometimes be made with texts from the Psalms, or with the Sermon on the Mount, or with 1 Corinthians 13. They could be interpreted in light of a hidden christological center that was secretly but ultimately their subject.

Three corollaries to this procedure are worthy of note. Each involved an extension of Barth's typological reading. Although Christ still functioned as the hidden center, he did so by way of certain mediating concepts.

First, consider the concepts of judgment and grace. For Barth these concepts were combined in the form of a dialectical unity. Although they stood in antithesis, they were not merely polar opposites, for each contained the seeds of the other. In principle, there was no judgment without grace, and no grace without judgment. The underlying reason could be traced back to Christ's cross and resurrection. No judgment could be more severe than the judgment suffered on the cross, and yet this judgment took place so that grace might abound. Likewise, no grace could be more triumphant than the grace of the resurrection, and yet this grace did not appear without the severity of the cross. Judgment and grace were ultimately inseparable in Christ, and the transition from the one to the other was paradigmatic, even for those biblical cases where the transition did not occur.

The fundamental cross/resurrection sequence — the transition from "negation" to "negation of the negation" — was construed as the template secretly governing all biblical stories of judgment or grace (and, by typological extension, all such instances throughout human life). These instances had to be viewed, so to speak, "stereoscopically." That is, they had to be read straightforwardly just as they stood, according to their manifest content, and yet also at the same time in light of their latent content as covert witnesses to Christ, their ultimate center and subject. When the latent content was inserted beside the manifest content, as in a stereoscope, a new hermeneutical perspective was opened up, we might say, from a two-dimensional to a three-dimensional image. Each image was valid in its own way.

Jesus Christ, crucified and risen, was therefore the real, mysterious, and governing factor in all other instances of judgment and grace. All other instances were finally centered in him and embraced by him. They did not stand alone, even when they seemed to stand alone. In Christ no instance of judgment, regardless of how severe, could remain unqualified by resurrection hope. Likewise, in and through him no instance of grace, regardless of how favorable, could transpire without judgment in a fallen world. Fragmentary instances of judgment or grace, as found in many biblical texts (and many human experiences), were regarded in terms of their secret overall template, as revealed and fulfilled in Christ, the ruler of all. He himself was their limit and their hope.

How Barth could achieve a christocentric reading through the lens of judgment and grace appears in this remark:

All the disasters of world history, all the persecutions and trials of the community, and above all the judgment on Israel which culminates in the destruction of Jerusalem, are only the great shadow of the cross falling on the cosmos, the Messianic woes which not even the cosmos can evade, the participation in the divine judgment, effected in the death of Jesus, to which even the cosmos is subject, though this judgment is to its salvation, to the salvation of Israel, the salvation of the community, the salvation of all human beings, and indeed of the whole cosmos. (III/2, 501 rev.)

Here all other judgments are ordered to the Cross of Christ.[1] They are ordered in a graded sequence with Christ at the center and extending outward to embrace the judgment that befalls Israel, the persecutions and trials of the Christian community, and finally all the disasters of world history — all wars, divisions, earthquakes, and famines, all "the deep shadows lying across the world" (III/2, 501). All these forms of negation are located under the great shadow of the cross. They all find their center in Christ so that they are all somehow in him and he in them. They all take part mysteriously, each in its own way, in the great judgment effected in his death. Therefore, not one of them is ever without him, nor is he without them. And therein lies their hope. The judgment effected in the cross was a judgment for the sake of salvation. All other forms of negation therefore stand also under the great promise of the resurrection. The negation of the negation effected in Christ reaches outward, beginning first with Israel and the Christian community, so as finally to embrace the whole world. All that participates in the one judgment in Christ participates also in the one grace of Easter hope.

A second hermeneutical move was closely related. It involved the idea of *simul iustus et peccator*, Luther's liberating concept of the justified sinner, as picked up and developed by Barth. Just as all other instances of divine judgment and grace were embraced, limited, and reconstituted by Christ's death and resurrection, so too, in another way, were "sinful" and "justified" reconfigurations of that same death and resurrection as their hidden center. For the believing sinner was someone who had been condemned in Christ's death and justified by his resurrection. This view of the believer's status generated a Christ-centered hermeneutic with more nearly anthropological implications.

In his commentary on Galatians 3:13, for example, Luther had employed this hermeneutic to interpret such figures as Paul the persecutor, David the murderer and adulterer, and Peter the blasphemer. In and through Christ they could each be seen as *simul iustus et peccator*. By means of the great exchange *(commercium admirable)*, Christ had made

---

1. Barth was well aware, of course, that not all forms of human misery and affliction could be ascribed to God's judgment upon sin. Here "the shadow of the cross" includes human suffering in all its forms. In dying for our sins, Barth believed, Christ had also made the world's sufferings his own. Therefore, all forms of judgment, misery, and affliction were somehow embraced by his cross so that they all found their hope in him. In this passage Barth presupposes the unity-in-distinction between sin and misery without making clear their distinction.

their sin and death his own in order that his righteousness and life might be conveyed to them. Despite being sinful in themselves, they were made righteous (not partially but totally) through their union and communion with Christ, which gave them their true and final identity, in spite of all that might seem to count against it. This was, for Luther, the central message of the Reformation.

Barth followed Luther's lead but took it a step further. In dealing with each term, whether *iustus* or *peccator*, he extended their reach. The two extremes, as he suggested in separated places, were represented by Judas and the Psalmist. On the one hand, not even Judas, the chief of sinners, could be placed with full certainty beyond the scope of Christ's resurrection. A margin of hope still remained that his negation by divine judgment might in turn be negated by grace. In principle, he was no different as *peccator* than Peter and the rest of the disciples.

On the other hand, the sin that still clung so closely ought not to rob believers of their proper self-confidence in Christ. The Psalmist's remarkable self-assurance in his own righteousness and the righteousness of his cause was not to be seen as a sign of hubris. It was rather the confidence of the justified sinner, who in Christ was fully righteous despite his ongoing sin. As *iustus* (by grace alone through faith alone), the Psalmist (in such a mood) displayed a healthy lack of anxiety about his own actual sinfulness. He was proleptically justified, in reality and in hope, because of Christ. Both Judas and the Psalmist, Barth suggested, were to be interpreted from a center in him.

The last hermeneutical move to be considered pertained to texts that seemed to be contradictory. In a seminal but little-noticed passage (I/1, 179-81), Barth examined four apparent biblical contradictions: (i) between conditional and unconditional covenants (Exod. 19–20 and Jer. 31), (ii) between prophecies of ultimate doom and of ultimate restoration (Amos and Hosea), (iii) between the picture of Jesus in the Synoptics and in John, and (iv) between the cross and the resurrection in Paul's preaching. The tensions evident in these materials, Barth argued, ought not to be resolved. Any efforts at harmonization or higher conceptual synthesis would be artificial. The tensions were valuable just as they stood, because they forced the reader to construe them dialectically. Barth's dialectical hermeneutic, as set forth at this point, was of immense importance for his entire theology.

In introducing these different blocks of material, each of which appeared to involve two irreconcilable trains of thought, Barth suggested that both were to be accepted as valid: "One of them is always true in experience and thought, and we must always believe the other that we do not see" (I/1, 179). It was a hermeneutic of dialectical inclusion. It meant moving back and forth without synthesis between the two trains of thought on the supposition that the two were compatible without being able to show how. The rationale for this procedure unfolded as Barth went along.

Barth began by discussing Exodus 19–20 in relation to Jeremiah 31. After reflecting on the two types of covenant — the one conditional and the other unconditional — he wrote:

> Now if we are to listen to both Ex. 19–20 and Jer. 31, we obviously cannot listen to both at the same time. A historical analysis of the two texts will in its own way show us at once that a systematic conspectus of both is impossible. Hence we can only listen either to the one or the other at the one time. Nor can it be a matter of harmonising exegesis but solely a matter of faith to see the validity of each covenant in the other, of the new in the old and the old in the new. (I/1, 180)

Faith affirmed that each covenant was valid in its own way, despite being unable to resolve the tension between them. The task of faith was to move back and forth within the tension, discerning the validity of each covenant in the other. For the new was somehow valid in the old, and the old in the new.

Barth then sketched two types of prophecy, the one of doom (Amos) and the other of deliverance (Hosea). How were they to be interpreted?

> We would say that prophecies of salvation and disaster, in the absolute sense in which they occur, were naturally impossible at the same time or in any inner connexion. There can thus be no system of prophetic utterance. It was either threat or promise. In this very one-sidedness it sought to be God's Word. To understand it there was and is needed what the New Testament calls faith, namely, the perception either way of what is not said. (I/1, 180 rev.)

Like Kierkegaard, Barth believed that God's Word could be "vigorously one-sided." It could accentuate one aspect very pointedly in order to speak truthfully to a specific situation. Lopsided situations needed to be shaken by one-sided interventions of God's Word. Faith, however, would know of the larger truth. It would be aware of what for a time was left unspoken. It would not only perceive the validity of the disruption, but also the truth of what remained unsaid. As schooled by the New Testament, faith would know how to deal appropriately with the occurrence of one-sided divine interventions. It was a matter of faith, however, as opposed to a rationally accessible synthesis, precisely because it allowed the antithesis to remain unresolved. Amos was vigorously one-sided, and rightly so, but he needed to be countered in the end by Hosea.

The tensions between the Synoptic Gospels and the Gospel of John in their depictions of Jesus were then outlined. Barth stated in conclusion:

> It is impossible to listen at one and the same time to the two statements that Jesus of Nazareth is the Son of God and that the Son of God is Jesus of Nazareth. One hears either the one or the other or one hears nothing. When the one is heard, the other can be heard only indirectly, in faith. (I/1, 180)

Over against the two types of covenant and the two forms of prophecy, this case involved the mystery of the Incarnation. Both the Synoptics and John, according to Barth, were written to attest that mystery, but they did so in opposite ways. In the Synoptics Jesus' humanity was in the forefront, whereas in John the forefront was taken by his deity. It is not as though the Synoptics were concerned only with his humanity, or John only with his deity. Both attested the one divine-human Jesus Christ in his indivisible unity, but they generally did so from very different vantage points. The two depictions were complementary. Neither could finally stand alone, and neither could offer a systematic conspectus of the mystery, which in the nature of the case would be impossible. The mystery could be presented only in the one way or in the other, either by putting Christ's humanity in the foreground and his deity in the background, or else by doing the reverse, with his deity in the foreground and his humanity in the background. Each presentation had to be heard on its own terms. Faith was a matter of fully attending to the one, while hearing the other only indirectly, and then of doing the same thing in reverse. There was no possibility of a higher synthesis. The Synoptics and John mutually supplemented and counterbalanced one another.

Barth's final example concerned the cross and resurrection of Christ in Paul's preaching. Here is his comment in full:

> Paul often used the two terms very closely together, but they always point in very different directions, whether with reference to Christ Himself, or with reference to the reality of salvation for Christians. Paul undoubtedly has both in view when he simply says Ἰησοῦς Χριστός [Je-

sus Christ] or ἐν Χριστῷ [in Christ], but it is worth noting that he can really say both only by this name. But this name is not a system representing a unified experience or a unified thought; it is the Word of God itself. In it the cross and resurrection are one, but they are not one — either for Paul, or his first readers, or us either — in what is said in explanation over and above this name. We can listen only to the one or the other, realising what is said by the one or the other, and then, in and in spite of the concealment, we can also in faith hear the other in the one. (I/1, 180-81 rev.)

The cross and resurrection of Christ, as proclaimed by Paul, were for Barth the paradigmatic case. They were what finally made necessary the procedure of dialectical interpretation. What held Christ's cross and resurrection together, he suggested, was not a concept but a name, not a system but a narrative. Their relation was beyond all unified experience and all unified thought. It was ineffable. Whatever might be said over and above this Name could only be a form of broken or dialectical discourse. No system could possibly contain it. The Name that held together this death and resurrection signified a kind of drastic apocalyptic interruption, so to speak, in the metaphysical status quo, a revolution that overturned the old order. It meant an end to metaphysical business as usual. It was an irruption of the new aeon into the old, and the old could not contain it. This Name was the event that could not be transcended, but transcended and embraced all things. The bearer of this Name was not determined by them, but they by him.

The unthinkability of what this Name represented suggested the paradigm by which to interpret other biblical conundrums dialectically. Tensions between the conditional and the unconditional covenants, between the prophecies of doom and of deliverance, between the humanity and the deity of Christ, were certainly not the same as one another nor as the death and resurrection of Christ. But when the latter was identified as the hidden center, a hermeneutical key was suggested by which the others could be interpreted without resolving the antitheses they represented. Just as Christ's resurrection was somehow implicit in his cross, and his cross in his resurrection, so each side of the other antitheses was reciprocally implicit, from the standpoint of faith, in the other.

Barth concluded:

These are just some of the great one-sidednesses of the Bible written and received as God's Word. It is a characterisation of the Bible as a whole when the Word of God is described (Heb. 4:12) as "sharper than a two-edged sword" (cf. also Rev. 1:16) and when it is then said to pierce asunder soul and spirit, joints and marrow, and to become judge of the thoughts and intents of the heart, so that no creature can hide from it, but everything is laid bare and held before its eyes. As we must say already at this juncture, it is this external one-sidedness of God's Word, resting on an inner one-sidedness not apparent to us, that makes faith faith, that makes it the apprehended apprehension — moving from the depths to the heights and the heights to the depths — of the ever invisible God who is beyond all experience and thought. From the Word of God faith has not only its existence but also this its nature. (I/1, 181)

To conclude: a great deal of Barth's biblical interpretation took place by thinking from a center in Jesus Christ. Thinking from Christ's centrality meant thinking most especially from his death and resurrection. The two together formed, so to speak, the center within the center. All hermeneutics proceeded outward from this center and then back to it again.

On this basis Barth could think typologically about biblical figures like David or Job. On this basis he could interpret the sorrows of Israel, the church, and the world under the signs of judgment and grace. On this basis he could hold out hope even for Judas and avoid moralizing about overconfidence in the Psalms. And on this basis he developed an ingenious dialectical hermeneutic that avoided the twin pitfalls of constructing either false harmonizations or false conflicts between diverse and apparently contradictory blocks of Scripture.

What held all these moves together was not a system but a Name. It was this Name and this Name alone that provided Holy Scripture with its unity. No doctrine or set of doctrines, no system or comprehensive scheme, no ideology or ontology, could perform this important unifying role for Christian hearers of the Word. The unity of the totality of Holy Scripture, and through it ultimately of all things, resided exclusively in the mystery of this Name. It was a Name whose utter ineffability transcended, relativized, and fractured every conceivable hermeneutics and every conceivable system of thought. "His eyes are like a flame of fire, and on his head are many diadems, and he has a name written that no one knows but himself. He is clothed in a robe dipped in blood, and the name by which he is called is the Word of God" (Rev. 19:12-13).

*   *   *

Over the past twenty years or so Barth studies have become increasingly technical. Although he saw himself as writing primarily for preachers, he has ever more become the captive of professors (mea culpa!). That is why it is usually better to read Barth than to read what is written about Barth. Nevertheless, because he is not always easy to understand, a little guidance every now and then can come in handy. While this book is a guide to his use of Scripture, it will succeed only if it whets the reader's appetite to read Barth.

Chapter 1, by Robert McAfee Brown, offers a refreshingly accessible introduction to some themes of this book. Brown wrote before the rise of academic Barthianism.

Chapter 2, by Katherine Sonderegger, beautifully explains how Barth saw Scripture as both reliable and inspired.

Chapter 3, on Rudolf Smend by George Hunsinger, the centerpiece of this volume, discusses what is probably the best essay ever written on Barth's interpretation of Scripture.

Chapter 4, by Hans W. Frei, is of interest not only for the light it casts on Barth, but also on Frei's own use of Barth in his influential proposals about "realistic narrative." This essay is published here for the first time.

Chapter 5, by Kathryn Greene-McCreight, displays Barth's typological exegesis in action. After Barth's reading of Leviticus 14 and 16 is deftly set forth, it is brought into conversation with Robert Alter and Jacob Milgrom.

Chapter 6, by A. Katherine Grieb, shows how Barth reads the Sermon on the Mount as possessing a hidden center in Christ.

Chapter 7, by myself, George Hunsinger, lifts up Hebrews 13:8 as a key passage for unlocking Barth's profound but elusive ideas about time and eschatology.

Chapter 8, by John Webster, shows that certain of Barth's distinctive views about the Gospel of John, which some have felt mark a shift in the development of Barth's theology, and especially in his 1942 doctrine of election, were already present as early as 1925.

Chapter 9, by Paul Molnar, measures several recent theologians against Barth on the question of Scripture and "religion." Special attention is devoted to Sallie McFague, Paul Tillich, and S. Mark Heim.

Chapter 10, by Paul Dafydd Jones, digs deeply into what makes Barth's christocentric interpretation tick. It serves as a fitting conclusion to the book.

The Appendices offer three brief excerpts from Barth himself. They are typical of the exegetical and theological riches to be found in his *Church Dogmatics*.

The second five chapters listed above were presented in May 2006 during a conference held at Princeton Theological Seminary on the theme "'Thy Word Is Truth': Reading Scripture Theologically with Karl Barth." The first five chapters have been added to round out the discussion.

I. Orientation

1. Scripture and Tradition in the Theology of Karl Barth

Robert McAfee Brown

Of all Protestant theologians on the contemporary scene, Karl Barth has taken Scripture with greatest seriousness, and he has thereby been forced to deal with the problem of Scripture and tradition with greatest fullness.

Barth is ecumenically important not only because Hans Küng has written a book about him, nor even because he may succeed in writing more words than St. Thomas Aquinas, but also because he has genuinely tried to reclaim a *distinctively* Christian faith for our day. When one reads his massive twelve volumes of *Church Dogmatics,* now well over six million words, one does not feel a sense of oppressiveness but of liberation. One is not trapped within "Barth's system," but released from any system — liberated to take seriously and yet joyfully the central affirmations of the gospel. If Barth emerges as the great heretic of our day, it will not be for emphasizing the dark side of the gospel (as was true of so many of his Calvinistic forebears), but precisely for being (if such a thing is really possible for a Christian) too hopeful.

I. The Central Christological Fact

Here is a man who really believes that something quite monumental happened back in the first century, and that it makes all the difference. The

---

The analysis in this chapter draws mainly upon Barth, *Church Dogmatics,* I/2 (Edinburgh: T. & T. Clark, 1956), pp. 457-740, 743-884; *Credo* (New York: Scribner, 1961), esp. pp. 173-203; and *The Knowledge of God and the Service of God* (New York: Scribner, 1939), *passim.* See also Barth's most recent statement of theological methodology, *Evangelical Theology* (New York: Holt, Rinehart & Winston, 1963), esp. Part I.

Christian message is that *God is for us;* that he has declared himself on our behalf; that he has taken what Barth calls "the journey of the Son of God into the far country" so that we might know, once and for all, what his disposition is on our behalf, namely that he loves us unconditionally; and that in Jesus Christ he has declared and enacted this love and grace. To be sure, there are powers and forces of evil at work in the world, but there is nothing more powerful than the grace of God. Indeed, in his latest and twelfth volume (which has the barbarous subtitle "Volume Four, Part Three, Second Half") he says that it is not enough to talk of "the triumph of grace," for that sounds too impersonal. The way we must characterize the message of the gospel is with the words "Jesus is Victor" (a phrase adopted from the Blumhardts) — victor over sin, over death, over all that could possibly threaten us.

Secure at that point, Barth does not find himself confined and tied down, but liberated and freed to look at absolutely everything else in the light of that one blazing fact. *Creation* can be accepted and enjoyed as the arena, the theater, in which this divine drama of victory has been enacted. *Men* can be seen not as dust destined for extinction but as those for whom Christ made the long journey, so that he could lift them up with him into the presence of the Father. *Sin* we have always with us, but in the light of the conviction that "Jesus is Victor" it cannot be taken with final seriousness, only with provisional seriousness. *The life of the Christian* is the life of gratitude, the life of joyful obedience, of glad thanksgiving, in which, as Barth says, *charis* can only lead to *eucharistia,* grace can only lead to gratitude. So it goes for volume after volume; secure at this central point — Christ as Alpha and Omega, as beginning and end — Barth can see everything afresh in the light of this fact.

Including Scripture and tradition. . . . The old Protestant orthodoxies until recently were imprisoned within Scripture. Roman Catholicism, it could be argued, until recently was imprisoned within tradition. Barth is imprisoned within neither; rather, he is freed by both, freed for the gospel, which comes to us through the agency of Scripture and through the channel of the church that brings Scripture to us. We are beholden to *tradition* as it explicates the meaning of Scripture for us, and we are beholden to *Scripture* as it sets forth the nature of what God has done.

This means that Barth can take tradition more seriously than any contemporary Protestant thinker has done, and yet not be constricted by it. One never finds him repeating the old orthodoxy simply because the tradition sanctions it. While he aligns himself at many points with the old orthodoxy, notably in his claims about the nature of the virgin birth and the resurrection, he also displays a remarkable freedom from it whenever that freedom is necessitated by his allegiance to the Word of God mediated through Scripture.

II. The Authority of Scripture

In order to clarify Barth's position on tradition, it is necessary to say something about his doctrine of Scripture.

Barth has been called every name in the book on this matter. Critics on the left accuse him of "biblicism" (whatever that means), and assert that he is so tied down to the Bible that he really lives in a private world of conventional orthodoxy where the air is stale and where there is no contact with living, breathing, twentieth-century man. But Barth is also under attack from the right, from those thinkers who find him even more dangerous than Nels Ferré finds Paul Tillich — and Ferré finds Tillich more dangerous than Father Tavard does. These critics find Barth dangerous because he "sounds" orthodox, but really isn't. He seems to be saying many orthodox things, they argue, but because he denies verbal inspiration and infallibility to the biblical text, he has really sold orthodoxy down the river.

We need to locate Barth somewhere in the midst of this crossfire. From the conservative critics let us learn that Barth is no fundamentalist, that he gives ample recognition to error within the biblical text, and that he is no enemy whatever of higher criticism, from which, indeed, he profits all through the exegetical portions of the *Dogmatics*. For Barth, in fact, it is extremely important that the Bible comes to us in intensely human form. God uses the biblical writers precisely as human beings. As he puts it:

> Every time we turn the Word of God into an infallible biblical word of man or the biblical word of man into an infallible Word of God we resist that which we ought never to resist, i.e. the truth of the miracle that here fallible men speak the Word of God in fallible human words. . . . To the bold postulate that if their word is to be the Word of God they must be inerrant in every word, we oppose the even bolder assertion, that according to the scriptural witness about man, which applies to them too, they can be at fault in any word, and have been at fault in every word, and yet according to the same scriptural witness, being justified and

sanctified by grace alone, they have still spoken the Word of God in their fallible and erring human word.[1]

In other words, God works through the human text, for "the fallible and faulty human word is as such used by God and has to be received and heard in spite of its human fallibility."[2]

How are we to know that these fallible pages are the Word of God? Here Barth finds himself in the same kind of circle in which all Protestants find themselves, though Protestants would assert that the circle need not be a vicious one. Unless we are prepared to vindicate the authority of the Bible by some authority external to it (such as an infallible church), thereby making *it* the ultimate authority, Protestants are placed in the position in which Barth finds himself placed, namely that the Bible's message to us is finally *self*-authenticating, and cannot be authenticated by any other norm. In typical fashion, Barth comments:

> The Bible must be known as the Word of *God* if it is to be *known* as the Word of God. The doctrine of Holy Scripture in the Evangelical Church is that this logical circle is the circle of self-asserting, self-attesting truth into which it is equally impossible to enter as it is to emerge from it: the circle of our freedom which as such is also the circle of our captivity.[3]

And again:

> For the statement that the human word of the Bible is the Word of God we can obviously give only a single and incomparable basis. This is that it is true. This basis either exists of itself or not at all. It is either already known and acknowledged or it is not accepted.[4]

I confess that I am always initially a little irritated by this kind of remark until I realize that there is no alternative to this kind of remark, which does not bind us to a *securitas* achieved on human terms, in which we finally make something binding on God. That is to say, the alternative to the position Barth sketches is to find a way of proving the case by some humanly constructed device. We will believe the Bible to be the Word of God, for example, because we can demonstrate that it has no errors and

1. *Church Dogmatics,* I/2, pp. 529-30.
2. *Church Dogmatics,* I/2, p. 533.
3. *Church Dogmatics,* I/2, p. 535.
4. *Church Dogmatics,* I/2, pp. 535-36.

therefore must be accepted. Or we will believe the Bible to be the Word of God because people with very persuasive credentials tell us it is. In either case, this becomes for the Protestant a kind of idolatry. Perhaps, after all, Barth is finally right when he says, "The Church does not have to accredit [Scripture], but again and again it has to be accredited by it."[5]

A basic decision is made at this point. Either the Bible occupies a unique status, or implicitly some coordinate authority is introduced alongside of it, which finally rises up, Barth would believe, to smother it and replace it. The decision of the church to set itself under Scripture remains the valid Reformation decision.

As Barth develops this doctrine of the authority of Scripture in his later writings, it becomes clearer and clearer that Scripture does not exist simply to witness to itself. In later volumes of the *Dogmatics* the term "Word of God" (so popular in volumes I/1 and I/2) tends to be replaced by explicitly Christological terms, so that any possible ambiguity is removed. The Word of God is not basically the words of a book; the Word of God is Jesus Christ, the Word made flesh. Scripture is so central for the church because Scripture is what Barth calls "the primary sign of revelation." But we are not to go back *to* a book, we are to go back *through* the book, to the One to whom the book basically witnesses, namely the God who has revealed himself in Jesus Christ. It is to bring us to him that the book is so necessary, for we cannot get to him apart from the book.

> The fact that the primary sign of revelation, the existence of the prophets and apostles, is for the Church book and letter, does not rob it of its force as witness. If the book rises and the letter speaks, if the book is read and the letter understood, then with them the prophets and apostles and He of whom they testify rise up and meet the Church in a living way. It is not the book and letter, but the voice of the men apprehended through the book and letter, and in the voice of these men the voice of Him who called them to speak, which is authority in the Church.[6]

So even Scripture itself is only a sign — but it is the indispensable sign, the primary sign, the sign without which the church cannot be the church. If the church, Barth says, "would see Jesus Christ, it is directed and bound to Holy Scripture."[7]

5. *Church Dogmatics*, I/2, p. 536.
6. *Church Dogmatics*, I/2, p. 581.
7. *Church Dogmatics*, I/2, p. 583.

Thus if the critics on the left want to insist that Barth takes his stand squarely on Scripture, they certainly have a point. That he will admit nothing into the understanding of the Christian faith that is not grounded in Scripture or cannot be consistently derived from the revelation of God found in Scripture — all this must be admitted. But that this makes him a "biblicist" in the pejorative sense in which that term is usually used, does not follow. Few men have taken with such radical seriousness the fact that if we are to know God we must look at the place where he gave himself to be known, namely in the Incarnation, access to which is cut off for us if we deny Scripture a normative place. And if Barth is right, as at this central point he seems to be, then any attempt on our part to take seriously the promises and the demands of biblical faith must align itself not too far from him in his concern to call the church once again to be *the listening church,* the church that hears what God has said and done, before it attempts to be the speaking and teaching church.

III. The Place of Tradition in the Light of Scripture

This raises, immediately, the science of tradition. The church listens, and then the church speaks. Its speaking is its "traditioning," its handing on, of what it hears. But a long time has passed since God acted in Jesus Christ on what Barth calls "the narrow strip of human history." By what critical standard is the traditioning process across those intervening centuries to be measured?

Barth had come to a fairly clear answer to this question as early as 1935, and dealt with the question of the relation of dogmatics to tradition in answer to questions posed for him by the Dutch clergy after he had given a series of lectures to them on the Apostles' Creed.[8]

Understanding "tradition" as "the sum total of the voices of the Fathers," Barth immediately repudiates the notion that this could be a second source of revelation, this being for him the historic Roman Catholic heresy that must be avoided. (Discussions at the first session of Vatican Council II on *De Fontibus Revelationis* would suggest that the Council fathers likewise wish to avoid such a conclusion.) Rather, in order to avoid what becomes the self-apotheosis of the church, "the Reformation Scripture-principle placed the Church *permanently* under the authority of the prophetic-

8. Barth, *Credo.*

Their own dogmas

apostolic Bible-Word."[9] *"Tradition,"* Barth goes on to assert in italics, *"is not revelation."*[10] He also points out that this does not mean jumping over the intervening nineteen centuries "to the Bible alone," as the orthodox thinkers of the eighteenth and nineteenth centuries tried to do.

> These determined "biblicists" had their contemporary philosophy in their heads, took it with them to the Bible and so most certainly read themselves into the Bible no less than Church Fathers and Scholastics. They were no doubt free of Church dogma but not of their own dogmas and conceptions.[11]

Far better, Barth seems to be arguing, that we approach the Bible in the light of what the church has thought about it than that we approach the Bible simply in the light of what contemporary philosophy says about something else. (One can see, back in 1935, the terms in which, two decades later, Barth will be taking issue with Bultmann.) The Bible must be read by the church. We cannot ignore what the church has said, even though we must not apotheosize it. In a vivid image, Barth continues:

> To my mind the whole question of tradition falls under the Fifth commandment: Honour father and mother! Certainly that is a limited authority; we have to obey God more than father and mother. But we have also to obey father and mother. . . . There is no question of bondage and constraint. It is merely that in the church the same kind of obedience as, I hope, you pay to your father and mother, is demanded of you towards the Church's past, towards the "elders" of the Church.[12]

In the selective process of dealing with the affirmations of the "elders of the Church," the norm, the standard, is clear:

> The norm that determines our choice is Holy Scripture. Holy Scripture is the object of our study, and at the same time the criterion of our study, of the Church's past. As I read the writings of the "Fathers," the witness of Holy Scripture stands continually before my eyes; I accept what interprets this witness to me; I reject what contradicts it. So a

---

9. Barth, *Credo*, p. 180.
10. Barth, *Credo*, p. 180.
11. Barth, *Credo*, pp. 180-81.
12. Barth, *Credo*, p. 181.

choice is actually made, certainly not a choice according to my individual taste, but according to my knowledge of Holy Scripture.[13]

This is not a matter that Barth has developed only as a principle. He has followed through on this criterion of selection in all of his subsequent writings, and it will be instructive to examine two examples of his attempt to do this: his treatment of the doctrine of election, and his attitude toward "church confessions."

A. The Doctrine of Election

Here is an interesting example of the way in which the relationship of Scripture and tradition is developed by Barth. In approaching a systematic setting forth of this doctrine, Barth, as a Reformed theologian, had expected to engage in a fairly conventional restatement of the traditional Calvinist position. As he put it in the preface to his volume on election:

> I would have preferred to follow Calvin's doctrine of predestination much more closely, instead of departing from it so radically. . . . But I could not and cannot do so. *As I let the Bible itself reach to me on these matters, as I meditated upon what I seemed to hear, I was driven irresistibly to reconstruction.* . . . It is because of the rather critical nature of the case that I have had to introduce into this half-volume such long expositions of some Old and New Testament passages.[14]

In other words, as Barth looked at his own theological tradition, and as he looked at Scripture, he saw a contradiction. He did not believe that what he read in Calvin on this matter was what he read in Scripture. (Let it be recorded that he is not the first person who has had this difficulty.) One source of difficulty, he felt, was the wrongness of the starting point of traditional theology. The starting point was too often some abstract notion of the omniscience or omnipotence of deity, from which certain logical conclusions were held to follow.

For Barth, this is wrong theological methodology. Christian theology, he asserts, can never move from the abstract to the concrete; it must begin and end with the concrete, the specific. If it wants to talk about God, it

13. Barth, *Credo,* p. 183.
14. *Church Dogmatics,* II/2, p. x, italics added.

must begin at the specific point where God has shown us who he is, namely in Jesus Christ. It must begin, in other words, with the God who has declared himself for us, and anything it says about election must proceed from the basic fact that *that* is the kind of God with whom we have to deal, namely that Jesus Christ is the electing God, who has sought us in love. And when one starts with the biblical contention that God is for us, that God has elected us in Christ from the foundation of the world (Eph. 1:4), then very different consequences follow from those that follow upon the conventional abstract starting point.

This is not the place to spell out all the implications that follow from such a starting point. All that can be stressed is that Barth's reformulation follows from his attempt to take seriously the full impact of the *biblical* revelation as that revelation focuses in Christ, and to engage in whatever reassessing of the *tradition* may thereby be made necessary. As a result, predestination is no longer a question of incomprehensible darkness, as it was for Calvin, but of incomprehensible light. It is not a question of an absolute decree, but of divine grace. It is not a question of consigning so many people to eternal perdition, but of recognizing that Christ desireth not the death of a sinner. It is a message of hope, pure hope; it is gospel, good news.

Barth will not accept the tag of "universalist." He insists that if the old orthodoxy was wrong to assert that most men must be damned, it would be equally improper for us to assert that all men must be saved. But it is nevertheless clear to him that there is one thing that is stronger than man's demonry, and that is God's grace, and that those who *are* called are called to acquaint the "others" with the fact that God's grace is for them too. No man, he says, who has been the recipient of God's grace can deny that it is in principle available to every other man. Certainly there is judgment, but the fact is that the judge himself has taken our place, borne the penalty, canceled out the debt. And to those who keep insisting that somebody must burn forever, Barth apostrophizes: *A strange justice.*

Peculiar Christendom, whose most pressing problem seems to consist in this, that God's grace in this direction should be too free; that hell, instead of being amply populated, might one day perhaps be found to be empty![15]

---

15. *Die Botschaft von der freien Gnade Gottes* (Zollikon-Zürich: Evangelischer Verlag, 1974), p. 8.

Against the logic-chopping of Calvin, and particularly the later Calvinist tradition, Barth is a liberating voice, simply because he tries to take seriously as his starting point the biblical affirmation that the reconciling act of God in Christ has actually taken place. The principalities and powers have been vanquished, for Christ has come. Jesus is Victor. As he put it to his students, speaking about Christology in the rubble at Bonn only a year after the war ended:

> Here we are standing at the centre. And however high and mysterious and difficult everything we want to know might seem to us, yet we may also say that this is just where everything becomes quite simple, quite straightforward, quite childlike. Right here in this centre, in which as a Professor of Systematic Theology I must call to you, "Look! This is the point now! Either knowledge or the greatest folly!" — here I am in front of you, like a teacher in Sunday School facing his kiddies, who has something to say which a mere four-year-old can really understand. "The world was lost, but Christ was born, rejoice, O Christendom!"[16]

B. The Place of Church Confessions

The nature of the biblical affirmation, then, determines what is to be done with subsequent tradition. Let us now see how Barth develops this point in terms of certain specific confessional statements of the past.

Barth has given a great deal of faithful attention to the previous confessions of faith of the church. His concern with Scripture does not lead him to try to bypass the intervening nineteen centuries. He reminds us that our approach to Scripture today is partly molded and influenced by our Christian heritage, and we must not try to assume that this is not so. We must listen to what the church fathers have told us, and what the church, in various places, has tried to offer us as a compendium of the faith, a guide to the meaning of Jesus Christ for the contemporary moment.

Barth has written, for example, three books giving expositions of the Apostles' Creed.[17] He has also given two series of lectures expounding the

---

16. *Dogmatics in Outline* (New York: Harper, 1959), pp. 66-67.

17. *Credo* appeared in 1935 at the height of the struggle over Hitler within the German church. *The Faith of the Church* (New York: Meridian, 1958) was a series of lectures given to French pastors in 1940-43. *Dogmatics in Outline* was given at the summer semester at Bonn in 1946.

content of the Heidelberg Catechism.[18] But his most ambitious attempt to deal with a given confession of faith is found in his Gifford Lectures for 1937-38, given at the University of Aberdeen, and structured in the form of a long running commentary on the Scots Confession of 1560.[19] We can use Barth's comments about the present worth of the Scots Confession to see specifically how he relates to "tradition" in the form of a church confession.

Barth takes his cue from a famous passage in the Scots Confession itself, which is surely one of the most significant utterances in Protestant church history. John Knox and his friends, while framing the original Confession, stated in the following terms the authority their confession was to have:

> Protesting that if any man will note in this our confession any article or sentence repugnant to God's Holy Word, that it would please him of his gentleness and for Christian charity's sake to admonish us of the same in writing; and we upon our honor and fidelity, by God's grace, do promise unto him satisfaction from the mouth of God, that is from his Holy Scriptures, or else reformation of that which he shall prove to be amiss. 3.20

The framers of the confession, Barth stresses, recognized its limited authority — it was to be followed only as it faithfully reflected the gospel found in Scripture. Wherever it could be demonstrated that it was *not* faithful to that same gospel, it was to be amended and reformed. To which Barth comments:

> That means manifestly that when we associate ourselves with this document, we must at the same time remain free in relation to it — free to give heed to the Scripture itself. The [Scots Confession] wishes to be read and understood as a signpost pointing to Scripture.[20]

18. *The Heidelberg Catechism for Today* (Richmond, VA: John Knox Press, 1964).

19. *The Knowledge of God and the Service of God* (New York: Scribner, 1939). These lectures, incidentally, represent the most remarkable theological *tour de force* of the century. The Gifford Lectures, according to Lord Gifford's will, must deal with natural theology. Barth does not believe in natural theology. Consequently, in his opening lecture he stated that believers in natural theology ought to be acquainted with the antithesis of their own position, and that he would therefore perform the function of describing for them that to which they were opposed. For the remaining 19½ lectures Barth made nary another reference to natural theology.

20. *The Knowledge of God and the Service of God*, pp. 11-12.

Again, toward the end of his second series of lectures, stressing the human quality of this and other confessional statements, he writes:

> Such a decision or confession of faith, as the Scottish Confession, cannot under any conditions wish to usurp the place of the Word of God. It cannot claim a validity which is absolute and obligatory for all time. . . . It cannot bind men's consciences, it is not in principle free from error. It is and remains simply a human decision. . . . But within its own limits the Confession can be a human decision of such a kind, *that through it the way will not be blocked but rather opened up for the Word of God. . . .*[21]

So two things happen. First, we are liberated, and the opportunity is given to us, as Barth says, "to utter in weak, fallible, human words, humbly but joyfully, a confession of faith in the Word of God."[22] But secondly, the process of liberation gives us the opportunity and obligation of a *critical* relation to the confession. The confession is not for us the last word, any more than it was for those who wrote it. As we read a confession, we must always ask ourselves whether it is or is not faithful to the gospel found in Scripture. And Barth at this point finds that confessions can sometimes help us to see the biblical faith more clearly — as, for example, at the point where both the Scots Confession and the Second Helvetic Confession rearticulate the doctrine of election in christological terms. He also finds that occasionally we will discover that the confessions have not been faithful to the biblical witness. In dealing with the Scots Confession's treatment of Israel, for example, Barth finds himself dissatisfied. The statements, he says, "require at this point to be supplemented, or rather to be qualified, if they are to be completely intelligible. We must go farther than our Confession. There is something else which the Old Testament tells us about Israel. . . ."[23]

So the confession is, in Barth's words, "a signpost pointing to Scripture." It must never be confused with Scripture, but by making use of it, our own understanding of Scripture can be enhanced.

Barth himself has had a hand in writing what may turn out to be an enduring "church confession." In 1934, at the Synod of Barmen, it became clear that the Confessing Church had to speak a definitive and decisive word against Hitler. And this was done by the members of the Synod in the so-called "Barmen Declaration," for the writing of which Barth was largely

---

21. *The Knowledge of God and the Service of God,* pp. 183-84, italics added.
22. *The Knowledge of God and the Service of God,* p. 155.
23. *The Knowledge of God and the Service of God,* p. 62.

responsible. The confession is solidly based on Scripture. And in confining itself almost entirely to theological statements, it turns out to be one of the most politically relevant documents the church has ever issued. It concentrates on the issue of Lordship. If Jesus Christ is Lord, as Scripture proclaims him to be, then we can give allegiance to no other Lord, no matter how pretentious or impressive his claims may be. Consequently, the first proposition reads:

> Jesus Christ, as He is attested to us in Holy Scripture, is the one Word of God, whom we have to hear and whom we have to trust and obey in life and in death.
>
> We condemn the false doctrine that the Church can and must recognize as God's revelation other events and powers, forms and truths apart from and alongside this One Word of God.

In other words, since Scripture tells us that Christ is Lord, Hitler cannot be Lord. Other "events and powers," such as Hitler, Nazism, or anti-Semitism, must be repudiated.

IV. Summary Statement

After these two extended examples of the relation of Scripture to tradition, let us now draw together more formally some of the things implicit and explicit in Barth's approach. Three things may be suggested by way of summary.

1. The *church fathers* must always be listened to with respect, but we must be careful not to give them a veneration that leads to idolatry. Barth describes a visit to Wittenberg, where he saw inscribed on a stove, "The Word of God and the teaching of Luther will never fail!" But if there is always a danger of that kind of idolatry of the past, there is also the danger of prematurely jettisoning what can be learned from the past. "We are not," Barth says, "to play truant from the school of Luther and Calvin until we are better instructed, but to learn in [that school] what there is to be learned."[24] This can never mean simply using their words, no matter how appropriate the words may have been in their own day. Barth makes the point in words that deserve quotation *in extenso*:

---

24. *Church Dogmatics*, I/2, p. 612.

There can be as little question of a repristination of the teaching of Luther and Calvin as of the orthodoxy of the seventeenth century in the present rediscovery and reacknowledgement of the authority of the Reformers. If there were, we would not be giving them the honor due to them, but refusing it. *Not those who repeat the doctrine most faithfully, but those who reflect upon it most faithfully so that they can then expound it as their own doctrine, are their most faithful pupils.*

But to reflect on their doctrine means to draw out the line indicated by them as it needs to be drawn in accordance with a new investigation of Scripture and the confession in reply to modern questions. As witnesses accredited by the confession of the Church of their day, they have ecclesiastical authority for the Church of today. Therefore the Church of today, with all the experience which it has since acquired, and the responsibility in which it itself stands, has to listen to them. This may mean deviation and contradiction as regards the historical form of their doctrine. The Church of today would not be accepting them if it were simply accepting or reproducing them in their historical form. It would be accepting them not as the Church of today, not as obedience to its own calling along the lines of the Reformation, but as an institute of antiquities — the worst dishonor of which it could be guilty for all its well-meant veneration.[25]

So tradition is not to be venerated for its own sake, and we are not called upon to repeat in our day exactly what the fathers said in theirs. However, we must listen to what the fathers said in their day, so that they can help to point us toward that to which they were pointing, namely the nature of biblical faith.

2. When we confront the past, we do not merely find the church fathers, we also find *the church confessions,* and the cumulative voice of the confessions speaks with greater effect than any individual theologian can do. Barth defines the conditions of a proper confession:

A Church confession is a formulation and proclamation of the insight which the Church has been given in certain directions into the revelation attested by Scripture, reached on the basis of common deliberation and decision.[26]

25. *Church Dogmatics,* I/2, p. 619, italics added.
26. *Church Dogmatics,* I/2, p. 620.

This means that a confession will be a kind of commentary on Scripture, "in the speech of its age." It cannot be anything more than a commentary; it must not try to stand on the same level as Scripture. It thus clearly has limits: it is limited by its origin and by its object. It has geographical and temporal limits, which is why new confessions will always be needed, in order to confess the faith afresh in a new situation. As Barth's translators rather ungrammatically render him, "In every case a new confession was needed which could not be a new one but only a new and preciser version of the old."

What then is the authority of a confession? The confession is authoritative as "a first commentary on Holy Scripture."[27] It is this as well as "a human word ranked before all other human words." Since nobody hears Scripture "purely," we have to test our hearing of Scripture against the confessions, but we also have to test our hearing of the confessions against Scripture. Since the Confession is "a signpost to Scripture," this means that a confession "becomes a constant antithesis, the horizon of our own thinking and speaking."[28] The confession confronts us with Christian history, it makes it necessary that we take into account what our forefathers have done and thought, it becomes a basis in terms of which we test our faith, and if we disagree with the confession, the burden of proof is always first of all upon us. We cannot "have done with the confession"; it is there to be reckoned with, even if we cannot fully accept it. If we go beyond such evaluations of a confession, Barth feels, we run the constant danger of equating revelation and church.

3. So the authority of the confession — and now of all "tradition" — can only be *a relative authority*. "What we know as dogma," Barth states, "is in principle fallible and therefore neither final nor unalterable." In the church confessions, he concludes,

> There can never be a final word, but only a word which is imperative and binding and authoritative until it is succeeded by something else. The Church confesses, and it also appropriates earlier and other confessions. But even as it does so, it remains open to the possibility that it may be better instructed by the Word of God, that it may know it better and therefore confess it better.[29]

27. *Church Dogmatics,* I/2, p. 649.
28. *Church Dogmatics,* I/2, p. 651.
29. *Church Dogmatics,* I/2, p. 657.

Thus, when it comes to the place where each of us is called upon to make his own confession, to declare how it stands with him, to witness to the faith he holds, the individual is not left simply on his own resources:

> Before I myself make a confession I must myself have heard the confession of the Church, i.e. the confession of the rest of the church. . . . I cannot thrust myself into the debate about a right faith which goes on in the Church without first having listened. . . . If I have not heard the Church, I cannot speak to it. . . . And for that very reason I recognize an authority, a superiority in the Church; namely that the confession of others who were before me in the Church and are beside me in the Church is superior to my confession if this really is an accounting and responding in relation to my hearing and receiving of the Word of God, if it really is my confession as that of a member of the body of Christ.[30]

V. Conclusion

In the difficult area of the relationship of Scripture and tradition, Barth has broken some fresh ground upon which new approaches can be constructed. He delivers us from what can be a very perverse notion of *sola Scriptura* that would assert that we go to the Bible and to the Bible alone, as though in the process we could really bypass tradition. He delivers us from a kind of biblicism that is content to rest simply with a parroting of the vindication, "the Bible says . . . , the Bible says. . . ." He confronts us with the necessity of taking tradition with utmost seriousness, and seeing it as a resource for the articulation of our own faith, so long as we keep it under Scripture and not alongside Scripture. He builds fences against the kind of subjectivism that is the morass of Protestant individualism, by pointing out that just as the church must first listen before it speaks, so must we first listen before we speak, and that when we do speak we may not jauntily set up our own private insights as though they had some kind of definitive worth simply because they are our insights. And he provides the supreme criterion by which all else, whether Scripture, tradition, church fathers, private insight, church structure, or whatever, must be judged — namely the criterion of the Lordship of Jesus Christ.

30. *Church Dogmatics*, I/2, p. 589.

Whatever witnesses to the Lordship of Jesus Christ we must retain. Whatever jeopardizes the Lordship of Jesus Christ we must discard. That the issue between what to retain and what to discard is momentous, constitutes both the glory and the risk of being a Christian.

2. The Doctrine of Inspiration and the Reliability of Scripture

Katherine Sonderegger

One of the steady themes in Karl Barth's long career was the centrality of the doctrine of Inspiration to proper theological and Christian reading of Scripture. Mentioned already in the well-known prefaces to the several editions of the *Epistle to the Romans,* this doctrine makes an explicit entrance in volume I, part 2 of the *Church Dogmatics* and is not far out of sight in any of the major *loci* of the four volumes, most especially in the fourth volume on the unified Person and work of Jesus Christ. I have been inclined in the past to see the doctrine of Inspiration as Barth's *answer* to the problem of historical criticism of the Bible, and as the *goal* of obedient, theological reading of Scripture as witness. Although I would not repudiate that interpretation, I am more inclined now to say that Barth has much deeper lessons to teach me here than that.

It is one of the remarkable characteristics of the *Church Dogmatics* that it seems to refine, reset, and redirect earlier interpretations of major themes: always there is something fresh, something more. The "something more" that I have caught sight of this time from the *Church Dogmatics* is the complex relation of Inspiration to the forms of Eternal temporality; and the even more challenging relation of the historical objectivity of Scripture to the doctrines of atonement and justification. In brief, what I think I saw earlier as an "answer" I now see diagnosed by Barth as a "conceptual puzzle" — an innocent playing with concepts, to borrow Hegelian idiom — and what I saw as "goal" now deepened by Barth into an existential encounter with temptation, disobedience, and Christ's own victory over both.

Let me begin with Barth's doctrine of Inspiration as "answer" or, better, as "conceptual puzzle." Perhaps a brief word of introduction will make my point clearer. In the first volume of the *Dogmatics,* Barth works through material he has wrestled with since his first move away from the theology of his youth. Deeply immersed in the Kantianism of prewar German academic theology, Barth was troubled by epistemic questions — How is true knowledge of God possible? How can the Bible be understood as revelation? — and these worries were brought forward into his dogmatic works, from his first lectures in dogmatics in Göttingen to his rewriting of the first volume of the *Christian Dogmatics* as our *Church Dogmatics,* volume I. In my view, the doctrine of Inspiration in I/2 still stands in the heavy shadow of these epistemological struggles. The result is a strong coloration of "dialectical" language and structure: the doctrine of Inspiration is the "event" of Spiritual disclosure of human words made conformable with the Divine Word; the relation of text to Divine referent is secured by the miracle of the Holy Spirit's working, the Capable on the incapable, the Truth to the reluctant and wayward human witness. Here is a sample:

> We believe in and with the Church that Holy Scripture has the priority over all other writings and authorities, even those of the Church. We believe in and with the Church that Holy Scripture as the original [*ursprüngliche*] and legitimate witness of divine revelation is itself the Word of God. The words "has" and "is" in these two sentences proclaim the same truth. . . .
>
> The "has" and "is" speak about a divine disposing, action and decision, to which when we make these statements we have on the one hand to look back as something which has already taken place, and on the other to look forward as something which has yet to do so. They do not speak, therefore, about a content [*Sachverhalt*] which we can see clearly or control. They do not say that we have the capacity and competence to ascribe to the Bible this priority, this character as the Word of God, and that this priority and character of the Bible are immediately clear to us. . . .
>
> If we say: the Bible has this priority, it is the Word of God, we must first replace the "has" by a "had" and "will have," and the "is" by a "was" and "will be." It is only as expounded in this way that the two words correspond to what we can actually know and say: we who are not in a position to carry through that divine disposing, action and decision or to handle them as though they were ours. (I/2, 502)

Barth's explicit treatment of the doctrine of Inspiration and its historical development turns on the event of God's free decision to reveal himself in human words, the testimony given in obedience by prophets and evangelists. Neither text nor author has the property of being inspired; indeed, for Barth, inspiration is like revelation: it cannot "now be before us in any kind of divine revealedness [*Offenbartheit*]" (I/2, 507). The strong note of recollection and expectation, sounded first in the Romans commentary, governs Barth's whole handling of the doctrine, such that the "indirect identity" claimed for the Bible with the Word of God can "only cause offense." As Word of God, the Bible will indirectly mirror the two natures of Christ, and in just this way, will be a scandal, offense, and stumbling block. The church is right to honor the testimony of the prophets and apostles, but right for a rather methodological reason. Form cannot be separated from content. To dismiss the form — God's "secondary objectivity," as Barth terms this in II/1 — in order to extract a timeless, essential content is to dabble in "myth" and "pagan religion." These themes will return to prominence when Barth has Bultmann in his sights, but here they reflect Barth's early encounters with D. F. Strauss and the more churchly "absolute idealists."

The concreteness and — to borrow an idealist phrase — the "plasticity" of Scripture cannot be peeled away to reveal the higher truths. Rather, as Barth says in a famous line:

> As truly [*gewiss*] as Jesus died on the cross, as Lazarus died in Jn 11, as the lame were lame, as the blind were blind, as the hungry at the feeding of the five thousand were hungry, as the sea on which Jesus walked was a lake many fathoms deep: so, too, the prophets and apostles as such, even in their office, even in their function as witnesses, even in the act of writing down their witness, were real [*wirkliche*], historical human beings as we are, and therefore sinful in their action, and capable and actually guilty of error in their spoken and written word. (I/2, 528-29 rev.)

Barth here endorses a strong doctrine of fallibilism in his doctrine of Scripture, where the error of the human nature of the Bible extends not only to historical and geographical details but to religious and theological teaching. These doctrinal errors point us indirectly to the miraculous nature of God's address to the church, and to suppress them, Barth warns, as did the Protestant scholastics, is to enter into the long ebb tide of "secularization" that seeks to give creatures control over the Creator, sinners over the free revelation of God.

Well, there is much to love in this doctrine of Inspiration. I myself am a fallibilist in epistemology and in my doctrine of Scripture. And there is nothing quite as energizing as watching Barth outflank the radicals on their own left side. But I think we have to ask whether Barth here has not allowed his epistemic preoccupations to distract him from the concrete, historical details of biblical texts, such that the *singularity* of the "secondary objectivity" of the Word does not have a lot of work to do in theological exegesis. It is a surprisingly formal treatment of Holy Scripture, and aside from the cardinal texts in 1 Timothy and 1 Corinthians, strikingly independent of Barth's close reading of the Bible, a signature of his later volumes. What kind of historical error can we tolerate, indeed welcome, in Scripture? What examples of doctrinal error should we accept as chastening reminders of our need for gracious redemption? Should all errors be equally conformable with the Truth of the Word, and all human sin be identical markers of the place of grace? Have we in fact joined "without separation, without division" the form of Scripture to the content of Divine Word? Would not any text, and all texts point to the same content: that God is gracious to sinners? This would amount to a form of occasionalism in the doctrine of Scripture. Do we not need, then, a "reliabilism" to accompany a strong doctrine of fallibilism, so that the particular shape and detail of a scriptural text can reliably guide the theologian in constructing doctrine, and the believer in constructing a Christian life? I believe that Barth was alert to this worry and increasingly in the *Dogmatics* addressed himself to the reliable contours of the scriptural witness. The Doctrine of Reconciliation, volume IV/1, provides a good example.

Among so many riches, we must choose; and we will not go far wrong with the transition section in Barth's doctrine of the atonement — Jesus Christ, the Lord as Servant, in Barth's phrase — titled "The Verdict of the Father" (IV/1, §59.3). Here Barth makes good on his promise to treat Christology and Reconciliation in a single, differentiated, but unified movement: the Person and Work of Christ is a living whole. Not surprisingly, then, Barth does not leave his discussion of the atonement, centered in Christ as Judge, judged in our place on the cross, without an extended reflection on Christ's resurrection as a moment in God's reconciling work. Barth's fullest treatment of the doctrine of resurrection will wait for the next part volume, Jesus Christ, the Royal Man. But here we see Barth take up the *locus* of resurrection under the idiom principally of juridical action: God the Father in the resurrection of Jesus Christ from the dead declares his verdict on the obedient Son, that Christ is our righteous Savior. We see the continuity to be sure with Barth's early treatment in volume I/2, especially in the christological *telos* of the doctrine. But the differences are instructive.

Here we are asked to consider how the victory won on Golgotha can be in fact as well as in truth, our own deliverance. We are asked to see both epistemically and metaphysically — noetically and ontically, as Barth puts it — that we are grasped, transferred from the kingdom of darkness to the kingdom of God's beloved Son. Holy Scripture relates the inescapable and irreplaceable history of the Son into the Far Country, telling the acts of this High Priest and Judge who called disciples, taught and healed, underwent temptation; then entered into his final temptation and torment, alone, utterly alone. The detailed analysis Barth gives of this singular narrative involves a renewed interest in the nineteenth-century radical critics, with Gotthold Lessing taking center stage, and the dialectical pairs, faith and history, outfitting themselves once again for battle.

All very familiar — yet with a fresh eye, not familiar at all! Barth will take the problem of the historical reliability of the text of Scripture — Lessing's famous "ugly ditch" spread between the contingent and necessary truths of the faith — and refuse to allow this nineteenth-century methodological crisis to take the upper hand. Indeed, Barth's treatment of Lessing is almost dismissive (more of that in a bit) and Barth's focus almost entirely metaphysical — that is, ontologically real — with only side glances at the wrenching conceptual struggles about the structure and warrant of true Christian belief. Barth is at his most dazzling here in his treatment of time and eternity; and despite this theme's famed abstractions, his analysis is fully concrete, earthbound, and particular. This is Barth's fully matured doctrine of Scripture, and I think it is here that we will see the doctrine of Inspiration not mentioned but *used*, demonstrated as a reliable and revolutionary force in doctrine and life.

Here is Barth on Lessing:

> How can that which has happened once, even if it did happen for us, be recognized today as having happened for us, seeing it does not happen today? . . .
>
> Put in this way, the problem is identical with one which was widely treated in the first decade of this century — the problem of faith and history. . . .
>
> In substance it is identical with Lessing's question concerning the relationship between the contingent truths of history and the necessary truths of reason. . . . It has the form of the problem of the historical dis-

tance between the being and activity of Jesus Christ in its own place and our being and activity in a different place. That there is this distance cannot be denied. . . .

But what is the mediation in which recollection becomes presence, indirect speech direct, history present-day event, the *Christus pro nobis tunc* [Christ for us then] and the *Christus pro nobis nunc* [Christ for us now], the Christ who meets us, the Christ who is our Savior not only as he is known and remembered historically but as he himself saves us today? The genuineness of this question cannot be disputed. (IV/1, 287, 288)

The echo of Barth's own question in volume I/2 is not, I think, unintended: we are now in fact revisiting the field once so carefully turned over by the young Barth. But now his own dogmatic distance from the "problem of faith and history" gives him a longer view: he now sees that there is another step that must be taken. Barth again:

How can we arrive at the perception (grounded in the being of Jesus Christ as the Lord who became a servant, and in his action as the Judge judged for us) that Jesus Christ belongs to us and we belong to him, that his cause *(Sache)* is our cause and our cause is his? We have already seen how this question arises and why it is so acute. Not in the fact of a temporal gulf between Jesus Christ and us, and the need to bridge it. This is one aspect of it, the aspect in Lessing's question. But on this aspect the difficulty is purely conceptual and can be overcome. We have seen that a concern for this difficulty is a movement of flight in an attempt to evade the real kernel of the question which arises in this context.

The kernel of the question is simply the incompatibility of the existence of Jesus Christ with us and us with him, the impossibility of the co-existence of his divine-human actuality and action and our sinfully human being and activity, the direct collision between supreme order and supreme disorder which we perceive when we start with the fact that our contemporaneity with him has been made possible in the most radical form — and not merely by the device of a concept of time which enables us to accept it. (IV/1, 348)

The tone as well as content is striking here. Barth holds that the higher-critical problem that demanded so much of his time and his generation's conceals a deeper, ontological crisis: that Christ as the Risen Lord is indeed the *Christus praesens* in our time and place, and we cannot abide the day of his coming. In this section Barth includes his customary string of questions, both rhetorical and dogmatic: Would it not be easier for us to think of Scripture as a riddle, a puzzle that absorbs our full conceptual powers, so that the distance we see in a historical text can be reinforced by our philosophical attempts to overcome it? He concludes with characteristic verve:

> The genuineness of Lessing's question cannot be disputed in that it springs from a very genuine need: the need to hide ourselves (like Adam and Eve in the garden of Eden) from Jesus Christ as he makes himself present and mediates himself to us; the need to keep our eyes closed at that about which we ask with such solemn concern, taking ourselves and our "honesty" [*Wahrhaftigkeit*] with such frightful seriousness; the need to safeguard ourselves as far as this movement of flight allows against the directness [*Unmittelbarkeit*] in which he does in fact confront us, against his presence and the consequences which it threatens. (IV/1, 292)

This is an *ad hominen* argument of the highest, dogmatic order. Barth has now replaced the dialectical, conceptual pairs of faith and history, eternity and time, with the christological and anthropological spheres, a metaphysical, realist pair grounded in Christ's person and work alone. In the passion, Scripture relates the facing and bearing of the final temptation — to refuse to be the obedient Son — in the garden of Gethsemane and the triumph over that testing in the cross, where fallen humanity truly comes to an end. Detailed exegetical work on the temptation narratives in Luke replaces the more abstract and generalized treatment of Scripture in the first volume, and the stark event-centered doctrine of Inspiration of volume I with a thoroughgoing confidence in the particular shape, sequence, and wording of the scriptural text and its christological referent.

The linchpin in Barth's later treatment is the exegesis and doctrine of Christ's resurrection from the dead. Here Barth understands the resurrection as the objective, concrete act of the Father: a divine "disposing, action and decision" — to borrow volume I's Spiritual language — to act when all creaturely actions are impossible. Like the virgin birth, the resurrection of Jesus is a historical event where the initiative and control of creaturely, historical agents are ruled out, and the divine agency manifested. Note here that the earlier categories of revelation are now made ontological and concrete: the event of disclosure is now the irruption of Christ's resurrection from the land of the dead. Not the actualist event of the Spirit's speaking but rather the presence of the Risen Lord is the mediation of God's reality with ours. Not a punctiliar moment of revelation in the midst of recollection and expectation, but rather the extended, temporal presence of Christ as Lord of his community, is the Word effective in human words. Barth's handling of the gospel narratives of resurrection shows how the christological content has come to dictate Barth's analysis of the form.

Christ's resurrection is told in a form determined by its content: it takes the shape of "saga" or "legend," or better, "prehistory." Barth encourages us not to shy away from the oddness of these accounts. Far from showing that we have now entered the realm of the visionary or mythological, the distinctive and alien form of the resurrection accounts demonstrate that they witness to a unique, transcendent fact. They are reliable accounts because they exhibit the form human words must take when they are addressed to and by a Divine Verdict. They exhibit, that is, the startling and threatening power of Christ's transcendent Lordship not against or beyond time, but *in it*. In Barth's idiom, the resurrection narratives in the Gospels are reliable depictions because they conform themselves to an Other Side made manifest on our side:

> Christ made known to the apostles this side of his (and their death) wholly in the light of the other side, and therefore he made known to them the other side, his (and their life) beyond, wholly in terms of this side, even as spoken in his resurrection from the dead, as the Yes of God to him (and therefore to them and to all men) concealed first under the No of his (and their) death. (IV/1, 352)

This manifestation is not an abstraction — a mediation of Eternity immanent with time — but rather a singular, concrete life, exhibited under the familiar habits of everyday life, eating and drinking, walking on the way, blessing, commanding, and teaching. This very life is the union of past and present, time and Eternity, contingency and necessity; this very life is the basis for the witness of the apostles and the basis of their testimony.

To understand the deepening of Barth's doctrine of Inspiration we have to reflect on this remarkable dogmatic and exegetical phrase: the Beyond made known wholly in terms of This Side. The "line of death," so menacingly prominent in the Romans commentary, still goes to work here: Christ demonstrates his life beyond death to those who can only have it still before them. The epistemic barrier, so prominent in volume I, still remains in place: we cannot know by our own powers our own death or the life that may stand on the other side. Yet these limits and boundaries do not now lead to a conceptual or dialectical resolution — this is now so much play with puzzles — nor is the chief dilemma the Kantian problem of noumenal transcendence or the higher critic's problem of historical uncertainty. Rather, Barth here sees the fundamental struggle in the fallen creature's flight from Christ's gracious and sovereign rule, and the fundamental ontological crisis of the presence of such a Lord in such a fallen world.

As in volume I, Barth affirms that these dilemmas can be overcome only by God and his in-breaking into the human word and world. But here, that Divine agency is not a moment but a whole life, Christ's risen life in which the words, actions, history, and conditions of creaturely reality are transformed to bear witness to Christ's life beyond the cross and grave. Christ himself is the "coinherence" of word and Word, the stable, available, and present Object to his community, the community where he is Lord. Holy Scripture is the record of those witnesses who have been called, commissioned, and instructed by the Present Christ. The goal of the doctrine of Inspiration cannot end now in proper reading, however faithful or attentive or confident; the goal rather is to be sent as were once the first disciples to speak these words about Christ's past because in them, his present Life — astonishing as it is! — abides with us, to chasten and to save.

3. Postcritical Scriptural Interpretation: Rudolf Smend on Karl Barth

George Hunsinger

I

An essay by Rudolf Smend titled "Postcritical Scriptural Interpretation," on how Karl Barth interpreted Scripture, has become a landmark in its field. Although it appeared nearly fifty years ago in a volume of essays written for Barth's eightieth birthday, it has stood the test of time.[1] I myself remember very vividly how Hans Frei once pulled that hefty *Festschrift* down from his shelf and opened it to Smend's contribution. He would later put into writing what he told me then, namely, that "it is a superb piece of work." It is, Frei remarked, "the best thing that I know of on Barth and historical criticism."[2]

When Smend wrote in 1966, he was just starting out as a young professor. Having studied at Tübingen, Göttingen, and Basel, he had completed his doctorate in Old Testament under Walter Baumgartner and then his habilitation thesis under Martin Noth. Nearly three decades later, toward the end of a distinguished career, he would return to his early interest, writing two more pieces on Barth's use of Scripture.[3] Since they do not substantially change the original picture that Smend painted, only his ini-

1. Rudolf Smend, "Nachkritische Schriftauslegung," in *Parrhesia: Karl Barth zum 80. Geburtstag am 10. Mai 1966,* ed. Eberhard Busch, Jürgen Fangmeier, and Max Geiger (Zürich: EVZ, 1966), pp. 215-37. Hereafter cited in the text as NS.

2. Frei in this volume, p. 54.

3. Smend, "Karl Barth als Ausleger der Heiligen Schrift," in *Epochen der Bibelkritik: Gesammelte Studien,* vol. 3 (Munich: Chr. Kaiser, 1991), pp. 216-46; Smend, "Der Exeget und der Dogmatiker: Anhand des Briefwechsels zwischen W. Baumgartner und K. Barth," in *Karl Barths Schriftauslegung,* ed. M. Trowitsch (Tübingen: J. C. B. Mohr, 1996), pp. 53-72.

tial essay will be examined here.[4] What gives it much of its power is not only its thorough acquaintance with Barth's writings, but also its having been written by a respected specialist in the history of modern biblical scholarship.

Smend begins by observing that although dogmatics is a different enterprise from biblical theology, Barth always intended his dogmatics to be "biblical." For him that meant adopting an essentially "biblical attitude." He sought to incorporate the "thought form" found in the Bible's witness to divine revelation (I/2, 816-22; cf. IV/3, 92-93). In fact, it has been estimated that the Index volume to Barth's great dogmatics includes roughly 15,000 biblical references and more than 2,000 instances of exegetical discussion.[5] Smend suggests that Barth fulfilled his project. "No theology was more biblical in sensibility than his" (NS, 215).

As a technical biblical scholar, Smend is aware that Barth's exegesis was not always flawless. "He certainly did his own brand of exegesis, and anyone who so desires can find any number of individual errors, but that does not detract from his monumental achievement" (NS, 215). Barth never regarded engaging with Scripture as something superfluous. He continually strove to let the sources speak on their own terms. "Who can say with confidence," asks Smend, "that Barth, despite his shortcomings, did not understand Paul (or Overbeck, or Mozart, or Anselm) more profoundly than many trained specialists?" (NS, 215). Although Barth may have been a dedicated amateur in some ways, he was often more insightful than card-carrying members of the exegetical guild.

Smend reviews the now-familiar debates between the early Barth and professional exegetes, like Jülicher and Schlatter, at the time of his Romans commentaries.[6] "He was not interested in narrow historicism," writes

---

4. In *Karl Barth: A Theological Legacy* (Philadelphia: Westminster, 1986), Eberhard Jüngel reports that Barth "firmly rejected" Smend's term "postcritical" because he regarded himself as having been a critical theologian all his life. Jüngel, who states that Barth did not quite understand what Smend was getting at, offers the term "metacritical" instead (pp. 73-74). In response to Barth and Jüngel, Smend would later lightly modify his terminology (though not his point) by suggesting that Barth's views showed a combination of "critical," "postcritical," and at times even "anti-critical" elements. See Smend, "Karl Barth als Ausleger der Heiligen Schrift," pp. 242-43, 246.

5. James A. Wharton, "Karl Barth and His Influence on Biblical Interpretation," *Union Seminary Quarterly Review* 28 (1972): 5-13; on p. 6.

6. See now especially Richard E. Burnett, *Karl Barth's Theological Exegesis: The Hermeneutical Principles of the Römerbrief Period* (Tübingen: J. C. B. Mohr, 2001). Contemporary critical responses, including Jülicher and Schlatter, may be found in *The Beginnings*

Smend, "but in the actual subject matter common to both Paul and the reader" (NS, 216). As far as Barth was concerned, the biblical scholars never got around to this all-important question. Instead they were content to break off after establishing and classifying merely what the text said. They failed to grapple with that which, for Barth, stood outside the limits of modern critical method:

> Applying criticism *(krinein)* to historical documents means, to me, measuring the words and phrases against the subject matter about which (if appearances do not deceive) they are inquiring. When documents contain answers to questions, then they need to be examined in relation to questions they are actually asking, and not to some other questions. Proper exegesis finally presses beyond the many questions to the one basic question by which they are all embraced.[7]

In this spirit Barth famously strove to unearth "the Word within the words." That, for him, was the essence of "critical theology." He therefore declared: "The historical critics need to be more critical!" If so, they would become, he continued, "more truly *historical*."[8] They would understand the Bible "as it understands itself, and indeed in the only way that it can be understood."[9] p 53

In these early remarks, as Smend rightly points out, the hermeneutic is already emerging that would guide Barth's later *Church Dogmatics*. It is not this hermeneutic, however, that mainly claims Smend's attention. He rather concentrates on the relationship between theological exegesis and modern criticism. He is interested in showing how Barth's practice of biblical interpretation at once affirmed historical-critical exegesis while also moving beyond it. To borrow a distinction used later by Barth, three phases were at stake here: *explicatio, meditatio,* and *applicatio. Explicatio* (technical exegesis) was essential but not enough. It needed to be supplemented and completed by *meditatio* (theological reflection) and *applicatio* (the consider-

of Dialectical Theology, ed. James M. Robinson (Richmond, VA: John Knox Press, 1962), pp. 61-130.

7. Karl Barth, *The Epistle to the Romans* (London: Oxford University Press, 1933), p. 8 rev.

8. Barth, *The Epistle to the Romans,* p. 8 rev. "Barth's problem with those who accused him of not taking historical criticism seriously enough . . . was that they had not yet taken the freedom of the Bible's subject matter seriously enough" (Burnett, *Theological Exegesis,* p. 241).

9. Barth, *The Word of God and the Word of Man* (New York: Harper, 1957), p. 53 rev.

ation of practical relevance) (I/2, 713-14, 722-40, 870-84, esp. p. 884).[10] Without *meditatio* and *applicatio, explicatio* was like a head without a torso.

It is a matter of some importance that in interpreting Scripture Barth never rejected modern critical methods. It was just that he did not place full weight on them. Beyond a certain point, they were not sufficient for the questions he found most pressing. Did this stance mean that Barth's approach to exegesis was merely naïve?

Although many commentators have thought so, the burden of Smend's essay is to show why this perception is not borne out. Barth's position, he contends, was certainly not naïve "in any vulgar sense" (NS, 218). Nevertheless, it was indeed "naïve" in a different, more sophisticated way. In a crucial passage Barth himself used the term "naïve" to differentiate two different eras of biblical interpretation, the one prior to historical criticism and the other after it (IV/2, 478-79). Before the advent of criticism the Scriptures were still read in a naïve fashion. Historical criticism would destroy this naïveté, though not in every respect. A postcritical stage would emerge in which the Scriptures could again be read naïvely. Barth's way of interpreting Scripture, Smend argues, represented precisely this "postcritical" possibility. It was not as though Barth had no conception of the second stage and was still operating merely in the first. On principled grounds, postcritical exegesis strove to put criticism to a certain degree behind it. It had passed through the fires of criticism while moving on to another level. At first glance "postcritical exegesis" might seem like just a slogan. But everything depends on what "criticism" means. To what extent, if any, could the results of modern criticism be transcended? In what sense might this criticism be limited in scope rather than all-encompassing (NS, 218-19)?

II

Barth believed in the necessity of historical criticism, because of Scripture's full humanity.

> The requirement that one must read, understand, and interpret the Bible *historically* is justified in its own right, and cannot be taken too seri-

---

10. Barth did not think of *explicatio, meditatio,* and *applicatio* merely as stages in a linear sequence, but as standing in a dialectical relationship in which they mutually circled back on and fructified one another.

ously. The Bible itself sets this requirement. At every point, even as it involves divine authority and inspiration, it is always a human word, which needs to be read, understood, and interpreted seriously as such. Any other approach would overlook the humanness of the Bible, and therefore the Bible as testimony to revelation. The imperative to understand the Bible "historically" means that it must be taken for what it obviously is and intends to be, namely, human speech as it arose from a certain people, at certain times, in certain places, in a certain language, and with a certain intention. Its interpretation must be informed by all the circumstances connected with it. (I/2, 464 rev.)

Historical-critical exegesis not only took the historical context into account, but also did justice to the humanity of the biblical writers. In this regard it was both commendable and indispensable.

At this point Smend introduces a distinction among three different types of hermeneutics. He associates the "grammatical-historical" method with Ernesti and Semler, the "grammatical-psychological" method with Schleiermacher, and, interestingly, the "*literary*-historical or literary-*historical*" method with Barth (NS, 220). Here Smend is astute to point out the "literary" aspect of Barth's exegesis. Reminiscent, perhaps, of someone like the English literary critic Frank Kermode, Barth often gleans his insights by paying close attention to the direct wording and literary structure of the texts. Smend's term "literary-*historical*," however, does not quite seem to strike the right note. Barth's anti-historicist impulses meant that he needed to work with a more complex notion of "history" than the one commonly presupposed by modern exegetes, a notion that could respect modern criticism while still making room for God. The term "literary-*theological*," or perhaps "literary-*narratological*" (or both), might therefore be closer to the mark.

Without introducing the idea of the "miraculous," though that is really what is at stake here, Smend notes that modern criticism sought to show that events as depicted in the Bible were impossible to the extent that they could be critically reconstructed. Furthermore, modern criticism dealt drastically with the fundamental contradiction between the biblical view of historical possibility and the modern one. Biblical events were systematically redescribed as occurrences that would fit within a modern, nonmiraculous understanding of historical possibility. This procedure seemed self-evident and beyond serious doubt.

Barth, however, would call this procedure into question. He worried that modern hermeneutics held to "a certain preconceived picture" of the "historical process as a whole" and of what might be possible or impossible within it (I/2, 725). It was this preconceived picture that he was prepared to challenge.

> [Modern or general hermeneutics] thinks it has a basic knowledge of what is generally possible, of what can have happened, and from this point of view it assesses the statement of the text, and the picture of the object reflected in it as the picture of a real, or unreal, or doubtful happening. It is surely plain that at this point an alien factor is exercising a disturbing influence upon observation. (I/2, 727)

The strange world of the Bible, Barth urged, should not be dismissed out of hand.

> Strict observation obviously requires that the force of a picture meeting us in a text shall exercise its due effect in accordance with its intrinsic character, that it shall itself decide what real facts are appropriate to it, that absolutely no prejudgment shall be made, and that it shall not be a foregone conclusion what is possible. If general hermeneutics does, in fact, hold this different point of view and work with a conception of what is generally possible as the limit which will be self-evidently presupposed for what can really have happened, it has to be said that this point of view is by no means inevitable and is not required by the essential character of hermeneutics. Biblical hermeneutics is not guilty of an arbitrary exception when it takes a different line. On the contrary, it follows the path of strict observation to the very end. Certainly, it does this because of its own definite presupposition. But it is to be noted that this presupposition does enable it to be consistent as hermeneutics. The same cannot be said of the presupposition of general hermeneutics. (I/2, 725)

Everything depended, Barth concluded, on "fidelity in all circumstances to the object reflected in the words of the prophets and apostles" (I/2, 725). Modernity may have called that object into question, with its strange and miraculous elements, but by the same token it must be prepared to be called into question by the singularity of that very object. Barth's commitment to that object yielded a distinctive way of reading Scripture, but the commitment of historical critics to naturalism did too. The simple point is that both were committed, but to different premises.

Smend, for his part, observes that historical criticism was not merely "negative" or debunking, as has sometimes been supposed. It also strove for a new kind of "positive" synthesis (NS, 220-21). It attempted to place the parts dissected by historical analysis into a new comprehensive whole that would stand up to criticism. In an age governed by historicism, this whole had to be one of critical history. In the process (and according to Smend this was crucial) literary analysis came to be eclipsed by efforts at historical reconstruction. Exegesis became the handmaid of historicism. The goal of modern criticism became that of reconstructing the cultural, religious, and literary history of Israel and earliest Christianity. Hans Frei would later describe this historicizing process as being obsessed with an interest in "ostensive reference" at the expense of a more literary-theological interest in biblical narrative. Little or no attention was devoted to narrative depictions of divine or human personal identities.[11]

According to Barth, the historicist reconstructions of modernity were then laid before the church with the words, "These are your gods, O Israel!" (I/2, 493 rev.). Smend allows that Barth was not entirely wrong (NS, 221). Reconstructed historical truth was the conspicuous (and often the only) result of modern biblical criticism, whether negative or positive. Nonmiraculous reconstructions were simply considered good form among the exegetes, and it should be remembered that for the most part they saw their work as theologically neutral. Modern faith and theology operated, on all fronts, within the bounds of the evidence as established by the rules of critical historical investigation. Apologetic arguments could then, in fact, be developed either way. Some would appeal to the results of modern criticism to support traditional theological views, while others would push them in the direction of skepticism and humanism. The question loomed all the more urgently, however, about whether theological exegesis and religious significance could be squared with a historical-critical approach to the Bible.

III

Radical scholarship had called into question the Bible's historical reliability. Two brilliant works in particular, as singled out by Smend, towered

---

11. Hans W. Frei, *The Eclipse of Biblical Narrative: A Study in Eighteenth and Nineteenth Century Hermeneutics* (New Haven: Yale University Press, 1974). It is not impossible that Frei's thesis about the importance of biblical narrative was influenced to some extent by Smend.

above the rest: W. M. L. de Wette's *Criticism of Mosaic History* (1806),[12] and D. F. Strauss's first edition of *The Life of Jesus* (1835).[13] De Wette and Strauss did not deny that actual events stood behind the stories of Moses and the Gospels. They simply rejected the idea that these events could be retrieved by critical historical methods. They believed it was impossible to reconstruct the history of either Moses or Jesus by these means. (It is note-worthy that on this point, at least, Barth would more or less agree with them: there were actual events behind the stories of Moses and Jesus, he believed, that modern criticism could not retrieve.) With such negative re-sults, historical criticism had done everything it could and ground to a halt (NS, 222-23).

It was De Wette's insight that the biblical writers were not merely inca-pable of writing history in the modern sense. More to the point, they had no intention of doing so.[14] What they really wanted was to portray God's action in the world in a way that would awaken faith. As De Wette argued, they were not concerned with history but with religion. The genre of the stories would be misunderstood if they were classified as historical reports. The overall effect of De Wette's analysis, however, was to cast doubt not only upon the stories' historicity, but also upon their religious views, as well as upon any modern hermeneutic that hoped to find religious mean-ing in them (NS, 223).

More recently, Smend observes, Old and New Testament studies have traveled much farther in this direction. They have come to ask about the religious interest behind every biblical text, and they have grown accus-tomed to dealing with historical questions only in this context. The idea that the oldest stratum would be the one most free of theological tenden-cies, and thus the most historically reliable, was found to have little basis in reality, whether for the Old Testament or the New. It became increasingly clear that from the very outset everything was told from a religious or theological point of view. By and large, in both Israel and earliest Chris-tianity, the biblical texts were always shaped by interests of worship,

---

12. W. M. L. De Wette, *Kritischer Versuch über die Glaubwürdigkeit der Bücher der Chronik mit Hinsicht auf die Geschichte der Mosaischen Bücher und Gesetzgebung: Ein Nachtrag zu den Vaterschen Untersuchungen über den Pentateuch* (Halle: Schimmelpfennig, 1806).

13. David Friedrich Strauss, *Leben Jesu, kritisch bearbeitet* (Tübingen: C. F. Osiander, 1835).

14. See Rudolf Smend, *W. M. L. de Wettes Arbeit am Alten und am Neuen Testament* (Basel: Helbing & Lichtenhahn, 1957), pp. 20ff. and 50ff.

preaching, and mission. The biblical texts were kerygmatic in character all the way down. That is precisely why they were spoken, sung, written down, transmitted, edited, and canonized (NS, 223).

"The appropriate use for them today (assuming that the communities then and now are roughly equivalent in character)," Smend suggests, "would involve the corresponding communal practices as well as the kind of theology written with such practices in mind" (NS, 223-24). At this point Smend resorts to the idea of witness. "The texts would thus be respected for their intention of bearing witness to God's actions with his people. They would be heard, understood, and interpreted not on the basis of an alien standpoint, but in terms of their own immediate subject matter" (NS, 224). However important and valid this point may be, it is still unclear how Smend would regard the relationship between "God's actions with his people" and actual historical events. Nor is it ever quite made clear how this relationship was understood by Barth. This omission is curious given its centrality to the theme of the essay.

Barth typically saw this relationship — namely, that between biblical texts and their extratextual referents — as being a matter of analogy.[15] He could allow, for example, that biblical narratives about Moses or Jesus involved legendary or fiction-like elements while still holding that they were not entirely fictional. He regarded them as sufficiently grounded in fact, even if the factual element was not accessible — as De Wette and Strauss also believed — to historical criticism. Barth differed from historical-critical skeptics, however, by not automatically discounting the existence of the miraculous at the factual level. How he did so is a complicated matter that can only be touched upon here. For Barth the heart of the matter, however, was that divine revelation itself — as grounded, centered, and fulfilled in Christ — was inherently miraculous by definition.[16] And that is the main reason why he assumed that the stories are sufficiently grounded in fact.

Biblical narratives that depicted miraculous occurrences could be sig-

---

15. See George Hunsinger, "Beyond Literalism and Expressivism: Karl Barth's Hermeneutical Realism," in *Disruptive Grace: Studies in the Theology of Karl Barth* (Grand Rapids: Eerdmans, 2000), pp. 210-25.

16. Barth defined "miracle" as follows: "the special new direct act of God in time and in history. In the form in which it acquires temporal historical actuality, biblically attested revelation is always a miracle, and therefore the witness to it, whether direct or indirect in its course, is a narrative of miracles that happened. Miracle is thus an attribute of revelation" (I/2, pp. 63-64).

nificantly legendary while still corresponding to some degree either to events as they had actually happened or else at least to the ultimate referent of those events as found in Christ himself (or, more usually, in some way to both). For example, the raising of Lazarus or of Jairus's daughter, as depicted in the Gospels, would be seen, on this view, as involving a kind of double referent. Although something analogous to what these stories depict would have occurred at the factual level, what they refer to and attest is, ultimately, the raising of Christ. The lesser miracles, though not unimportant in their own right, would be seen as enacted parables of the one great miracle, which is Jesus Christ, Incarnate and Risen. On a case-by-case basis, the Gospel miracle stories could be allowed to have varying degrees of factual veracity (all the way, say, from very little to rather great) while still referring, taken as a whole, to the one great miracle of Christ. The various miracle stories would stand in an analogous factual relationship to what they immediately depict as well as to what they ultimately attest. What makes it possible to give this kind of measured, sophisticated credence to the Gospel stories is faith in the Risen and Incarnate Christ. If the Great Miracle stands, then the lesser miracles, and the stories that depict them, have their place. While occasionally gesturing in this direction, Smend never quite brings this aspect of Barth's thought into focus.

Drawing from De Wette's work, on which he is an acknowledged expert, Smend regards the kerygmatic nature of the biblical texts as an opening for theological exegesis (NS, 224). When the biblical writers are taken seriously on their own terms, exegesis is properly theological. Smend cites from Barth:

> But when we do take the humanity of the Bible quite seriously, we must also take quite definitely the fact that as a human word it does say something specific, that as a human word it points away from itself, that as a word it points towards a fact, an object. In this respect, too, it is a genuine human word. What human word is there which does not do the same? We do not speak for the sake of speaking, but for the sake of the indication which is to be made by our speaking. We speak for the sake of what we denote or intend by our speaking. (I/2, 464)

The biblical text was to be respected, by contrast to a kind of

> hearing in which attention is paid to the biblical formulations but not to what the words signify. In this sort of listening, what is said by the

texts is not heard or overheard. The words are interpreted merely in terms of their immanent linguistic and historical context, as opposed to what they say, and what we hear them say, in and beyond this context. The result is an exposition of the biblical words that in the last resort consists only in an exposition of the biblical authors in their historical reality. (I/2, 466 rev.)

Given the validity of historical-critical exegesis, Smend suggests, modern criticism had to develop into theological exegesis if it did not wish to remain incomplete. Between historical and theological exegesis, no final opposition could remain.

According to Smend, De Wette attempted to carry through a critical understanding of the Old Testament by pursuing this kind of exegesis (NS, 224). De Wette wanted to develop a line of criticism that would make itself superfluous. With energy and radicality, he pressed relentlessly toward completing the critical task in this way. "In the critical investigations of modern biblical scholars," Smend quotes De Wette as writing, "numerous historical sources have been disputed with regard to their immediate authenticity and credibility. But a complete, thoroughgoing criticism would show that not a single historical work of the Old Testament has any historical value to it."[17] Criticism as such should stop with this negative judgment. "Any positive thing that it might suggest could only be precarious."[18] But this conclusion cleared the way for something else. "If we were to toss all the historical materials together at random, mixing together the early and the late, the historical and the mythological," De Wette wrote, "then, above the confusion, the spirit of religion would rise up and soar, unspoiled, clear and pure, disclosing itself to worthy eyes."[19]

Observing that Barth shared something of the same radical, critical views as De Wette, Smend draws a remarkable conclusion:

The true follower of De Wette as a theological exegete was not Julius Wellhausen, but Karl Barth.[20] Wellhausen, for his part, renewed De

---

17. De Wette, *Aufforderung zum Studium der hebräischen Sprache und Literatur* (Jena/Leipzig: Gabler, 1805), p. 28.

18. De Wette, *Aufforderung zum Studium*, p. 32.

19. De Wette, *Aufforderung zum Studium*, p. 31.

20. A comment perhaps equally as striking as this one about Barth and Wellhausen had been made forty years earlier by Rudolf Bultmann: "By 1926 . . . Bultmann was . . . comparing the significance of Barth's accomplishment in the field of theological exegesis to that of

Wette's negative criticism, making it the starting point for a positive reconstruction of ancient Israel's history. De Wette might even have agreed with the results. In any case, with respect to the lineage of Old Testament criticism, Wellhausen (by way of Vatka) was the true successor of De Wette, just as in New Testament criticism Baur was the successor of Strauss.[21] But this was not so in theology. Karl Barth believed that modern criticism did not fully appreciate what its radical results had accomplished.[22] However, that was not entirely true of the young De Wette. Although he was consciously a figure of the second phase of exegesis, in which one could no longer remain naïve, he wanted to plunge headlong into the third, post-critical phase. He anticipated the kind of exegesis that Barth would actually practice a hundred years later. But even if he had carried it out himself, he would not have done it in the same way as Barth. In any case, a key presupposition for them both — regardless of the great differences in their cultural and intellectual milieux — was that verifiable history as such no longer had to function as the supreme norm. In the view of Rudolf Bultmann, who was not far from Barth at this point, the Christian message or kerygma was not something that could be validated by historical criticism. (NS, 225)

From this point of view, theology would be immunized against historical criticism, so as no longer to be undermined by it. It could then go about its proper business of interpreting Scripture (NS, 226).

Modern criticism serves faith best, Barth believed, when it kicks away a prop that is no prop at all.

> Critical historical study signifies the deserved and necessary end of the "foundations" of this knowledge which are not really foundations, because they were not laid by God himself. He who still does not know (and we all still do not know it) that we no longer know Christ accord-

---

F. C. Baur's in the field of historical exegesis. . . . Because of Barth's contribution to our understanding of the exegetical task, Bultmann declared: 'we stand at a new beginning'" (Burnett, *Theological Exegesis*, pp. 93-94). To this, we may add the remark of Gerhard von Rad on the occasion of Barth's death in 1968: "What a miracle that one should appear among us who did nothing else than to take God at his Word" (quoted by Smend, "Karl Barth als Ausleger," p. 216).

21. Cf. Smend, "De Wette und das Verhältnis zwischen historischer Bibelkritik und philosophischem System in 19. Jahrhundert, *Theologische Zeitschrift* 14 (1958): 107-19; on pp. 112-13.

22. See Robinson, ed., *Beginnings of Dialectical Theology,* p. 180.

ing to the flesh may let himself be told this by critical biblical scholarship; the more radically he is terrified, the better it is for him and for the subject matter. And this may well be the service that "historical knowledge" can render the real task of theology.[23]

Here knowing is a certain non-knowing, and the most radical biblical scholarship is a useful negative discipline (NS, 227). Again, Barth:

The theology of the Reformation did not need this negative discipline because it still had the courage *not* to avoid the offense of revelation and therefore did not raise at all the question of a historically knowable middle point of the gospel. *We need* it because in our flight from the offense we have fallen into this impossible question.[24]

The Reformation served as an antidote against all false forms of security that sought a foundation for faith apart from grace.

During the era of De Wette and Strauss, Smend observes, the legendary elements of the texts were carefully distinguished from the historical elements (NS, 228). Since then, the questions have been refined and further discriminations have been made. Along these lines Barth appended an important "hermeneutical note" to his exegesis of the story of Israel's spies (Num. 13-14).

Various elements can be picked out in the story of the spies. There is a "historical" element in the stricter sense (the persons and cities and localities mentioned). An element of saga is evident (the account of the branch of grapes carried by two men, and of the giants who inhabited the land of Canaan). There is also a conflated or composite view (fusing past and present almost into one), which is so distinctive a feature of historical writing in Old and New Testament alike. It is to the latter elements that we must pay particular attention in our reading of these stories if we are to understand them, for they usually give us an indication of the purpose which led to their adoption into the texts. (IV/2, 479 rev.)

As Smend points out, here negative criticism goes behind the text, not to verify but to interpret it (NS, 229).

---

23. Robinson, ed., *Beginnings of Dialectical Theology*, p. 170 rev.
24. Robinson, ed., *Beginnings of Dialectical Theology*, p. 180.

IV

As understood by Barth, the function of biblical criticism was mostly pre-liminary (NS, 233). It pertained to history in the modern sense of the term. It allowed various elements of the texts to be distinguished, whether they be historical, or legendary, or conflations of past and present occurrences. Critical distinctions like these had to be made. But after they were made, wrote Barth, "they can be moved again into the background, and the whole [text] can be read, with this tested, critical naïveté, as the totality it professes to be" (IV/2, 479 rev.).

Historical and non-historical elements flow together at this point (cf. III/1, 80-81). Verifying the miracles historically ceases to be of great importance. What matters is the sort of events being reported: events that are incomparable and mysterious.[25] "The ill-advised hunt for a historical truth *supra scripturam* [prior to Scripture] is called off," wrote Barth, "in favor of an open investigation of the *veritas scripturae ipsius* [the truth of Scripture itself]" (I/2, 494 rev.). What emerges as the sole object of exegesis, from a theological standpoint, is the texts themselves. No other option makes sense if the following is true: "Revelation stands, no, it happens, in the Scriptures," wrote Barth, "and not behind them. It happens. There is no way around this in the biblical texts — in their actual words and sentences — given what the prophets and the apostles, as witnesses to revelation, wanted to say and have said."[26]

Theological exegesis is determined by this picture of the attested events (NS, 234). It tries to respect what it finds in the texts. It operates with a hermeneutic that allows them to correct our ordinary picture of what is and is not possible.

> Scriptural exegesis rests on the assumption that the message which Scripture has to give us, even in its apparently most debatable and least assimilable parts, is in all circumstances truer and more important than

25. Cf. Barth, *Evangelical Theology: An Introduction* (New York: Holt, Rinehart & Winston, 1963), pp. 65-67.

26. Barth, *Christliche Dogmatik* (Munich: Chr. Kaiser, 1927), p. 344. Smend cites this relatively early passage without noting that in I/2 Barth later distinguished more carefully between the "objective" and "subjective" aspects of revelation, namely, revelation as it happened objectively in Christ once for all, and then as it happens in the Spirit subjectively for us again and again. In other words, for the later Barth, what happens through the Scriptures here and now is grounded in what happened apart from us in Christ there and then.

the best and most necessary things that we ourselves have said or can say. In that Scripture is the divinely ordained and authorized witness to revelation, it entails a claim to be interpreted along these lines; and if this claim be not duly heeded, it remains at bottom inexplicable. (I/2, 719 rev.)

Exegesis stands before the necessity of this reorientation, as does faith.

[The Bible] can be received as a witness of revelation only by a human spiritual world whose inner security has been shaken, and whose attitude has become yielding and responsive to the biblical spiritual world. It will then be manifest at once that the spiritual world of the Bible is not itself an unshaken quantity, but a moving, living force existing and functioning in a very definite service. . . . This service consists precisely in the communication of the witness to revelation which is proper, not to our world, but to the Bible and its world. (I/2, 719 rev.)

The complicating factor, by which our spiritual world is shaken, is the immanence of the transcendent God, or more precisely the immediacy of God to history and of history to God.

Not all history is "historical." . . . In its immediacy to God every history is in fact "non-historical." That is, it is underivable and incomparable, and therefore impossible to perceive, comprehend and describe by ordinary means. But that does not mean it ceases to be genuine history. And for this very reason it can only be the object of a "non-historical" . . . depiction and narration. (III/1, 80 rev.)

In addition to the "historical" there has always been a legitimate "non-historical" . . . view of history and its "non-historical" . . . depiction in the form of "saga." (III/1, 81 rev.)

To put it cautiously, [the Bible] contains little pure "history" and little pure "saga," and little of both that can be unequivocally recognized as the one or the other. The two elements are usually mixed. In the Bible we usually have to reckon with both history and saga. (III/1, 82 rev.)[27]

27. "Saga" or legend was a term Barth used over against "myth" and "history." "Myths" were stories that embodied timeless truths while "history" in the historicist sense excluded God on principle from its accounts. "Sagas" or legends, by contrast, were stories about actual, unrepeatable events in which God could be depicted (whether directly or indirectly) as

Smend states that "Barth simply *believed* that history itself is determined by this transcendent dimension, whereby the word 'simply' should not be misunderstood" (NS, 234). In this connection, Smend continues, Barth spoke of the need for exegetical "impartiality." However, as explained above, though left vague by Smend, Barth also believed that legendary elements at the literary level could correspond by way of analogy to miraculous elements at the factual level.

> It must be a consideration of what the texts say (and do not say) as they attest revelation, without measuring them by an imported picture of the world and history, without reading them through these alien spectacles, without prejudice as to what is possible or impossible, good or less good, without prescribing what they have to say and what they cannot say, without imposing questions which they themselves do not ask, but entering into their own questions and remaining open to their own replies, which, if our thinking is to be genuinely "historical," must have precedence over our own attitude (which we naturally reserve). (IV/2, 150 rev.)

"'Historical' knowledge in this impartiality," Barth noted, "can never be simple and self-evident, because none of us is really impartial" (IV/2, 150).

V

From the days of his Romans commentaries on, Barth continually pressed for a reconsideration of what counts as "historical" with respect to the biblical texts. "What modern study has to ascertain as the *historical truth is the true meaning and context of the biblical texts as such*. Therefore it [historical truth] does not differ from the biblical truth that has to be established" (I/2, 494 rev.). Barth was thinking at this point of the biblical texts "in their unity and totality" (IV/2, 479). As Smend rightly notes, "Unity and totality were

---

the central acting subject. On the human side, sagas involved elements of theologically informed intuitions (*Vorstellungen*) as well as imaginative or poetic depictions (*Darstellungen*) of events that were in some sense beyond ordinary depiction. Although grounded in actual occurrences, sagas were not primarily reports, but witnesses to divine revelation. Barth used the term "saga," for lack of a better term, in order to bring out the special literary genre of biblical stories about the world's creation, the Virgin Birth, Christ's resurrection, and other such ineffable occurrences. It represented a kind of critical realism that was unacceptable to historicists for its audacity and to literalists for its reticence.

not merely a question of historical and non-historical elements. The unitary testimony of Scripture consisted in innumerable individual testimonies that became more difficult to bring under a common denominator, the more carefully criticism laid them out" (NS, 234).

Barth did not dispute the existence of contradictions, Smend continued, nor did he regret that they had come to light (NS, 234). The biblical testimony, Barth declared, could never be "sufficiently dissected by historical criticism."[28] Harmonizing exegesis was ruled out. For example, regarding the Yahwist and priestly creation accounts, he wrote:

> Our best course is to accept that each has its own harmony, and then to be content with the higher harmony that is achieved when we allow the one to speak after the other. Hence the second account must be read as if it were the only one. And superfluous though it may seem after reading the first account, the whole problem and theme must be reconsidered from a new angle. (III/1, 229 rev.)

Diversity in the texts held a greater significance for Barth than the problem of historicity. Diversity could not be glossed over by the practice of theological exegesis. "A biblical theology can never consist in more than a series of attempted approximations, a collection of individual exegeses" (I/2, 483).

At this point, Smend develops an interesting comparison between Barth and von Rad. "It is noteworthy," he writes, "that everything we have seen so far corresponds, in its essential intentions, to von Rad's theology of the Old Testament" (NS, 235). Von Rad distinguished between two pictures of Israel's history, the one as depicted by ancient Israel, and the other as reconstructed by modern criticism. For von Rad only the first was the object of theological reflection, although the second remained important for exegesis. But the "object of reflection" — an idea that more or less corresponded with Barth's idea of revelation as the "subject matter" of scriptural witness — was thought to be mediated through a whole range of diverse testimonies. Von Rad argued that these should not be suppressed when the interpreter "re-narrates" them.[29] Otherwise, according to von Rad, they would be "overwhelmed and interrupted" by preconceived ideas.[30] Along these lines Barth and von Rad formed a common front.

28. Robinson, ed., *Beginnings of Dialectic Theology*, p. 178 rev.
29. Gerhard von Rad, *Old Testament Theology*, vol. 1 (New York: Harper, 1962), pp. 123-28.
30. Von Rad, *Theologie des Alten Testaments*, vol. 2 (Munich: Chr. Kaiser, 1969), p. 11. (Omitted from the ET.)

They both wanted the biblical word to be heard without interference and without being mingled with extraneous elements. That was the main point of their respective hermeneutics. The word of the Scripture, Barth maintained, in order to be understood, "wants not to be mastered by us, but to lay hold of us" (I/1, 471 rev.).

As Smend points out, Barth and von Rad both paid considerable attention to how Scripture could be construed as a unity in the midst of its very real diversity (NS, 235). For von Rad, Israel's unity was something to be affirmed, as long as it was recognized that this affirmation was a *credendum,* in other words, an article of faith. It was a unity that von Rad felt became visible only "in the interval between a promise and a fulfillment."[31] He found it much harder to speak about a "midpoint," or unifying center, for the Old Testament than for the New.[32] No such "midpoint," von Rad argued, was to be found. Barth's views were not far from this position. He, too, could find no single concept or principle that would unify the diversity of Scripture. What the biblical texts ultimately attested, he argued, was not a concept but "revelation."

> Now revelation is no more and no less than the life of God himself turned to us, the Word of God coming to us by the Holy Spirit, Jesus Christ. But in our thinking — even in our reflection on the biblical texts — it is only improperly, i.e., only in the form of our recollection and expectation, that we can "presuppose" Jesus Christ and then add to this presupposition other thoughts, even those which derive from our exposition of the texts. (I/2, 483 rev.)

Not being a principle, revelation did not stand at human disposal. It was not merely an idea in a conceptual scheme (NS, 236). "Even the biblical witnesses themselves cannot and do not try to introduce revelation of themselves. They show themselves to be true witnesses in that they speak of revelation only by looking forward to it and looking back at it" (I/2, 483 rev.). Likewise, theological exegesis could only look backwards and forwards to the living God about whom testimony was given. In that way it refused to silence the witnesses. "How else can we understand their testimony except by going with them into the remembrances, *their* remembrances, and the expectancy, *their* expectancy? Only through a hermeneu-

---

31. Von Rad, "Offene Fragen im Umkreis einer Theologie des Alten Testaments," *Theologische Literaturzeitung* 88 (1963): 401-16; on p. 406.

32. Von Rad, *Old Testament Theology,* vol. 2 (New York: Harper, 1966), p. 362.

tic of openness — and not by some misguided attempt to do what they supposedly failed to do — will our interpretation of their testimony suit the case" (I/2, 484 rev.).

Viewed from the standpoint of faith, diversity pointed to a higher if ineffable harmony — if only by way of unresolved antitheses, which bore witness dialectically to the self-revelation of God in its irreducible mystery and complexity (I/1, 179-81).[33] On this basis Barth rejected all attempts to minimize the diversity of materials within the scope of the canon (I/2, 483). A particularly striking case can be seen in his portrayal of Jesus as the "Royal Man" (in IV/2), which is set forth through a series of numerous conjunctions of opposites. These countervailing tendencies, Barth suggested, represented "how he was seen by the community in which the New Testament arose" (IV/2, 247). Barth intended to follow suit: "And this is how we have been trying to see him, adopting, to the best of our knowledge and conscience, the same standpoint as that from which he was seen in the New Testament" (IV/2, 247-48).

> In order to carry out this project, critical exegesis had to be placed to one side. We have thus refrained (again deliberately) from any critico-historical construction or reconstruction. . . . In so doing we have consciously accepted . . . that the standpoint from which they saw Jesus and told us about him lies beyond the temporal limits of his life; that they saw and attested him in the context of events which took place after his death and which they described as his resurrection and ascension and the impartation of his Holy Spirit to the community. (IV/2, 248)

As Smend points out, Barth was aligning himself with the standpoint of the post-resurrection witnesses as mediated by the New Testament (NS, 236).

> From this standpoint they saw and represented the totality of his life as that of a Royal Man, not with the intention of adding something to the truth of his historical existence, or in any way glossing it over, but with the intention of causing the one and only truth of his historical existence, as it later disclosed itself to them, to shine out in the only way which is at all commensurate with it. We have simply followed them in this. (IV/2, 248 rev.)

---

33. See my discussion in the Introduction to this volume, pp. xv-xix above.

Christ's resurrection, as so attested, was at once hermeneutically indispensable and yet also beyond the scope of critical method.

> Our position in relation to the New Testament, and therefore to Jesus himself, is not one which is adopted in abstraction from his resurrection. We make no attempt to see and understand his life prior to his death as if it were not illuminated and interpreted, as if it were unsatisfactorily or mistakenly interpreted, by what happened after his death, as if we were later free to see and represent it either in this light, in one like it, or in a very different light. Neutrality of this kind is quite illegitimate when it is a matter of expounding the witness to Jesus in the New Testament. . . . This witness may be accepted or it may be rejected. But it must always be heard in the form in which it grew up and by which it stands or falls. (IV/2, 248 rev.)

The identity of Jesus Christ was to be understood in light of his resurrection or not at all, if it was to be understood in light of the apostolic witness.

Smend arrives at his conclusion: Barth's hermeneutic was adopted "not naïvely, but deliberately and consciously" (IV/2, 248). It operated postcritically, in other words, from the standpoint of a "second naïveté." Postcritical interpretation accepted but deliberately relativized not only modern critical findings pertaining to the history of Israel, Jesus, and early Christianity, but also all historicizing approaches to Old and New Testament "introduction." It reconfigured not only "literary-*historical*," but also "*literary*-historical" analysis. The reception of Barth's groundbreaking hermeneutical efforts, whether in agreement or dissent, will be shown less at the level of theory and more at the level of practice. Will biblical interpretation after Barth continue to domesticate and disintegrate the texts, or will it seek to recover the true unity and mystery of its object?[34]

---

34. For a recent discussion of Barth's influence on Old Testament studies, see Mark S. Gignilliat, "Barth and the Renaissance of Old Testament Theology in the Early Twentieth Century," in *Karl Barth and the Fifth Gospel: Barth's Theological Exegesis of Isaiah* (Aldershot, UK: Ashgate, 2009), pp. 1-24. For a survey of the growing interest in theological exegesis, as it arises directly or indirectly under the influence of Barth, see Daniel J. Treier, *Introducing Theological Interpretation of Scripture: Recovering a Christian Practice* (Grand Rapids: Baker Academic, 2008).

4. Scripture as Realistic Narrative: Karl Barth as Critic of Historical Criticism

Hans W. Frei

A Dantesque Vision

I was struck by the theme of the conference this year: *Beyond the Theology of Karl Barth.* It made me wonder just what there is beyond Karl Barth. May I make a moderate proposal?

I think all of you who have found yourself not simply studying Barth but then finding his thought congenial will have noticed how difficult it is not to fall into the same language patterns as Barth, to use the same vocabulary, sometimes even the same kind of syntax; and you will have noticed that it sounds terribly awkward and secondhand when it comes from people other than Karl Barth himself. A friend of mine, a theologian, was asked by a particularly fine student, who is a devoted Lutheran, and who has worked hard on Barth, "If one is simply *not* a Barthian what does one finally learn from Barth?" And my colleague, who is neither a Lutheran nor in any sense a Barthian, thought for a minute and then he said,

> It surely has been a long, long time since anyone has had a comic vision of the world, the sense, that is to say, of a vision of reality which is inherited from the tradition that is so profoundly embodied in Dante's

This lecture was given at the meeting of the Karl Barth Society of North America in Toronto, Spring 1974, and contains Frei's explanation of Barth's hermeneutical procedure and his stance towards historical criticism and factual claims; it also contains a fine description of Barth's Anselmian and Dantesque sensibility. Frei spoke from notes rather than from a full text, but the lecture was taped, and a transcription has been made and edited by Mark Alan Bowald.

Divina Comedia, the sense of reality being in the deepest way a divine comedy.

And it seems to me that this is particularly fitting when one recalls the way in which Barth as a Calvinist was always correcting, and being corrected by, Lutheran colleagues. We remember the Calvinist-Lutheran controversies and discussions that were revived in him — on the *extra Calvinisticum* against the *inter Lutheranum* (that is to say the question of the tension between the transcendence of the Divine Word over its own Incarnation, whether or not there is such a transcendence) or again the relationship between law and gospel, or again the relationship between justification and sanctification. In all these matters, where there really is no right or wrong and no final adjudication (but which are themselves, as Barth would have said, "beautiful problems") Barth proceeded from so different a vision from his Lutheran friends and colleagues, even though, nonetheless, they were in such close contact with each other. The Lutheran finally proceeds always from a *religious* position, that is to say, he finds himself cast into the question of how he as a man under law, a sinner in a regulated world, can find a gracious God and how he can either solve or live fruitfully in the tension between his existence under law and his existence under gospel. How different this is from Karl Barth who, even when he states the same issues, is proceeding from a totally different basis. He is proceeding not from, first of all, a basic situation of a *religious* problematic but a basic affirmation of a *reality.* He finds himself in a real world that everywhere manifests, first in the historical process in which mankind is engaged, but secondly even in nature itself, wherever he looks, the divine grace that emerged in the history of Israel and emerged for all mankind in the crucifixion and the resurrection of Jesus Christ. His basic affirmation is that this is the picture of reality. The real world is to be talked about this way; Barth proceeds from this vision, and whatever problems may arise are problems that arise in reflection on this reality.

Recall that for Barth it was always true that the history of the covenant, that particular history, was paradigmatic. It was almost as if — indeed, one would want to say it *was* as if — that history was the one real history of mankind, and all history (all other history that historiographers, or as the Germans say, "scientific historians," construct; all *Historie* in contrast to *Geschichte,* as Barth himself said) is to be regarded as a figure of that covenant history. All other history is a history in its own right, yes, and to be seen as having its own meaning, yes, but nonetheless, finally, its reality is to be understood as a figure in that one history into which we are — not only as members of secular history but also in our own experience — to include ourselves also, as figures in that one history. All of Barth's theology was the constant sketching out in regard to particular doctrines or particular stages of that one history, this story as the vision of all reality. This was the vision of a *Divina Comedia*.

In the middle of the twentieth century the boldness and daring of that is so enormous and so right and so fitting that one cannot repeat it; one can simply either do something like it oneself, or go one's own way in respectful disagreement. How do you compare, how do you modify basic visions of the world?

And how consistent it was! Do you recall the one aspect of Barth's theology where he showed his consistency most of all? He used a peculiar German term that comes from the early nineteenth century. It comes, as a matter of fact, from Christian Wolff's vocabulary as traced through Kant and then through Hegel: *anschaulich,* or "intuition," which always meant a kind of a concrete preconceptual grasp on the real tactile world. He used that word and with the early Heidegger he gave it a reverse twist, and he suggested that we are to ourselves *unanschaulich.* We really don't, even in our most apparently direct apprehensions of ourselves, have a direct glimpse of ourselves. And do recall that in the tradition not only of Schleiermacher but of all early-nineteenth-century German philosophy one of the basic affirmations was that self-consciousness, direct presence to oneself — either immediately or, for Hegel, in a mediate way — is the essence of selfhood. And recall also that the early Barth, the Barth of the second edition of the commentary on Romans, had suggested that this is *so* true — it is so true that we are directly present to ourselves, directly conscious of ourselves — that it is precisely for that reason that all contact with the divine escapes us. For, in contrast to the liberal theologians, he said, there is no presence of God included in our direct presence to ourselves. The presence of God is precisely the radical other of our presence to ourselves; because we are, for the early Barth, *anschaulich* to ourselves, therefore God is totally *unanschaulich* to us. And recall how gradually first in the *Christian Dogmatics*[1] and then when he scrapped that in the first volume of the *Church Dogmatics* and then, increasingly consistently (I would maintain) from II/1 on, he reversed that picture. The reality of our history with God is so real, it is so much the one real world in which we

---

1. Barth, *Die Christliche Dogmatik im Entwurf* (Zürich: TVZ, 1982).

live, that what is *anschaulich* to us is really that: our life with God — to such an extent that we are not really *anschaulich* to ourselves. We do not know, we do not grasp ourselves.

So consistent was he in this, you see, that he suggested that our very knowledge of ourselves as creatures, but even more our very knowledge of ourselves as sinners (which is, again, the Lutherans' basic experience) is a knowledge, an apprehension, a tactile direct contact that has to be *mediated* to us. We have to learn it, in an almost Wittgensteinian way. (And there is, incidentally I think for me, a lot of relationship, a lot of similarity between the later Wittgenstein and Karl Barth.) We have to learn in an almost Wittgensteinian way how to use the concepts that apply to the way we know ourselves, because the world, the true, real world in which we live — the real world in which the Second World War took place in which Barth was so much engaged, in which the conflict with Nazism took place, in which the conflict or the *adjustment* with Communism took place later — that real world is only a figure of an aspect in that one overall real world in which the covenanted God of grace lives with man.

A Dialectical Relationship to Historical Criticism

That, then, brings me more directly to the thing that I am supposed to talk about. For the early Barth, you see, was the Barth of a radical negative criticism of historical criticism for whom, in line with the unintuitability of God, the *unanschaulich* of God and the *unanschaulich* therefore of the real subject matter of the Bible, the most self-destructive historical criticism was the right kind of historical criticism.

You remember what he said in the first edition? It was (and it is one of the few sayings from the preface of the first edition that I think he held to all his life) that he was happy he did not have to choose between historical criticism and the old doctrine of inspiration, but that if he did he would choose the old doctrine of inspiration. He held to that. He held to that through thick and thin. He felt he did not have to choose. But he also felt that the priority belonged to something like the old doctrine of inspiration (although it had to be carefully modified) — the doctrine of inspiration that genuinely pressed you to the subject matter of the Bible that was in the text, rather than to the peripheries that were behind the text, which was what historical criticism did. During the dialectical period, in the twenties, the way he held the doctrine of inspiration together with historical criticism, the way he avoided literalism, was by understanding that historical criticism must be radical. In the second edition preface and again in his acrid discussion with Adolf von Harnack, he insisted that the critics are not radical enough, and at least through to the 1930s, at least through volume I/2 of the *Dogmatics,* he preferred those critics who suggested that all reliable historical knowledge fails us, particularly in regard to the New Testament texts and particularly those that bear on the origin of earliest Christianity, and of course particularly those that bear on the destiny as well as the teaching of Jesus Christ.

Barth, the early Barth, the Barth of the dialectical period of the 1920s, had a deep stake in the kind of thing that Bultmann was doing in indicating that we know precious little about the life of Jesus Christ — that, as Bultmann was to say in that famous ungrammatical expression of his, the *that* is all we know about Jesus Christ, or, if not all, then essentially most of what we know about him. Barth had a stake in that because it indicated to him that one could not go beyond the text if one was to read the Bible for its subject matter, if one wants to read the Bible, if I may use the word, genuinely *religiously.*

Similarly, he (probably without knowing it) had a stake in the writing of Albert Schweitzer; certainly Schweitzer's *Quest of the Historical Jesus*[2] was in one sense thoroughly congenial to him. That is to say, it was congenial in the sense that a radically Christian, radically eschatological orientation (in the sense of Barth's own strange eschatology of the 1920s) allows a use of the text only in the way that the form critic suggested it was to be used, or at least in a very similar way: the texts are reports of preaching, they are kerygmatic. Therefore, if they are to be understood, if they are to be interpreted, they must be interpreted *kerygmatically.* To use the kind of terminology that we have learned from Donald Evans,[3] self-involving language can only be understood in a self-involving way. And it cannot be understood scientifically or objectively-historically.

The early Barth had therefore, I say again, a stake in the most radical kind of criticism, and if he found it possible to have historical criticism and the doctrine of inspiration together it was by virtue of the fact that the best historical criticism had, in effect, a self-destruct mechanism built into

2. Albert Schweitzer, *The Quest of the Historical Jesus: A Critical Study of Its Progress from Reimarus to Wrede,* trans. W. Montgomery (London: A. & C. Black, 1954).

3. Donald Evans, *The Logic of Self-Involvement: A Philosophic Study of Everyday Language with Special Reference to the Christian Use of Language about God as Creator* (London: SCM, 1963).

it. That is to say, then, that there was no *positive* relation between historical criticism and theology but only a *negative,* mutually exclusive one. But in that sense they were highly compatible; there was indeed a remarkably strong negative dialectical relationship between the two.

An *Ad Hoc* Relationship to Historical Criticism

As Rudolf Smend observed in an article in the festschrift for Barth's eightieth birthday, *Parrhesia* (and, by the way, the article that Smend wrote is the best thing that I know of on Barth and historical criticism; it is a superb piece of work),[4] Barth at that stage did not have a *nachkritische* exegesis, a *post*-critical exegesis, but rather a *nebenkritische* exegesis: the two things (exegesis and criticism) were *juxtaposed,* side by side. They were not stages on the way of exegesis but simply rested there side by side.

But in the 1930s, you see, it seems to me at any rate that a radical revolution occurred, although it was gradual. It was a revolution in exegesis that goes thoroughly with that reality vision of his, with that insistence that the world must be looked at historically, that the only way we know the world is historically. And when Barth began to talk that way, then he also began to talk in his hermeneutics about a new analytical category that he felt applied to the right kind of exegesis, and he called it "literary-historical." And that is in a certain sense an extremely accurate description of what he now proceeds to do and how he now proceeds to relate himself to historical criticism.

It is, in a way, thoroughly parallel to another series of reflections he had. You may recall that he had in the 1920s a polemic (a very sympathetic, profoundly sympathetic polemic) against Ludwig Feuerbach, in which he said that this notion of Feuerbach's that religion is just an illusory projection of our own self-apprehension is a profound threat to liberal theology but that it ignores two basic aspects of the human individual, that is to say, that he is a sinner and that he does not know his own limitation, namely death. Anybody who knows himself to be a sinner and anybody who knows that he is radically limited by death will never allow even the species notion of man to be projected into deity. And at that point, all you can do

---

4. Rudolf Smend, "Nachkritische Schriftauslegung," in *Parrhesia: fröhliche Zuversicht: Karl Barth zum 80. Geburtstag am 10. Mai 1966,* ed. Eberhard Busch, Jürgen Fangmeier, and Max Geiger (Zürich: Evangelischer Verlag, 1966), pp. 215-37.

after being profoundly sympathetic to Feuerbach is simply to laugh him off. But when Barth took up the polemic against Feuerbach again in the *Dogmatics* several times, especially in volume IV/2, it was on a totally different basis. It was not on a negative basis. He couldn't do that any longer because, you see, we don't even know our own sinfulness and our own radical limitation in the face of death. We don't even know that, really, directly. We know it only as communication from God. Then alone do we know what sin and real death mean. And so the only way you can polemicize against a man like Feuerbach who would raise man to the level of God is, as it were, by ignoring him, as it were by putting over against him a positive vision.

The reason I mention this, you see, is that from now on Barth's relation to historical criticism is of the same sort. You look steadily at the text and what the text says, and then you utilize, on an *ad hoc* basis, what the historical scholars offer you. You cannot state systematically or in a general theory what the relation between theological exegesis and historical criticism is. You could do that in the dialectical period of Barth, when there was a general theory, namely a negative compatibility between historical exegesis and theological exegesis. Now you cannot do it anymore. The point however is that you must always be a theological exegete, and then in particular cases of texts you will find an *ad hoc* relation, maybe negative, but maybe positive, with the always tentative results of historical criticism.

Reading Naïvely

In the *Church Dogmatics* IV/2, Barth has an exegesis that Smend, and Eichholz in the essay on Barth in *Antwort*,[5] both consider very important, as does James Wharton[6] in a fine talk that he gave at the Barth Colloquium at Union Theological Seminary two years ago. He has an important exegesis of Numbers 13 and 14, the story of the spies in the land of Canaan, the Israelites by the land of Canaan; and he precedes it by a prefatory hermeneutical remark because he says that this story should be called a *history*. And then he goes on:

5. G. Eichholz, "Der Ansatz Karl Barths in der Hermeneutik," in *Antwort: Karl Barth zum siebzigsten Geburtstag am 10. Mai 1956*, ed. Ernst Wolf (Zürich: Evangelischer Verlag, 1956), pp. 52-68.

6. James A. Wharton, "Karl Barth as Exegete and His Influence on Biblical Interpretation," *Union Seminary Quarterly Review* 28 (Fall 1972): 5-13.

The term "history" is to be understood in its older and naïve significance in which — quite irrespective of the distinctions between that which can be historically proved, that which has the character of saga, and that which has been consciously fashioned, or invented, in a later and synthetic review — it denotes a story which is received and maintained and handed down in a definite kerygmatic sense.[7]

Notice that there are certain distinctions here. First, *that which can be historically proven* — that is to say, empirical history, history to which our fact questions are relevant. As my son said to me after coming home from a Sunday school lesson on the story of the resurrection when he was twelve years old, "What's the evidence for that one?" It's that kind of history: "What's the evidence for that?" that Barth speaks of first of all, that which can be historically proven. The word he uses there is not *geschichtlich* but *historisch;* that's *historisch* history, that for which evidence is relevant.

Secondly, *that which has the character of saga.* And by saga he means a history-like story, but a history-like story that is poetic and therefore has grown up, as it were, through an oral tradition.

And finally, *that which has been consciously fashioned or invented.* That is to say, what a later and sophisticated redactor will have put down, never mind whether something happened or not. And I would propose to you here that the nearest equivalent to that in modern terms is what we speak of as the novelist. The realistic novel is something history-like but it is at the same time invented. Now the novel is history-like in two ways. First, the author seems to be saying, "I'm not giving you myth, I'm not giving you a fable or an allegory because a fable or an allegory always has a distance between the story, the representation, and what it means, the thing represented — whereas the representation is what I mean; I don't mean something else. I mean what I say. I am being literal." And Barth, incidentally, wanted the text always to be literal in that same fashion: it means what it says. It is to be taken literally *whether or not* something happened. The novel is history-like in a literal way: just as history is rendered literally, so a novel is rendered literally. And that means then, secondly, that such an account speaks about the interaction of persons and temporal incidents in such a way that these two things render each other and by their interaction render the story and the meaning of the story. The *meaning* of the story is not something detached from the story, but emerges out of these temporal

7. CD IV/2, pp. 478-79.

connections of character and incident with each other, which mean each other and nothing else. Whereas, of course, in myth in particular the interaction of character and circumstance in time is only a surface element — and this is not so in a novel and, Barth says, not so in the Bible.

So Barth speaks, you see, of three sharply distinct things that do however have a common generic or literary-historical character. And thus, you see, what Barth can do now is to suggest that in a certain way we *can be critical.* We are no longer at the same stage as the naïve precritical forebears. We are no longer there. We do not read Genesis in the same way our forebears did. And yet it has the same character for us — the same literary-historical character in which we can read it as thoroughly sophisticated critics. Barth did not deny the truth or (in a peculiar, hard-to-get-at sense) the *historicity* of Genesis. He always vehemently insisted that the creation accounts are *Geschichte* but he insisted equally strongly that they are not *historische-Geschichte.* First of all, nobody was there, and therefore the evidence is ludicrous. But secondly, an event that is an immediate rather than a mediate relationship between God and man is something to which our notion of factual temporal event is not adequate, so that we cannot say how creation is a temporal event — or, shall we say, we can only think of it *analogically* as a temporal event. As such we must think of it as a temporal event, but our category for thinking of it as a temporal event must be analogical to our *historisch* category of event; it cannot be literally the same.

In these ways, then, Barth is indeed, you see, in the position to suggest that we must be as naïve as our forebears were before the rise of criticism in the interpretation of the Bible and as naïve as the Bible itself. There must be between us and the text a direct relationship, a direct relationship that is really, if you wanted to put it this way in a very broad sense, literary. We read naïvely. We understand the texts without any schematism coming between us and the reading, and yet we do not do it in the same unsophisticated way as they did it. We do it as those who are perfectly well aware that there is such a thing as criticism. But we have now, you see, unlike the historical critic, Barth claims, gone beyond it.

Let me then go on in the same passage:

In relation to the biblical histories we can, of course, ask concerning the distinctions and even make them hypothetically. But if we do so we shall miss the kerygmatic sense in which they are told. Indeed, the more definitely we make them and the more normative we regard them for the purpose of exposition, the more surely we shall miss this sense. To do justice to this sense, we must either not have asked at all concerning these distinctions, or have ceased to do so. In other words, we must still, or again, read these histories in their unity and totality. It is only then that they can say what they are trying to say. To be sure the history of the spies does contain different elements. There is a "historical" (*historisch*) element in the stricter sense. [Quite possibly these were, in our sense of the word, real persons. Certainly, judging by the archeology, the names were those of real cities and real localities. So there is a *historisch* element there.] . . . There is also an element of saga (the account of the branch of grapes carried by two men, and of the giants who inhabited the land). There is also the element which has its origin in the synthetic or composite view (fusing past and present almost into one) which is so distinctive a feature of historical writing in Old and New Testament alike.[8]

(It is also, by the way, a feature of the novel, isn't it? From the very beginning in the eighteenth century, literary critics who were trying to understand this new genre always suggested that the novel must be about something contemporary to the writer, contemporary to our manners, contemporary to the world we lived in, even if it took the shape of, and succeeded in reproducing the atmosphere of the old. The novel has its own peculiar way of synthesizing the old and the new, past and present time, successfully. Barth suggested that the same thing is very true of Old and New Testaments.)

It is to the latter elements then, that we must pay particular attention in our reading of these stories if we are to understand them. For they usually give us an indication of the purpose which led to their adoption into the texts. But in relation to them, if we are discerning readers we shall not overlook the historical elements or even jettison those which seem to have the character of saga.[9]

We look for the common literary character in all of it. The meaning of it is clear, he suggests, and it is the text. The Bible is largely and centrally realistic narrative. He was of course well aware of the disjunctions and the distinctions of the Bible, but the comprehensive frame for Barth, the most important thing, which lends it unity more than anything else is that it is

8. CD IV/2, p. 479.
9. CD IV/2, p. 479.

realistic narrative. And please bear in mind that that is not the same thing as that obscure and wretched notion called *Heilsgeschichte.* It is not the same thing. But as realistic narrative it is *clear.*

The truth of it, when we raise that question, and we have raised it for the philosopher at any rate, is a quite distinct question. Though for Barth, it must be added, that distinction does not really arise. Remember that, for Barth, it depicts the one real world in which we all live so that to understand the meaning of it is the same as understanding the truth of it. If you understand it rightly you cannot *not* think of it as real, what is depicted there. That strange, marvelous little book on Anselm's proof for the existence of God[10] is in a peculiar sense also applicable to Barth as an interpreter of the Bible as realistic narrative. He didn't make that application himself, but it is clearly consonant with what he does. Bear that in mind.

So then, "in relation to them, we shall never overlook the historical elements or even jettison those which seem to have the character of saga" because we can't hold them together literally. How he concludes, then, is by saying, "When the distinctions have been made," and we must make them, "they can be pushed again into the background and the whole can be read," and — here comes the marvelous phrase — "with this tested and critical naivety as the totality it professes to be."[11]

That was what Barth's ambition was, to be a *direct* reader of the text, and not of some hypothetical subject matter behind the text. The subject matter is the text. But he did it not as an uncritically naïve reader but as a critically naïve reader, and as a result he felt confident that, even though he could state no general theory about the relationship between theological exegesis and historical criticism, there was no conflict, and given individual texts you would find how the two related themselves to each other, provided always that historical-critical exegesis was not the governess but was in the service of the theological exegete. Even though he could never distort its results, nonetheless he must use it as a handmaid rather than either a mistress or a mother.

10. Karl Barth, *Anselm: Fides Quaerens Intellectum; Anselm's proof of the existence of God in the context of his theological scheme,* trans. I. W. Robertson (London: SCM, 1960).

11. Barth, *Anselm: Fides Quaerens Intellectum.*

Questions

QUESTION: How does Barth handle passages like the one in Paul where Paul deals with the resurrection by trying to point to what looks like to me some empirical evidence where he says, "Look, over 600 people saw Jesus after he was raised from the dead"? Now there we see right in Scripture we have some effort being made to tie one of the Christian truths to empirical evidence of some sort.

FREI: Quite candidly I don't remember. The trouble is, one of the reasons I am hesitant to reply to questions is that I am in the presence of greater experts than myself. I should say that, although I read avidly in sections of IV/1, IV/2, I/2, and III/1 this time for this particular presentation, it has been some time since I really read in Barth, so I will have to call on the experts to correct me here. But Barth's position is perfectly clear. He says in reply to Bultmann that it is perfectly obvious that in the biblical text the resurrection is something that happened to Jesus and not to the disciples. It is the right response to make. Whether true or not, the story has it happening to Jesus. But that limits one's options. And even though one has certain stories that affirm *Geschichte*, it is a *Geschichte* that is an immediate relationship between God and time, unlike most *Geschichte* that we know, which is a mediated relationship, and therefore we are not in a position to make dogmatic statements about the relevance of concepts of fact and evidence to that. However, we go by the text and we do know that the relationship between notions of factuality and historical evidence should be related positively rather than in opposition to this divine-human history. And therefore to the extent that one can make it, in exegesis, come off, that there is as positive a relation as Paul's testimony claims — to that extent, we follow it and we obey it. Nonetheless, on the other side, there is the word of Paul also, that indicates to us, that warns us that we should not speculate. And I am now talking not about the Barth who wrote the book on the resurrection of the dead, but the later Barth of the *Dogmatics*. We should not speculate. None of us know really what a spiritual body is. We are not given an evidential witness scene of what a resurrection is like, and thus no matter how positive the evidence, the event itself remains, though strongly to be affirmed, an evidentially indescribable, rather than a describable event. And it is not surprising therefore that here empirical testimony becomes not absent, but utterly confused. The Gospel accounts are confused and confusing, and to go behind them even with the aid of Paul's testimony, to go behind them to see the "factual thing in itself" is therefore an impossibility. I think that's fair, though I stand subject to correction. I do believe that it makes good sense to talk that way.

QUESTION: [Largely inaudible on the tape; the question is directed to clarifying the perception that early in Barth's career he maintained a separate and adversarial relationship between theological exegesis and historical criticism. The question ends with a reference to Barth's *Credo*,[12] which made this point pungently.]

FREI: Yes, he used to do that sort of thing all the time. As you know he was a wonderful, delightful, and perverse man who could make a point often by exaggeration. Remember, somebody asked him once whether the snake really talked in the garden, do you recall? And he said, "I don't know whether it talked or not, it's far more important what it said." And then he added, "Yes! It talked!" I'm tempted to let it go at that. All I can say is that he was working on I/2 and doing preliminary work on II/2 at the same time that he was writing the appendices to *Credo,* and I think what he did there was to make a point by exaggeration. He was no longer really, if you read the sections on hermeneutics in I/2, that simplistic and separatist about the two things, theological and historical exegesis. But take the audience into account. He could not be subtle. He had to be direct and driving to make his point.

QUESTION: Professor Frei, your presentation has done a magnificent job of showing the difference between the uses of *Geschichte* and *historisch.* I get constantly impatient with, for instance, James Barr — and there have been a whole number of others — saying that this distinction between *historisch* and *geschichtlich* is all just one big blur of confusion. I think, Dr. Frei, that you have made a real contribution in the way you have brought out the importance of this distinction in Barth's thought. On this matter of his tending to downplay the historical question, I think one has to recognize that Barth saw almost the whole of historical scholarship concerning itself with historical questions and hardly anybody except himself bothering about the theological question, and that he didn't tend to so emphasize the historical just because this was the thing worth worrying about.

FREI: Yes, I do agree with that, particularly in view of the fact that he, when

12. Karl Barth, *Credo: A Presentation of the Chief Problems of Dogmatics with Reference to the Apostles' Creed,* trans. J. Strathearn McNabb (London: Hodder & Stoughton, 1936).

he saw other people doing theological exegesis, especially as the 40s and 50s progressed, he thought that they were doing it in a hair-raising, *unhistorical* way. One of the greatest objections he had to the whole existential syndrome, that whole malaise, if I may so call it (and in Germany I gather they now regard it as something of a foolish wild mercury) was that it was totally unhistorical. It had nothing to do with the real world of outward events in which selves and political event, selves and ordinary history interacted. And he was desperately concerned with that all the time, and he thought proper theological exegesis had to be concerned with that; so not only did he see historical critics doing no theological exegesis but even the theologians who were doing theological exegesis weren't doing what he regarded as the proper kind of historical-theological exegesis.

I do agree completely, but may I make one point with regard to Professor James Barr, since with some hesitation I shall have to admit to being something of an admirer of James Barr's work. I read his books assiduously. I just wish there weren't so many of them. There are now three that say much the same thing. He and I have had some correspondence. You are absolutely right in what you say about Barr's reading of Barth. I think he may be coming around. (You know how that is: when one talks to somebody who doesn't agree with one, one always thinks they may be coming around. He probably isn't at all.) But I have suggested the reading of Barth that I have just given you to Professor Barr and pointed out to him that again and again in the first third or so of *Old and New in Interpretation,* the second of his books, he hammers home a literary theme, namely, that while it is extremely awkward to think about the Bible as history, the history of the mighty acts, the history of God's self-revelation (all those terms that Barth did use, which Barr has put so heavily into question as hermeneutical devices), nonetheless one of the marks of the Bible is that it is a cumulative narrative, literarily. And I suggested to him that he has been misreading Barth, that this is an understandable misreading because everybody else has been doing the same thing as far as I can see, and that Barth ought to be read from his literary-historical texts as an exegete. Perhaps not as a theologian, but as an exegete. I suggested that, in effect, he was saying the same thing as Barth was saying there. Barr said that that seems very likely and that therefore he would like to rethink his position on Barth, about *Historie* and *Geschichte.*

QUESTION: I find the question of the whole point of view of the novel on realistic narrative very congenial itself, but one can see the reintroduction of another historical problem since the realistic narrative with which we are dealing is millennia old and the novel is, I think, only a few hundred years old in its present form. We don't have, for example, the great historical problem when we read *Middlemarch,* but we have the tremendous historical problem of the texts we read when we read Matthew, Mark, Luke, and John. Could you comment on this?

FREI:[13] The text of an ancient document is always subject to a variety of critical evaluations, like attestation, happenstance, source, form, and redaction criticism. Let us recall that these procedures, revisable as they are, and their conclusions even more revisable, are thoroughly appropriate, but that they say nothing either way about a direct reading of the text. They tell us about these texts in their cultural contexts, mayhap even the intention of the author and the redactor. But is there anything that tells us that the text cannot be looked at also in its own light if it makes syntactical sense, grammatical sense, and if it appears that you could show forth a kind of structure in the text itself, not simply in the thought of the redactors? In other words — the proof of the pudding is in the eating.

---

13. [The beginning and end of Frei's response are difficult to make out on the tape, and what can be made out sounds rather garbled. Only the relatively clear middle part of his answer is given here.]

II. Exemplification

5. "A Type of the One to Come":
Leviticus 14 and 16 in Barth's *Church Dogmatics*

Kathryn Greene-McCreight

Barth's *Church Dogmatics* has been described as "nothing other than a sustained meditation on the texts of Holy Scripture."[1] Certainly, this is partially true. However, does this aesthetic assessment really lend us a "thick description," as anthropologist Clifford Geertz would say, of Barth's exegetical "method"? Barth's dogmatics are clearly "exegetical," but to posit this is not to say all that much. Even the least experienced of theological students can readily discern "sustained meditation on the texts of Holy Scripture" throughout the *Church Dogmatics*. To describe his *Dogmatics* thus is not entirely a helpful observation.

In fact, one could argue that two of the most theologically fruitful aspects of Barth's own exegesis in his *Church Dogmatics* are:

- His reading of the Old and New Testaments as a canonically interconnected whole. The Bible is read as a single text, theologically interdependent, which bears the communication of the Holy One. For Barth, this is a theological reality to be confessed, not a historical judgment to be tested in the fires of criticism.
- His postcritical qualification of modern criticism. In the Preface to the Second Edition of his *Epistle to the Romans,* Barth rebuts those critics who accuse him of refusing to engage the historical-critical method.[2]

1. F. Watson, "The Bible," in *Cambridge Companion to Karl Barth,* ed. John Webster (Cambridge: Cambridge University Press, 2000), p. 57.

2. "I have been accused of being an 'enemy of historical criticism' . . . I have nothing whatsoever to say against historical criticism. I recognize it, and once more state quite definitely that it is both necessary and justified. My complaint is that recent commentators confine themselves to an interpretation of the text which seems to me to be no commentary at

Later in the same Preface, he makes his celebrated statement that the "critical historian needs to be more critical."[3] In order to deal with the Bible responsibly on its own terms, Barth argued, historical criticism was indispensable, but not enough.

If we consider Barth's exegesis within the theological task as he understood it, we need to have these points illustrated for us from his *Dogmatics*. Is it a historical-critical investigation, or a close textual reading, or something else entirely? Surely other theologians of the twentieth century, not to mention now of the twenty-first century, "care" about the Bible, "use" the Bible, and "reflect" on biblical themes in their systematic work. So, how exactly does Barth listen to and read the words of and meditate on themes of Scripture in a way that most other modern and contemporary theologians simply do not? If Barth can be said to have methods regarding the use of Scripture in theology, what are they? And how would such methods, if indeed he brings such to his dogmatic task, impact both his theology and its exegesis? Is Barth in fact an exegete at all, or as his critics accuse, is his reading better described as eisegesis?

As did those from the earliest Christian tradition up until the dawning of the Enlightenment, Karl Barth shares with them a reading of Scripture that attends a canonical Rule, or the Rule of Faith[4]. In addition, Barth em-

---

all, but merely the first step towards a commentary." Barth, *The Epistle to the Romans,* trans. E. C. Hoskyns (New York: Oxford University Press, 1968), p. 6.

3. Barth, *The Epistle to the Romans,* p. 8; Brevard Childs, *Biblical Theology of the Old and New Testaments* (Minneapolis: Fortress Press, 1993), p. 215. So Barth: "The interpretation of what is written requires more than a disjointed series of notes on words and phrases. The commentator must be possessed of a wider intelligence than that which moves within the boundaries of his own natural appreciation. . . . Criticism applied to historical documents means for me the measuring of words and phrases by the standard of that about which the documents are speaking — unless indeed the whole be nonsense." Brevard Childs: "I would suggest that it was Karl Barth who has captured the true insights of the Reformers when, in response to Bultmann and his legacy, he argued for a far more radical position regarding the nature of the Bible, namely, to be 'more critical than the critics'! In a word, all scripture suffers from human frailty; there is no untainted position."

4. On the Rule of Faith and the interpretation of the plain sense, or literal sense, of Scripture, see Kathryn Greene-McCreight, *Ad Litteram: How Augustine, Calvin and Barth Read the "Plain Sense" of Genesis 1–3* (New York: Peter Lang, 1999). See also the following remark: "In my judgment the church's Rule of Faith is narrative in shape, trinitarian in substance, and relates the essential beliefs of Christianity together by the grammar of christological monotheism." R. W. Wall, "Reading the Bible from within Our Traditions: The 'Rule of Faith' in Theological Hermeneutics," in *Between Two Horizons: Spanning New*

braces the fruit of the biblical criticism of the modern period, as he insisted was the case. The question is this, however: How does he do this, and to what result? Is Barth simply readapting traditional figural exegesis? He certainly makes use of the older exegesis, and incorporates the newer. Yet ultimately he reads the text far more closely than either the older or the newer exegesis offers. This means that even his closest reading of the biblical text can in fact issue in typological reading, in a figurative linking of both Testaments, and in relating the text and the reality *(die Sache)* to which it bears ultimate witness: the crucified and risen Christ. How is this?

While Barth clearly gives a close hearing to both Testaments, in some respects his dogmatic, or better yet, his kerygmatic, reading of the Old Testament can be more illustrative of what makes up a distinctly critical (or postcritical) yet ruled reading. To show how Barth's interpretation of Scripture is similar to, yet ultimately distinct from, both the "older" traditional exegesis, as Barth calls it, and the critical modern exegesis, indeed "more critical than the critics," we will now turn to Barth's treatment of Leviticus 14 and 16 in *CD* II/2, *The Doctrine of God*, in paragraph 35, *The Election of the Individual* (357ff.).[5] Then we will be able to compare Barth's reading to some of the traditional exegesis on these passages. After that, we will hold up against the prism of Barth's reading two examples from the contemporary conversation: a classic historical critic and conservative rabbi (Jacob Milgrom) and a narrative textualist (Robert Alter). I choose contemporary figures with the hopes that we, a century Barth's junior, may stumble onto his careful listening to Scripture and learn from him.

The exegetical section we will examine is found in II/2: *The Doctrine of God*; chapter VII, par. 35: *The Election of the Individual*; subsection 2, *The*

Testament Studies and Systematic Theology, ed. J. B. and M. T. Green (Grand Rapids: Eerdmans, 2000), pp. 88-127. I would agree with Wall, but would add that the Rule of Faith binds canonically the Old and New Testaments in interpretation.

5. What interests me particularly here is not Barth's hermeneutics in general, nor even his interpretation at specific points of the New Testament. Here we can look to M. K. Cunningham, *What Is Theological Exegesis? Karl Barth's Interpretation and Use of Scripture in His Doctrine of Election* (Valley Forge, PA: Trinity Press International, 1995); P. McGlasson, *Jesus and Judas: Biblical Exegesis in Barth* (Atlanta: Scholar's Press, 1991); and B. Bourgine, *L'Herméneutique Théologique de Karl Barth: Exégèse et Dogmatique dans le Quatrième Volume de la Kirchliche Dogmatik* (Leuven: University Press, 2003). I am interested specifically in Barth's use and interpretation of the Old Testament, which itself reveals something unique about Barth's exegesis that his reading of the New Testament may not necessarily do. See in specific Otto Bächli, *Das Alte Testament in der Kirchlichen Dogmatik Karl Barths* (Neukirchen-Vluyn: Neukirchener Verlag, 1987), pp. 170-74.

Elect and the Rejected, beginning on p. 341. We will follow Barth's dogmatics here, specifically examining how he sketches the biblical depiction of
God's election and rejection of the individual. Barth points out that "we
do not need to confine ourselves where there is explicit mention of election, where the terms *baḥar* or ἐκλέγεσθαι are therefore used." Barth understands this doctrine, or maybe better, theme, of Election to run
exegetically throughout the Old and New Testaments. He sees that it "belongs to the very air" breathed there, and is not keyed simply to vocabulary
or terminology. Barth mentions characters that are not usually thought of
in terms of election: Abel and Cain, as well as the *loci classici:* Abraham,
Isaac, and Jacob; Moses and David; and all the prophets. Barth observes:
"[They] do not stand for themselves but for God. They live and speak and
work in the name of God" (II/2, 343). They are God's elect, chosen by God
to witness to his works.

But what is the meaning of divine election for Barth? Is it that everyone is simply chosen by God, a unity in diversity? Do all possess the Holy
Spirit? Are they all of the lineage of Abraham? Not necessarily. In some respects, Barth speaks in the voice of Paul here, and yet gives the doctrine of
election his own hearing. "This, then, is how the elect and others differ
from one another: the former by witnessing in their lives to the truth, the
latter by lying against the same truth. It ought to be clear that to this extent
they belong together" (II/2, 346). They belong together in the sphere of the
divine election of grace, the former in obedience and the latter in disobedience. All is grace. Our response determines how we line up or not against
that grace, and this is determined itself by God's electing action throughout the history of Israel and the church.

Later, in the comparatively short section where Barth turns to the specific matter of the interpretation of Leviticus, he is so bold as to preface it
by saying, "We have to consider in greater detail the witness to Christ in its
first and basic form as prophecy and announcement: the witness to Christ
in the Old Testament" (II/2, 354). In the ritual laws of Leviticus, this becomes all the more striking than in the patriarchal narratives of Genesis,
which Barth has just shown at some length.

He thus turns to the interpretation of the ceremony for pronouncing a
leper clean in Leviticus 14:4-7. In this ceremony, the priest takes two living
birds, along with cedar, scarlet, and hyssop. One bird is killed under running water and the blood is collected in a clay pot. The other bird is dipped
in the blood of the first, and the leper to be cleansed is sprinkled seven
times in this blood. The second and living bird is allowed to fly away.

The second ritual Barth considers at this point is from the Day of Atonement, in Leviticus 16:5ff., in which two goats are treated in the following manner: they are both first placed before the Lord, at the opening of the Holy Tabernacle. Then Aaron casts lots over the goats, one for the Lord and the other for Azazel. Aaron offers the goat over whom the lot is cast as a sin-offering. The blood of the first goat is sprinkled seven times on the mercy seat of the sanctuary and then on the altar outside. Aaron then lays his hands on the head of the live goat, and confesses over him all the sins of the children of Israel, putting them on the head of the goat, then sending the goat via the hand of a fit (or "prepared") man into the desert. The sins of the people thus are cast away into an uninhabited land.

Reading these chapters separately and then together, Barth notes that the following narrative elements and form are common to both Leviticus 14 and 16. Two creatures in each story, exactly alike in species and value, are dealt with in completely different ways. The selection of the animals is different: in Leviticus 14 the selection seems to be made by the priest, while in Leviticus 16 the selection is done via lots. Barth says at this point, "In both cases it is obvious that the selection is inscrutable, and that it is really made by God Himself" (II/2, 357). This is important for Barth theologically, of course, in his doctrine of election. One creature is sacrificed and the other is allowed to go free. The ceremonies are "obviously" (so Barth says) a comment on the history of Israel as a history of the differing choices, as we have already seen in Barth's interpretation of the stories of Abel and Cain, Isaac and Ishmael, Jacob and Esau, etc.: election throughout the history of Israel whereby that which is not properly Israel is chosen as Israel.

Barth also points out that the ceremonies both attest a purification. In Leviticus 14 the priest acts as a medical expert in the confirmation of the healing of leprosy, and Leviticus 16 attests the healing of the sins of the whole nation, actions that have already taken place but now are merely attested. "Neither the priest, nor Aaron, but God, is its author" (II/2, 358). The common content emphasizes the inner differences. "The use and non-use, the slaying and releasing of the two creatures are common to both rites, but they possess a different meaning in each case." In the second account, the reconciliation is necessary. "The death of the one goat, full of grace and salvation, is accompanied by the life of the other, which is in fact, the essence of desolation, indeed of death itself" (II/2, 359). "This is where you properly belong," it is said in effect to the nation in the treatment of this second goat, in its banishment to the desert. The second goat is the image of the non-elect, just as Cain stands apart from Abel, as Ishmael stands apart from Isaac, as Esau stands apart from Jacob. But, notes Barth, both goats, and not only the first goat, are "placed before the Lord."

As regards Leviticus 14, Barth says that thanks to the fact that the first bird has yielded its life and blood for the purification of the second bird, the latter is actually pure, and freedom may and must be given it; and when the healed leper is sprinkled with the same blood, he is told that he is now removed from the realm of the divine wrath, and is once more a free member of the congregation. "This bird undoubtedly signifies the resurrection, the grace of God directed to man, the freedom given to him, the life restored to him, his radical purification and renewal, for the sake of which he himself must first and inexorably die" (II/2, 361). The one bird has to die that the other may live; what is done to the first is to the advantage of the second one. Barth concludes this analysis of Leviticus 14 and 16:

> Let us gratefully know ourselves to be elect in the picture of the first goat of Leviticus 16 — grateful that we are accepted to sacrifice ourselves, grateful that we may suffer the saving judgment of the wrath of God, which is the wrath of his love, as only the elect can and may do! But let us with equal gratitude recognize ourselves as the non-elect in the picture of the second bird of Leviticus 14 — grateful because there is ordained for us the life for whose painful birth the other is elected, the resurrection for whose sake the elect must go to his death! (II/2, 361)

Barth now turns from the narrative form of the passages to their commonalities in content. Both are concerned for humanity, for the leper and for the nation as a whole. Both death and life — first death, then life — are decreed by God for humanity. But Barth has already said, and says again here, that we cannot yet speak of Jesus Christ: "We do not know the man of whose death it can be said that it is this saving sacrifice, and who can on this account be described as the elect of God" (II/2, 362). It is too early at this point in exegesis to speak of Jesus Christ. The text must be read more thoroughly.

But once the inner correspondences of the text are worked out more carefully, Barth comes to the conclusion that, either the Old Testament has no subject matter, but points into the void, so that there is nothing to see (II/2, 363), or else the subject of the Old Testament may be accepted as identical with the person of Jesus Christ. Barth admits at this point that it is not a purely exegetical matter, purely a textual observation, but that something else is at work here. "The choice between these two exegetical possibilities is not an exegetical question; it is a question of faith . . . to be distinguished from exegesis. But it is inescapably posed by [exegesis]" (II/2, 363-64). In other words, while the ultimate reality of Jesus Christ can be seen only through faith in him, the text clearly points in this direction.

Barth speaks of the "older Christian exegesis," none of which unfortunately he quotes directly other than Calvin, saying that it is correct in its judgment that the Old Testament election stories and Leviticus 14 and 16 are to be read christologically. This he states even though until now he has not mentioned the name of Jesus Christ, as did this older exegesis almost immediately upon reading the texts. "So far we have not followed the example of this older exegesis. For we have kept the name of Jesus Christ in the background, preferring to let the Old Testament text, which could not utter his name, speak by and for itself" (II/2, 364). But only the positive decision of faith in Jesus Christ, which is really the only way to know him anyway, can "vindicate the older Christian exegesis of these texts as prophecies of Christ" (II/2, 364). This makes the older exegesis not only "vindicated" but also necessary. The Old Testament can only halt with a "penultimate word" as it encounters the subject matter of the text, which stands not in it, but over against it. "In the decision of faith, then, we have an advantage over the exegesis which does not know this decision, or which thinks to be non-committal in the matter" (II/2, 364).

What is this "older exegesis"? While Barth does not mention what examples he has in mind, the older exegesis is, without a doubt, fascinating. Hebrews sets the stage: "For the bodies of those animals whose blood is brought into the sanctuary by the high priest as a sacrifice for sin are burned outside the camp. Therefore Jesus also suffered outside the city gate in order to sanctify the people by his own blood" (Heb. 13:11-12). After that, chronologically speaking, readings start to heat up. For example, Cassiodorus makes a similar link but more explicit: the hyssop being dipped in the sacrificial blood, sprinkled seven times on the body of the leper, "revealed by way of anticipation that inward stains of sins could be effectively removed by the precious blood of the Lord Savior."[6] The exegetico-thematic link here is the blood of the sacrificed animals.[7]

But there are links made outside of this: Justin Martyr equates the of-

---

6. Exposition of the Psalms 50.9; ACW 51:501.

7. John of Damascus makes a link between this "episode" from Leviticus 14 and baptism. This is one of the four baptisms prefigured before Christ. The first baptism was the flood of Noah, the second was the Red Sea, the third is Leviticus 14, and the fourth is that of John. Notice here that the first three are OT while the fourth is NT. Figural reading does not necessarily "bridge" OT and NT. *Orthodox Faith* 4.9; FC 37:346.

fering of the flour with a "prototype" of the eucharistic bread, "which our Lord Jesus Christ commanded us to offer in remembrance of the passion he endured for all those souls who are cleansed from sin."[8] Tertullian and Theodoret of Cyr understand the two goats of Leviticus 16 to represent the two natures of Christ.[9] Caesarius of Arles takes the phrase of Leviticus 16:29 that "you should afflict yourselves and shall do no work" and does not even read this christologically, but interprets it as referring to the good spiritual effects of fasting.[10] Origen reads both chapters christologically,[11] and he was mediated in the Middle Ages by Hesychius and thereby entered various glossae. Bede also was an influence on this tradition of reading Leviticus 14 and 16 christologically.[12]

Let us turn briefly to Origen, to try to tease out the difference between what Barth is doing and what the "older exegesis" did, at least some of it, and certainly the very influential. In Homily 8 on Leviticus,[13] Origen starts out by saying that the "two hens" resemble the two rams, since one is offered to the Lord and the other released "into the field." In other words, Origen too, like Barth, notices structures in the texts of Leviticus 14 and 16 that correspond to each other. The cedar wood refers to the wood of the cross, without which no one can be cleansed from sin. This is no great contribution: wood everywhere in the biblical text conjures up the wood of the cross in patristic exegesis. Likewise Rahab's scarlet cord throughout patristic exegesis is taken to indicate the blood from Christ's side. Again, no great novelty here. But Origen does make links between Leviticus and Genesis (in the commonplace of Rahab's scarlet cord), within the Old Testament, and not only from the Old Testament to the New. While this may not be entirely novel, it moves from Old to the New Testament, but also from book to book within the Old Testament itself.

Origen then goes on to speak of the two lambs to be offered by the leper.[14] Why does Barth not pick up on this? In Origen's Homily Nine, an-

---

8. *Dialogue with Trypho* 41; FC 6:209-10.

9. Tertullian, *Against Marcion* 3.7.7; ANF 3:327. Theodoret of Cyr, *Dialogue* 3; NPNF 23:226.

10. Caesarius of Arles, *Sermon* 197.1; FC 66:45.

11. See his Homilies on Leviticus, Sources Chrétiennes.

12. Many thanks for this information to Ephraim Radner, who wrote the theological commentary on Leviticus for the Brazos Press series in Scripture and Theology.

13. Origen, *Homilies on Leviticus 1–16*. Fathers of the Church: A New Translation by G. W. Barkley (Washington, DC: Catholic University of America Press, 1990), p. 168.

14. Origen, *Leviticus*, p. 173.

other form of the two rams being offered is the two robbers on either side of Christ at the crucifixion.[15] Christ is the "prepared man," and goes into Hell for us as the scapegoat goes into the desert. Origen sees in the scapegoat the concept of rejection somewhat as Barth will, although just in a snippet of thought as opposed to an overarching structure.[16] Origen equates to Barabbas the goat sent "living into the wilderness," while the goat that was offered to God to atone for sins is Christ, and Pilate is the "prepared man" who led the goat into the wilderness.[17]

Barth is in line with the tradition in his more modest christological interpretation. This has led him to the conclusion that in the final analysis the "text leaves us with an enigma . . . that it is not to be met with in the human realm of Old Testament events and ideas" (II/2, 364). Barth insists that one cannot say that these passages are prophecies of Jesus Christ just because one is stuck with an enigma, as if to pull Christ out of the hat to perform the rabbit trick. One cannot begin exegetical investigation assuming the *presence* of Jesus Christ, but in the correspondences of the text to the life of Israel and to the life of Jesus Christ, this identification is powerful.

Is this the only difference Barth exhibits from the "older exegesis"? Is it only that he defers talking about Jesus Christ until having shown the patterns within the Old Testament text into which Jesus Christ then "fits"? "So far we have not followed the example of this older exegesis," for the name of Jesus is kept in the "background" (II/2, 364). Barth prefers to let the Old Testament speak for and by itself, that Old Testament which could not utter the name of Christ. But even in doing this, the text leaves us with this "enigma," the "riddle" to which the solution is Jesus Christ.[18] He is that "open secret" of the Old Testament, the exegesis of which "can only halt with a penultimate word as it encounters the subject of the text, which as such does not stand in the text but, so to speak, over against it" (II/2, 364). Jesus is the "unknown quantity" whose emergence is only through

15. Origen, *Leviticus,* p. 184.

16. Origen, *Leviticus,* p. 188.

17. Origen, *Leviticus,* pp. 204-5.

18. "Moses transmitted *principles and rules;* successive generations transmuted them into laws. What are the principles which lie behind the tradition in the Torah? . . . The book of Leviticus and many of its sometimes contradictory laws can be understood as the various manifestations of the principles of the Ten Commandments, or Decalogue." J. Milgrom, *Leviticus: A Book of Ritual and Ethics* (Minneapolis: Fortress Press, 2004), p. 2. Milgrom himself sees in the text of Leviticus something *other* than the text. This is his own way of making sense of the relationship between Mosaic authorship and Oral Torah.

exegesis, but could still be explained differently if it were not from the "positive decision of faith." Only this can vindicate the "older exegesis." "In the decision of faith, then, we have an advantage over the exegesis which does not know this decision" (II/2, 364).

The presupposition with which Barth proceeds is this: the elect individual in the Old Testament is always a witness to Jesus Christ, and is in fact a type of Christ himself. "It is He, Jesus Christ, who is originally and properly the elect individual." In this sense, declares Barth, Jesus Christ is each of the four animals of Leviticus 14 and 16. They are "prophecy" and as such cannot speak yet of fulfillment in Jesus Christ, just as the Old Testament prophecy cannot yet speak of the New Testament fulfillment. Here is one of the major differences between Barth and most of the "older exegesis": Jesus Christ is the subject matter of the text, but in fact as the content of prophecy cannot be properly spoken of without reference to *faith* in him.

At this point, Barth turns to the New Testament, showing where it speaks prophetically of Jesus Christ. 1 Peter 1:20 points to Jesus Christ as "destined before the foundation of the world, but was revealed at the end of the ages for your sake." Hebrews 13:12 indicates, according to Barth, that Jesus Christ, like the second goat, "must suffer the sin of many to be laid upon him . . . in order that he may bear it away" (II/2, 365).

Barth finally engages in the "older exegesis" that reads in the story the two natures of Christ, not in the older exegesis that saw in the wood the cross, in the scarlet and the animals' blood the blood of Christ, but rather the two natures alone. "In him, who was very God and very man, in perfect unity, the glory and the shame and abandonment were reality, one reality" (II/2, 365). So, says Barth, the older exegesis was right because of this fit with the New Testament. In Romans 4:25 the prediction of Leviticus 14 is fulfilled: "Jesus Christ was delivered for our offenses and was raised again for our justification." This is a remarkable reading, for nothing in the Leviticus 14 text serves as a "catchword." Barth also sees in the first bird, along with the older exegesis, a "deeply hidden honour . . . which properly belongs to the man Jesus Christ . . . because in his obedience he is so pure and consequently so usable an offering" (II/2, 365).[19] Indeed, he thereby steps into the place of the leper, dying the death without which the leper cannot be purified. But Jesus Christ is also the cured leper, the second bird "lifting

---

19. *KD* 403: ". . . die tief verborgene Ehre, die dort dem ersten Vogel, die in Wirklichkeit den Menschen Jesus Christus angetan wird."

itself into freedom." He rises from the dead (Rom. 1:4) so that all with him might walk in newness of life (Rom. 6:4).

Barth points out what one of his students, Hans Frei, later takes as one of his overarching theses: this Jesus is the "unsubstitutable" (Frei's term) presence of God. There is no other man delivered up as Jesus is. There would be no value in the sacrifice of any other. This one, as God incarnate, man divine, "in him, who was at the same time very God and very Man, the humiliation and exaltation were reality, one reality" (II/2, 365). Barth does, then, agree with the older exegesis of each set of animals signifying the depths of the Chalcedonian formula (II/2, 366), but when he finally suggests this, he has so thoroughly examined the inner correspondences of both Leviticus 14 and 16 (which the older exegesis does not do) that it does not seem to be eisegesis but a true exegesis.

Barth challenges his reader that if this exegesis of the passages is not proper and appropriate, then a better reading must be found. "Those who think they must reject this as the final word in exegesis of Leviticus 14 and 16 must either undertake to prove another and better final word in explanation of these passages, or they must admit that they do not know of any, and therefore that ultimately they do not know to what or to whom these passages refer" (II/2, 366). Not only the birds and the goats are types of Christ in his election and rejection, but so are Abel and the very different Cain. Barth is eager to follow his exegesis with the conclusion that each of these types of Jesus Christ is different from its counterpart, and each is set off from the next. The types come in dualities, and the dualities are bound to each other, and yet the partners of each are unique, one set from the other in their "historical multiformity."

> In other words, we have to recognize Jesus Christ not only in the type of Abel [*in dem Typus Abel*] but also in the very different type of Cain; not only in the type of Isaac and his sacrifice, but also in the very different type of Ishmael and his expulsion and miraculous protection; not only in the type of the chosen stock of Leah but also in the very different chosen stock of Rachel [notice the rare use of women in the typology!]; not only in the type of the Israelite nation but also in the very different type of the excluded and yet not utterly excluded heathen nations. (II/2, 366)

That is, none of the types are formed as though from identical cookie-cutter stamps. None of them give quite the same witness, nor do the types simply repeat the witness of the others. Exegesis of these types cannot be "reduced to a formula" or "simplified." But this "multiformity of historical appearances is best observed and maintained if here too the final word in exegesis is actually the name of Jesus Christ" (II/2, 366).[20] In other words, the narrative of the Old Testament text is best maintained and respected if we see the ultimate interpretation to be prophetic of the name of Jesus.

At this point, I would like to turn to the modern commentary of Jacob Milgrom[21] and compare some of what Barth does with Milgrom's work. The obvious differences must be stated up front: Barth writes of Leviticus 14 and 16 within the context of his *Dogmatics* within his discussion on Election. This, of course, affects and enables his theological reading of the stories. Milgrom writes a historical-critical commentary on the whole of Leviticus, a different genre of work entirely from where Barth's exegesis appears.

Can we call Milgrom's work "exegesis" when we compare it with Barth's? Posing such a question of a historical-critical scholar's reading of the Bible may be surprising. However, even a simple glance at Milgrom's commentary quickly reveals to us a work that it is far from a "close reading" of the biblical text itself, given Barth's earlier words about his own work's relation to historical criticism. Of course, any biblical scholar would consider the building blocks of exegesis, or at least its first steps, to be a close reading of the text. However, Milgrom's impressive scholarly work resembles a conventional series of observations of the prehistory of the text. Milgrom's commentary will be useful to us in illuminating key features of Barth's own exegesis by showing up any similarities and many differences between the two.

Milgrom, first of all, does not choose to read the two texts of the birds and the goats, Leviticus 14 and 16, together as does Barth. They are not of the same origin, even though they are both from Israel's pagan past.[22] "The bird rite . . . is extraneous to the Priestly system of impurity and is a residue of a pagan exorcistic rite. . . . Indeed, it is most likely the pagan origins of this rite that motivated Israel's priesthood to take charge of its execution. In large measure the priests succeeded in excising, and failing that in blunting, the most blatant pagan elements of the rite."[23]

---

20. *KD* 404: "Aber gerade für die Erhaltung und Beachtung der Mannigfaltigkeit der geschichtlichen Erscheinungen wird dann am besten gesorgt sein, wenn das letzte Wort der Exegese auch hier tatsächlich der Name Jesus Christus ist." See also *CD* 389.

21. Milgrom, *Leviticus.*

22. Milgrom, *Leviticus,* p. 135.

23. Milgrom, *Leviticus,* p. 133.

Milgrom does, however, lead us into some interesting observations that happen to substantiate some of Barth's claims about the texts. Milgrom does notice the similarity in structure of the bird rite and the goat rite, but he leaves this observation without further comment.[24] He simply adds that "[t]he transformation of the bird rite into a practice compatible with Israel's monotheism was more successful than the similarly structured scapegoat rite in which the name of the original divine recipient of the animal, Azazel, was preserved."[25] Barth clearly has made more exegetical and hermeneutical hay here than this. Indeed, Milgrom actually suggests that the bird rite was retained because the "(mostly, non-monotheistic) masses insisted on it" [!], but also because "from the priestly point of view it presented vividly and forcefully the very battle and victory of life over death."[26]

In addition, Milgrom notes as does Barth the "binary opposition between holiness and impurity, which symbolize [sic] the forces of life and death, respectively."[27] Milgrom notes that all the elements in the rite connote life, the *live* wild birds, the *live* spring of water, the *lifeblood* and the bloodlike signifiers of the red cedar and the red yarn. "In opposition to this life-affirming ritual stands the scale disease, which itself so clearly illustrates the forces of death. . . . [This] is a rite of passage, marking the transition from death to life."[28] Milgrom thus notes the symbolism here, while Barth presses on to the significance of the symbolism. This is in part because Barth's reading of the texts of Leviticus 14 and 16 is holistic; that is, he is willing to read the biblical canon as both theological and historical backdrop, and thus can read of the resurrection of Jesus Christ as signified by the elements of the rite.

As for Milgrom's observations on Leviticus 16, he notes some of the fascinating similarities and differences between the Babylonian New Year

---

24. Milgrom, *Leviticus*, p. 133.

25. Milgrom, *Leviticus*, pp. 133-34.

26. Milgrom, *Leviticus*, p. 134. "Indeed, that the bird rite turns out to be extraneous to the rest of the Priestly ceremony proves that it has been borrowed from Israel's anterior cultures and it was retained not because Israel's priests wanted it but probably because the people at large demanded it, practiced it, and would not have tolerated its deletion. For them, this rite of exorcism was indispensable" (p. 136). Milgrom offers no evidence here to back up these claims. Apparently he is importing a playfully inversed Marxist understanding of religion here.

27. Milgrom, *Leviticus*, p. 134.

28. Milgrom, *Leviticus*, p. 134.

Festival and Israel's Yom Kippur.[29] He also points to the similarities and differences between the Azazel rite as it appears in Leviticus, and the Azazel and elimination rites in the Ancient Near East, and he concludes that "Israel's monotheism and priestly doctrine of collectiveness are the major contributing factors in transforming the elimination rites of the Ancient Near East into those of Yom Kippur."[30] He also argues that chapter 16 really follows on chapter 10 chronologically, and that chapters 11–15 are an editorial insert. Part of his reasoning is that, since Leviticus 19 is (or should be seen to be) the center of Leviticus, if one removes chapters 11–15, chapter 16 is brought closer to the center, indeed to the center of the Pentateuch. Milgrom also notes that the Priestly source wants to show Moses to be the true prophet over against Aaron, who plays a major role here.[31]

Milgrom does indeed offer "traditional" readings. A later rabbinic source does in fact, according to Milgrom, preserve the "best evidence of the original nature" of the Day of Atonement (Rabban Simeon b. Gamaliel).[32] This "original" reading of the Day of Atonement, however, cuts across the plain sense of the narrative at Leviticus 23:23-25, which shows the "dreary" nature of the holiday as it is now celebrated. Again, an "early rabbinic tradition" holds that a red ribbon was tied to the horns of the live goat, as a way of identifying the one goat from the other, since they had to be intentionally identical. Milgrom notes that this practice has ancient parallels, and he points to parallels within the Bible where red ribbons are used as marks of identification (Gen. 38:28; Josh. 2:18).[33] How-

---

29. Milgrom, *Leviticus,* p. 164.

30. Milgrom, *Leviticus,* p. 167.

31. Milgrom, *Leviticus,* p. 170. "It can hardly be overlooked that the Priestly source, as represented in Leviticus 16, is set up in deliberate contrast with the narrative tradition of Mount Sinai. . . . Whereas Moses penetrated the divine cloud, Aaron stands in front of the (incense) cloud — a discernible sign that the Priestly source concedes that the prophet (Moses) is superior to the priest (Aaron)."

32. Milgrom, *Leviticus,* pp. 162-63. "This day [the tenth of Tishri, the culmination of Israel's ancient New Year's festival] then, was marked by feasting, merriment, and the dancing of maidens in the vineyards, which, no doubt, resulted in many marriages throughout the land — a far cry from the practice of 'self-denial' that characterizes this day's successor to the present time. The transformation may have occurred when the emergency contingency for purging the sanctuary was abolished and its somber, mournful aspect was transferred to the 'once a year' purgation of the sanctuary on the tenth of Tishri, whose original jubilant character was replaced by fasting and penitence."

33. Milgrom, *Leviticus,* p. 169.

ever, this is simply stated as though "true," and no religious or ethical significance is offered.[34]

While Milgrom can therefore be said in some respects to read the text closely, he is more interested in the prehistory of the text as forming the present text than he is in reading the actual words themselves. Even the rabbis are interesting to him mainly for the way in which they agree with the former structure and religious context of the present text. However, something other than the narrative of the biblical text functions as the subject matter, *die Sache,* or *res,* of interpretation. The assumption is that this "something other" which is now taken to be the subject matter is in fact the *prehistory* of the text.

This tendency blocks Milgrom from reaching to the religious or ethical *significance* of the narratives of Leviticus 14 and 16, other than to offer a reading that Moses is greater than Aaron. And so, we might feel, the Lion of Judah does not roar. Of course Milgrom's religious community would be appalled if he, like Barth, were to push out from the shores of the Hebrew Bible into the foreign waters of the New Testament. There, they would hear the unpalatable (to their ears) confession of Thomas, who, when invited to put his finger into Jesus' post-resurrection wounds, declares: "My Lord and my God" (John 20:28). To this confession, of course, the Synagogue has said and continues to say no. At the same time, the Christian might ask whether Milgrom's religious community would feel ethically encouraged by this rabbi's notes on the prehistory of the Torah.

Finally, we will consider yet another contemporary interpreter of Leviticus, Robert Alter. Alter's genre is unique to him among the other two readers whom we have considered. Unlike Barth's *Dogmatics* and Milgrom's *Continental Commentary,* Alter writes of Leviticus 14 and 16 in the context of his *Five Books of Moses,* where his own interests lie presumably not in the prehistory of the text but in the textual nature and in the process and strategies for translating the canonical text. The work is, and describes itself as, a translation with a running commentary underneath.

The work of Alter, which has previously been so interested in the nar-

---

34. Milgrom, *Leviticus,* p. 170: "Thus the rabbi's exegesis of v. 13 must be correct: the ark is covered by 'the cloud' and not by 'the incense'. . . . Thus it can hardly be overlooked that the Priestly source, as represented in Leviticus 16, is set up in deliberate contrast with the narrative tradition of Mount Sinai. . . . Even then a difference is maintained. Whereas Moses penetrated the divine cloud, Aaron stands in front of the (incense) cloud — a discernible sign that the Priestly source concedes that the prophet (Moses) is superior to the priest (Aaron)."

rative of the Hebrew Bible, would lead one to expect much from the commentary in *The Five Books of Moses*.[35] Yet Alter may be more successful with narrative than with ritual. While his translation of Leviticus 14 and 16 is fresh, he does not have much to offer in the way of commentary, certainly less than Barth and even than Milgrom.

Alter's comments on the bird ritual of Leviticus 14, which Barth reads as a literary and theological parallel or comment on Leviticus 16, end up, perhaps surprisingly, as if echoing Milgrom's concern for the prehistory of the text. Alter looks to Milgrom on the details of the cedar wood and crimson for the "interpretation" that these elements are used in this rite of purification for their red color, "linked with blood, which also functions as a purifying agent."[36] At verse 5, he links the "live" bird with the "living water" (although he translates it as "fresh water"). He does not refer to Milgrom here, yet follows him. He notes at verse 6 how the Hebrew syntax "highlights the living bird in contrast to the slaughtered bird." And at verse 7 he notes the parallel between the releasing of the bird with the releasing of the scapegoat in chapter 16, but does not make any further comment on this "obvious analogy."[37] In addition, without crediting Milgrom (possibly since the comment is so used), Alter says that "there is something clearly archaic about this entire ritual, and scholarship has detected antecedents in Mesopotamian rites of magical purgation." Even here, he does not add Milgrom's comment about the specific use of such Mesopotamian rites when enfolded within the faith of the Hebrews.

In the ritual of the scapegoat, at Leviticus 16:8, Alter comments that ancient inscriptions and seals tell us something about how we should translate *laYHWH* and *la ʿazaʾzel*, that these words are the actual texts written on the two lots. In addition, Alter suggests that "Azazel is a goatish demon or deity associated with the remote wilderness. The name appears to reflect *ʿez*, goat."[38] The lots were in all likelihood pulled out of a box or urn. At verse 9, he notes again the similarity between the bird ritual and the goat ritual, but gets nothing out of the observation except this: "Approximate analogues to the so-called scapegoat ritual, using different animals, appear in several different Mesopotamian texts. The origins of the practice are surely in an ar-

---

35. I am thinking in particular of Robert Alter, *The Art of Biblical Narrative* (New York: Basic Books, 1981) and *The World of Biblical Literature* (New York: Basic Books, 1992).

36. Robert Alter, *The Five Books of Moses: A Translation with Commentary* (New York: W. W. Norton, 2004), p. 599.

37. Alter, *Five Books*, p. 600.

38. Alter, *Five Books*, p. 612.

chaic idea — that the polluting substance generated by the transgressions of the people is physically carried away by the goat."[39] He goes on to say that "an unapologetic reading might make out the trace of a mythological plot, even if it is no more than vestigial in this monotheistic context."[40] Alter also mentions the interpretation of the early rabbis at this point, but it gains his commentary no cohesion nor does it move it forward: the early rabbis imagined the goat as being pushed off a high cliff.

While Alter seems to have more success at reading the purer narrative texts of the Hebrew Bible, when it comes to the narratives of ritual, he is in danger of becoming banal. This is particularly interesting in light of his comments in his introduction: "But as I got caught up once again in this endlessly fascinating text, it struck me that there were important features that by and large had been given short shrift in the modern commentaries. . . . There were whole orders of questions, it seemed to me, that had been neglected or addressed only intermittently and impressionistically by the modern commentators."[41] It seems ultimately that Alter has succumbed to the indifference of modern commentary; and whatever the "whole orders of questions" may have been that he envisioned, we as readers of his text do not discover them. It is true that Alter is a consummate translator and maybe his "commentary's" achievements should be looked for here: "The present translation, whatever its imperfections, seeks to do fuller justice to all these aspects of the biblical style in the hope of making the rich literary experience of the Hebrew more accessible to readers of English."[42]

In any case, it can be seen that Milgrom and Alter, each with his own emphasis, do not come near the success that Barth has with the unfolding of the literary and theological qualities of these ritual narratives. Certainly one may object to Barth's use of the typology of "the One to Come," or his inserting of his own Chalcedonian concentration into the narratives,[43] and his claim that the Old Testament qua Old Testament points nowhere except into the abyss.[44] Indeed to read these texts as prophecy may seem it-

---

39. Alter, *Five Books,* p. 613.

40. Alter, *Five Books,* p. 613.

41. Alter, *Five Books,* p. xlvii.

42. Alter, *Five Books,* p. xlv.

43. See, for example, George Hunsinger, *How to Read Karl Barth: The Shape of His Theology* (New York: Oxford University Press, 1991), pp. 85-86, and "Karl Barth's Christology: Its Basic Chalcedonian Character," in Webster, ed., *Cambridge Companion to Karl Barth,* pp. 127-42.

44. I use the term "Old Testament" here advisedly and soberly. It was usually the term Karl Barth chose over against the term "Hebrew Bible." The contemporary political and

self a slip in genre. And yet it is clear that Barth makes more "sense" of the stories of these rituals than does either Milgrom or Alter. As for this kind of reading by which Barth makes more "sense" of the ritual narratives of Leviticus 14 and 16, which we might call typology just for convenience, Barth clearly feels that it is superior to the critical exegesis.

Frances Young, referring to the work of David Dawson, has suggested that even historical-critical exegesis (and also liberation and feminist readings) are forms of allegory.

> Even the once dominant historico-critical reading, against which such readings have reacted, may be regarded as in some sense allegorical in that it enabled the domestication of ancient texts to modern apologetic needs. It said, "You used to read these texts as being obviously about dogma, but really they are about something else." Every critical reading shares something with allegory according to Dawson; every attempt at entering the world of the text, or seeing the text as mirroring our world and reflecting it back to us, involves some kind of allegory.[45]

We have seen this tendency with both Milgrom and, surprisingly, with Alter.

So does Barth's exegesis involve this kind of allegory?[46] The word *typology* might be more appropriate, insofar as it follows Barth's use of

---

theological use of the term "Hebrew Bible" instead of "Old Testament" is anachronistic, of course, when dealing with Barth. I am certain though, that if he had lived to see the political and theological day, he still would have chosen "Old Testament" over "Hebrew Bible."

45. F. Young, "Allegory and the Ethics of Reading," in *The Open Text: New Directions for Biblical Studies?* ed. F. Watson (London: SCM Press, 1993), pp. 116-17. This is clear also in the earlier Milgrom quote above on the Levitical texts being "really" in some way about the Ten Commandments and his comments about the rites being "originally about" Mesopotamian purification rites. See also D. Dawson, *Allegorical Readers and Cultural Revision in Ancient Alexandria* (Berkeley: University of California Press, 1992).

46. Even though Barth does say something close to this: "No one reads the Bible directly; we all read it through a pair of glasses, whether we wish to or not." Barth, *Unterricht in der christlichen Religion: Prolegomenon* (Zürich: TVZ, 1985), p. 279. See also: "In this sense, we all pursue allegorical exegesis; that is, we make use of some key, some schematism of thought, in order to come along [with the text]." Barth, *Die christliche Dogmatik im Entwurf,* ed. Gerhard Sauter (Zürich: TVZ, 1982), p. 525. See also B. McCormack, "Historical-Criticism and Dogmatic Interest in Karl Barth's Theological Exegesis of the New Testament," in *Biblical Hermeneutics in Historical Perspective,* ed. Mark Burrows and Paul Rorem (Grand Rapids: Eerdmans, 1991), p. 335. I see Barth as engaging (at least here in Leviticus 14 and 16) in typology, and would think that he would agree. I understand his "key" or "schematism" to be the Rule of Faith. See Greene-McCreight, *Ad Litteram.*

typus or *type*. However, can one in fact assume an airtight distinction between allegory and typology? For Barth, the Old Testament contains or is built on a rich set of complex typological or figural correspondences, fully funded according to the text's immediate exegetical context. Even so, Barth suggests that the Old Testament points to the void without the Word of faith in Christ. The New Testament, as read by the church, concurs; and thus the person of Jesus Christ in his full deity and full humanity appears in type in the Old Testament and in the antitype of the One to Come, who has come and who always comes, in the New. Is this pattern of argument true of Barth's Old Testament exegesis elsewhere? And what of his New Testament exegesis? That would require another essay.

What is it then that functions as the *res* of Scripture for Barth? What does he look for in reading the Bible? Clearly here it is not merely historicity, although it is that in part. Neither is it only "original meaning," nor "original context," nor "prehistory" of the text. Barth focuses on *the way the words go,* the textual sense, and allows a ruled reading to guide him.[47] This policy means that ultimately Barth focuses on prophecy and announcement in the Old Testament. In Scripture Barth looks for, and indeed finds, the reality of the crucified and risen Christ, whom all Scripture is thought to attest. In the Old Testament, the reality of Christ appears only as *type,* as a supposition of faith, without which the Old Testament liturgies of Leviticus 14 and 16 would finally appear hollow and void. But with this kind of close reading and a ruled reading, Barth sees the substance of election and hope.

---

47. Greene-McCreight, *Ad Litteram.* "The way the words go" is used to translate Aquinas's *circumstantia litterae.* Cf. *De pot.* 4.1.r; 4.2.r; Bruce Marshall, "Absorbing the World: Christianity and the Universe of Truths," in *Theology and Dialogue: Essays in Conversation with George Lindbeck* (Notre Dame: University of Notre Dame Press, 1990), p. 101, n. 38.

6. "Living Righteousness":
Karl Barth and the Sermon on the Mount

A. Katherine Grieb

Introduction

In a conversation I once had with Stanley Hauerwas, he described his newly completed commentary on the Gospel of Matthew[1] as the hardest work he'd ever done in his life. This is a series that invites theologians to reflect on biblical texts directly, without engaging matters of historical and other kinds of higher criticism. Stanley said, "So I did away with the Synoptic Problem. Matthew is just writing by himself. And there's no distance between Matthew and Jesus: we're reading Jesus *with* Matthew, not through or against Matthew. And there's no distance between Matthew and us: I assume Matthew was writing to and for us." I said, "Of those three assumptions, the third is the least controversial from a New Testament point of view. Matthew was probably writing for anyone who would listen, so, arguably, for us." He said, "The critics are going to kill me." I said, "Hopefully not. You followed the rules of the game as defined by this project." In fact, I look forward to reading his commentary and I expect to learn a great deal from it.

But, as I have argued elsewhere with respect to 1 Corinthians in particular[2] and to Scripture in general,[3] Karl Barth's theological exegesis

---

1. Stanley Hauerwas, *Matthew*, Brazos Theological Commentary on the Bible (Grand Rapids: Brazos Press, 2007).

2. A. Katherine Grieb, "Last Things First: Karl Barth's Theological Exegesis of 1 Corinthians in *The Resurrection of the Dead*," *Scottish Journal of Theology* 56 (2003): 49-64.

3. A. Katherine Grieb, review of Richard E. Burnett, *Karl Barth's Theological Exegesis:*

This paper is dedicated to the memory of Jaroslav Pelikan (1923-2006), who combined history and theology with grace and vigor.

and his approach to reading Scripture theologically, at least in the mature writing of the *Church Dogmatics,* does not bracket out the historical framework, word studies, or literary analysis that is the meat of most biblical scholars. Barth is clearly interested in those questions as well. What is different about Barth is that he consistently refuses to *limit* himself to those questions, as so many biblical scholars do, as if the biblical scholar had one task to do and the theologian had another task to do. Barth deals with historical, philological, and literary questions as he needs to, often in an introductory way, framing the questions as he moves more deeply into the passage, brings it into conversation with other biblical texts, reflects on tendencies in the history of interpretation that have proved helpful or harmful, engages other interpreters of the passage either directly or indirectly, and finally gives us a reading that is profoundly christological, so that we come away from reading the biblical text with a sense of our relatedness to Jesus Christ through it.

Following Barth's own pattern, I want to spend a few minutes (1) recalling what is known about the Sermon on the Mount from a historical and literary point of view, before (2) turning to an overview of the history of its interpretation, with attention to important precursors and conversation partners behind Barth's reading, and then (3) I will discuss, at least briefly, Barth's reading of the Sermon as it appears in a short section of fine print in II/2. I will (4) argue that Barth's reading of the Sermon on the Mount makes some exegetical moves that are characteristic of his theological exegesis in general and that an important difference between Barth and Bonhoeffer is evident here. By way of conclusion, following Jaroslav Pelikan, whose recent death prompts me to dedicate this paper to his memory, (5) I will add a brief rhetorical comment about Barth's reading of the Sermon, before (6) closing with some observations about why Barth's theological exegesis, including historical, linguistic, and literary analysis, remains important for contemporary studies of the Sermon on the Mount.

1. The Sermon on the Mount: A Quick Overview and Review

First, then, a few brief reminders about the Gospel of Matthew, its overall structure, the place of the Sermon on the Mount within it, and the struc-

---

The Hermeneutical Principles of the Römerbrief Period (Tübingen: Mohr-Siebeck, 2001), in *Review of Biblical Literature* at Society of Biblical Literature website (Fall 2003).

ture of the Sermon itself from a literary point of view. Almost all New Testament scholars think the Gospel of Matthew was written sometime between 70 and 100 CE, perhaps in the mid-80s, based on Mark's Gospel as well as other traditions about Jesus available to the evangelist we name Matthew, following the tradition of the early church.[4]

Although there are alternative ways to outline the Gospel of Matthew, one of the most persuasive has been that suggested by Benjamin W. Bacon in 1930.[5] Bacon described a preamble (1:1–2:23) consisting of genealogy and infancy narratives, an epilogue (26:3–28:20) consisting of the passion narrative and accounts of resurrection appearances,[6] and between them a structure of five books, modeled on the Pentateuch, the five books of the Torah. Each of these five books has a narrative component paired with discourse material.[7] The end of each discourse is clearly marked by a phrase referring to Jesus finishing these sayings or parables. The end of the fifth and last discourse is marked by the phrase "When Jesus had finished saying *all* these things," which is followed by a final passion prediction and the passion narrative itself.

The Sermon on the Mount is the first of these discourses. The scholarly consensus is that this is not the transcript of an actual sermon delivered by Jesus, but rather a collection of sayings and teachings assembled, perhaps by Matthew, from smaller units of Jesus tradition. Combined with the place of privilege of being the first discourse of the five, is the literary framing device that has Jesus go up "the mountain" at its beginning and come down at its end. The generic reference to "the mountain" is widely interpreted by scholars, including Barth, as a reference to Moses' ascent of Mt. Sinai to receive the Torah. So Matthew 5:1-3 (NRSV) reads, "When Jesus saw the crowds, he went up the mountain; and after he sat down, his disciples came to him. Then he began to speak, and taught them, saying:

4. The four canonical Gospels were written anonymously and the traditional names of the evangelists come from early church tradition. Some scholars think Matthew and Luke shared a common tradition (or even text) not available to Mark ("Q"), but such a tradition/text is not needed to account for the interesting similarities and differences between Matthew's "Sermon on the Mount" and Luke's "Sermon on the Plain."

5. Benjamin W. Bacon, *Studies in Matthew* (London: H. Holt & Co., 1930).

6. Nils A. Dahl, in *Jesus in the Memory of the Early Church* (Minneapolis: Augsburg, 1976), questioned whether the passion narrative and resurrection appearances were not more central to Matthew's Gospel than the term "epilogue" implies.

7. Book 1: narrative 3:1–4:25; discourse 5:1–7:29; Book 2: narrative 8:1–9:35; discourse 9:36–11:1; Book 3: narrative 11:2–12:50; discourse 13:1–53; Book 4: narrative 13:54–17:21; discourse 17:22–19:1a; Book 5: narrative 19:1b–22:46; discourse 23:1–26:2.

Blessed are the poor in spirit, for theirs is the kingdom of heaven. . . ." (a phrase that occurs thirty-two times in Matthew's Gospel) and we're into the Beatitudes or blessings. There are nine of them, also carefully structured, with the longest at the end. The disciples are then compared to salt, light, and a city on a hill before Jesus solemnly warns them that he does not come to abolish the law but to fulfill it, that not one stroke of a letter will pass from the law until all is accomplished, and that unless the righteousness of his disciples exceeds that of the scribes and Pharisees, they will never enter the kingdom of heaven. Six antitheses follow, built on the pattern: "You have heard it was said . . . but I say to you . . . ," which includes some of the most strenuous commands in the Bible. We will return to these. The antitheses end with the difficult conclusion usually translated: "Be perfect, therefore, even as your heavenly Father is perfect."

Chapter 6:1-18 gives instructions on how the community of disciples is to practice its righteousness (the NRSV's word "piety" obscures the ongoing stress on righteousness throughout the Sermon); how to give alms, how to pray, how to fast. In the section on prayer, the "Lord's Prayer" appears, without the doxology added by the later church and with commentary underlining the need for forgiveness and forgiving. The rest of the chapter (6:19-34) concerns the singlemindedness of discipleship and injunctions not to worry about money, food, or clothing. The disciples are to seek first God's kingdom and its (or his) righteousness; they are not to worry about tomorrow; today's worries are enough for today.

Chapter 7:1-12 deals with judging, discernment, and reliance on God in persistent prayer. Verse 7:12 appears to serve as a summary: "In everything, do to others as you would have them do to you; for this is the law and the prophets." The rest of chapter 7 (vv. 13-27) builds on the proverbial doctrine of the two ways: one leads to destruction and one to life. False prophets come like wolves in sheep's clothing but will be known by their fruits. Jesus warns that not all those who call him "Lord" will enter the kingdom of heaven, but only the one who does the will of his Father in heaven. The others, even though they do deeds of power in Jesus' name, will be called "workers of lawlessness." The Sermon ends with Jesus' startling parable: the one who hears these words of mine and does them is like a wise man who builds his house on rock; it survives the floods and storms; but the one who hears these words of mine and does not do them is like a foolish man who built his house on sand; the winds and floods destroyed it and great was its fall. The discourse ends with Matthew's marker formula "now when Jesus had finished saying these things" and the framing device of his descent from the mountain. In between these is the important statement that "the crowds were astonished at his teaching, for he taught them as one having authority, and not as their scribes."

2. History of Interpretation: Important Precursors and Conversation Partners for Barth

That very quick review of the Sermon on the Mount and its key placement in Matthew's Gospel shows clearly that, as written in the first century of the Christian era, it was of some importance to the evangelist and to his community, but it was important as part of the larger Gospel with its prologue, its other narrative and discourse sections, its passion narrative and its resurrection stories. Dale C. Allison, who with W. D. Davies has written a three-volume extensive commentary on the Gospel of Matthew, rightly — from a strictly exegetical point of view — protests against lifting Matthew 5–7 out of the larger context supplied by Matthew 1–4 and 8–28.[8] It is Augustine who is generally credited with (or blamed for) coming up with the name "The Sermon on the Mount" (De Sermone Domini in monte) and for writing the first book (or rather two books) on Matthew 5–7 as a unit sometime between 392 and 396 CE. Augustine begins his commentary on the Sermon by referring to it as "the highest morals, the perfect measure of the human life."[9]

Augustine was not the only one of the church fathers to value the Sermon on the Mount or to comment upon it. "No portion of the Scriptures was more frequently quoted and referred to by the Ante-Nicene fathers than the Sermon on the Mount. The fifth chapter of Matthew appears more often in their works than any other single chapter, and Matthew 5–7 more frequently than any other three chapters in the entire Bible."[10] This summary of Jesus' ethical teachings was useful for the project of apologetics, defending Christianity by appealing to the high moral standards of its founder. As a result of the formation of the New Testament canon and the privileged place awarded to Matthew, the first Gospel, "the

---

8. Dale C. Allison, *The Sermon on the Mount: Inspiring the Moral Imagination* (New York: Crossroad, 1999), p. xi. See also his three-volume commentary, with W. D. Davies, *A Critical and Exegetical Commentary on the Gospel According to Saint Matthew*, International Critical Commentary, vol. 1 (Edinburgh: T. & T. Clark, 1988).

9. Warren S. Kissinger, *The Sermon on the Mount: A History of Interpretation and Bibliography* (Metuchen, NJ: Scarecrow, 1975), p. 13.

10. Kissinger, *The Sermon on the Mount*, p. 6.

church's Gospel," the Gospel most commented on by patristic, medieval, Renaissance/Reformation, and modern scholars, the Sermon on the Mount has become almost identified with the teachings of Jesus for the church throughout the ages.

Even modern skeptics who have become alienated from the church, its liturgies, and its creeds (its "dogma") have insisted that they were loyal to the person of Jesus of Nazareth and to his authentic message as summarized in the Sermon on the Mount and epitomized in its Golden Rule, "in everything do to others as you would have them do to you" (Matt. 7:12). To take just one example from many possibilities, the American poet Henry Wadsworth Longfellow devoted the "Prelude" of his *Tales of a Wayside Inn* to such a modern disciple and expositor of that message:

> Skilful alike with tongue and pen,
> He preached to all men[11] everywhere
> The Gospel of the Golden Rule,
> The New Commandment given to men,
> Thinking the deed, and not the creed,
> Would help us in our utmost need.[12]

From within the church, the Jesuit poet Gerard Manley Hopkins challenged: "Nowhere in literature is there anything to match the Sermon on the Mount: if there is, let men bring it forward." It has been called "the sermon of sermons" and "a standard by which all religious speech may be measured."[13]

And yet the Sermon on the Mount has posed a challenge for the church for most of its history and especially in the modern period. As G. K. Chesterton quipped, "The Christian ideal has not been tried and found wanting. It has been found difficult and left untried."[14] Jesus' teach-

---

11. The problem of honoring the specific words of an author who wrote before the conventions of language changed to become more inclusive without at the same time prejudicing modern readers against the author remains difficult. I have chosen to leave quotations written in English alone, but have modified translations (especially of Barth) where it could be done easily, leaving the rest. Barth scholars have long recognized the need for a new translation of the *Church Dogmatics* into the contemporary English idiom.

12. Jaroslav Pelikan, *Divine Rhetoric: The Sermon on the Mount as Message and as Model in Augustine, Chrysostom and Luther* (Crestwood, NY: St. Vladimir's Seminary Press, 2001), p. 37.

13. Pelikan, *Divine Rhetoric,* pp. 35-36.

14. A. E. Harvey, *Strenuous Commands: The Ethic of Jesus* (London: SCM Press, 1990), p. 1.

ing in the Sermon on the Mount is expressed in imperatives: it appears to lay down rules for which obedience is commanded. These commands seem to be radical, uncompromising, and (at times) extreme. It has been suggested that they cannot be totally and generally "obeyed" by any community of people living in the world as we know it. Does that mean that all of these would-be followers of Jesus are condemned to be perpetually in the wrong?[15]

Yes, answers one school of thought; all potential followers of Jesus Christ are condemned by the Sermon on the Mount. That is the whole point of the Sermon: to reveal to us our total depravity and disobedience to God's will and to force us to throw ourselves upon the gracious mercy of God.[16] This use of the Law is preparation for the Gospel. For Martin Luther and other Reformation commentators, the Sermon on the Mount plays the rhetorical role of Romans 1:18–3:20, a perfect and complete indictment of all humanity before God.

No, answers another school of thought; these commandments were never intended for everyone, but only for those who are free to adopt a life of total renunciation.[17] (See Thomas Aquinas, *Summa* 2.1 q. 108, art. 4 for a clear articulation of this double standard.) Some exegetes appeal to the story of the rich ruler who turned away from following Jesus as support for this position. Jesus had said to the man, "If you would be perfect, go, sell what you have and give to the poor, and you will have treasure in heaven; and come, follow me" (Matt. 19:21). There is already a hint of this tendency in the *Didache*, an early Christian writing that may have appeared shortly after Matthew and in the same general area of Syria. At 6:2 it says, "If you are able to bear the whole yoke of the Lord, you will be perfect; but if you are unable, do what you are able to do." The same sort of distinction between more and less advanced disciples was probably already known to the Essenes at Qumran, and was attested by the Manichees, the Bogomils, and the fourth- or fifth-century Syrian *Book of Steps*.[18]

Another school of thought argues that to read the Sermon on the Mount as requiring specific obedient actions is to misread it. Jesus was speaking not of acts but of inward dispositions. We "obey" when we discipline our wills to be ready to undertake such courses of action *if required*.[19]

---

15. Harvey, *Strenuous Commands*, p. 22.
16. Harvey, *Strenuous Commands*, p. 22.
17. Harvey, *Strenuous Commands*, p. 22.
18. Allison, *The Sermon on the Mount*, p. 3.
19. Harvey, *Strenuous Commands*, p. 22.

Once again the story of the rich man is appealed to, this time in conjunction with the counsel of 1 Timothy 6:10 that not money but the *love* of money is the root of all evil. The rich man could have been saved, perhaps even with his riches, if he had learned to free himself from his inordinate love of money. The antitheses of the Sermon on the Mount focus on our inner states, as in Psalm 51:6, "You desire truth in the inward parts." This was the view of Abelard and more recently of Wilhelm Herrmann (who taught both Barth and Bultmann) and E. F. Scott. Martin Dibelius has summarized the position as follows: the Sermon "does not demand of us that we *do something* but that we *be something*."[20] Allison points out that this reading works better with some parts of the Sermon than with others. It may help with adultery and anger, with almsgiving, prayer, and fasting, but it cannot accommodate the ruling on divorce. Indeed, one famous difficulty with the Sermon is that it does *not* consistently separate the inward from the outward, being from doing, intention from performance. One minute it commends an attitude; the next it requires an action.[21]

Yet another school of thought insists that these commands were appropriate only to the time when Jesus was speaking them: presumably his intentions for us would have been quite different.[22] There are several versions of this argument, but two of them are particularly important for us. The first is the Dispensationalist position associated with the nineteenth-century anti-liberal movement here in the United States (John Nelson Darby, the Plymouth Brethren, the Scofield Reference Bible) with its (usually seven) dispensations or ages of humanity. In this reading, the Sermon belongs either to "the age of Man under Law," from which Christians are exempt, or to "the age of Man under the Personal Reign of Christ," which will not arrive until after the Millennium. So Donald Grey Barnhouse says: "The offer of the Kingdom as made in the Sermon on the Mount is now definitely past. The age of grace runs its course. We are not to make the mistake of trying to force the Sermon on the Mount to a literal fulfilment today. It will be fulfilled literally, but not until the age in which we live comes to a close and the Lord shall be dealing once more with his people Israel."[23] In other words, the Sermon on the Mount is not our problem.

---

20. Martin Dibelius, *The Sermon on the Mount* (New York: Charles Scribner's Sons, 1940), p. 137, quoted in Allison, *The Sermon on the Mount*, p. 6.

21. Allison, *The Sermon on the Mount*, pp. 6-7.

22. Harvey, *Strenuous Commands*, pp. 22-23.

23. Donald Grey Barnhouse, *His Own Received Him Not* (New York: Fleming H. Revell, 1933), pp. 38, 40-41, quoted in Kissinger, *The Sermon on the Mount*, pp. 63-64.

The same happy results are achieved by another anti-liberal response, one that would be horrified to be linked with the Dispensationalists. I mean the "consistent eschatology" and "interim ethic" of Johannes Weiss and Albert Schweitzer. Against the Protestant liberalism of the nineteenth century, found in Wilhelm Herrmann and Albrecht Ritschl to be sure, but epitomized perhaps by Adolf von Harnack and his Kantian distinction between the "husk" of the Sermon on the Mount which could be discarded and the "kernel" of truth which must be kept, reducing the righteousness of God to the "brotherhood of man," Weiss and Schweitzer rightly argued that no such rationalistic distinction or reduction was possible. Jesus intended a radical, uncompromising ethic for himself and his followers for the particular brief interim time before the eschaton to prepare his disciples for the advent of the reign of God, which would come any moment. In fact, when it didn't come as soon as Jesus thought it should, he went and got himself crucified in Jerusalem to trigger God's apocalyptic vindication in the coming kingdom. He was, of course, tragically mistaken, says Schweitzer, though it was a reasonable belief for a messianically oriented Jew of his time. It would, however, be a category mistake for us to assume that the Sermon on the Mount, written under those unique circumstances, would apply today, when the reign of God seems as far away as ever. Once again, the Sermon on the Mount is not our problem.

There were several responses to Weiss and Schweitzer, among them C. H. Dodd's stress on the realized eschatology of the kingdom, but there are two more readings that are important to get on the table because they are Barth's immediate precursors and dialogue partners. These are Reinhold Niebuhr and Dietrich Bonhoeffer, both of whom come out of the Lutheran tradition and carry on Luther's own complex readings of the Sermon in very different ways.

Reinhold Niebuhr's treatment of the Sermon on the Mount as an absolute ethic is clear from the following quotation from *Christianity and Power Politics*: "The injunctions 'resist not evil,' 'love your enemies,' 'if ye love them that love you what thanks have you?' 'be not anxious for your life,' and 'be ye therefore perfect even as your Father in heaven is perfect,' are all of one piece and they are uncompromising and absolute."[24] His own solution to the problem is found in his essay "The Relevance of an Impossible Ethical Ideal," a chapter in his book, *An Interpretation of*

---

24. Reinhold Niebuhr, *Christianity and Power Politics* (New York: Charles Scribner's Sons, 1940), p. 8.

Christian Ethics.[25] Here Niebuhr explains that the prophetic ethic of Jesus goes beyond the demands of rational universalism. It represents a more "impossible possibility" than the universalism of Stoicism. "The faith which regards the love commandment as a simple possibility rather than an impossible possibility is rooted in a faulty analysis of human nature," since the human being remains a finite creature. "Jesus thus made demands upon the human spirit which no finite man can fulfil."[26] The Sermon thus leads us to "repentance, the gateway to the Kingdom." Out of despair, faith arises. Niebuhr reads the Sermon on the Mount in conjunction with Romans 7:19, "For I do not do the good I want, but the evil I do not want is what I do."

This very brief sketch of the history of modern biblical interpretation is designed to help you to see that most of this history of the interpretation of the Sermon on the Mount is the history of attempts to get rid of it if possible or at least to isolate it somehow, so that it can be valorized and honored in theory but not expected, for one reason or another, to be obeyed. The most notorious exceptions to that pattern are Leo Tolstoy, a long stream of Anabaptist interpreters, and Dietrich Bonhoeffer.

Bonhoeffer took Reinhold Niebuhr's phrase and turned it on its head when he spoke of "the impossible possibility" of simple obedience to God's "mandates," but it is also helpful to understand his thought in relation to Barth. Andreas Pangritz claims, in *Karl Barth in the Theology of Dietrich Bonhoeffer,* that the theological differences between Barth and Bonhoeffer have been overstated.[27] Upon Bonhoeffer's return to Germany in 1935, the Sermon on the Mount moved into the foreground of his thought and here, according to Eberhard Bethge, he did not yet find anything helpful in Barth. Already in 1934 Bonhoeffer had written to Erwin Sutz about the German church conflict: "You know, I believe — and perhaps you are surprised by this — that the whole matter will be resolved through the Sermon on the Mount." "I am currently trying to preach on it, very simply without pretension. And I speak always for *keeping* the commandment and against evading it." Similarly, he wrote to Reinhold Niebuhr, "The dividing line lies . . . with the Sermon on the Mount." To Sutz, he described his plans for the underground seminary at Finkenwalde:

25. Reinhold Niebuhr, *An Interpretation of Christian Ethics* (London: SCM Press, 1936), pp. 113-45.

26. Niebuhr, *Interpretation,* pp. 128-29.

27. Andreas Pangritz, *Karl Barth in the Theology of Dietrich Bonhoeffer* (Grand Rapids: Eerdmans, 2000), pp. 51-57.

"The entire training of the budding theologians belongs today in church, monastery-like schools in which pure doctrine, the Sermon on the Mount, and worship can be taken seriously." To his brother Karl Friedrich he spoke of "the uncompromising attitude of a life lived according to the Sermon on the Mount in the following of Christ."[28]

Writing to Sutz, Bonhoeffer commented that Barth's theology "both delayed once again . . . but also made for" the realization "how everything comes to a head through the Sermon on the Mount." Bethge notes that at this stage in Bonhoeffer's questions, Barth did not take him far enough. When he himself provided the answer he sought in *The Cost of Discipleship*, it was only after his death that Barth expressed the agreement and approval for which he longed.[29] Instead of Barth, Bonhoeffer turned to Søren Kierkegaard and his stress on the loneliness of the "individual" Christian over against "the idea of the church." Barth had been preoccupied with Kierkegaard at the time of his second edition of *Romans* in 1922, but had moved away from his "pietism." For Bonhoeffer, on the other hand, after Barmen, Kierkegaard's stress on the way that Christianity could not fit into the world was a word in season. Bonhoeffer's distinction between costly "grace as answer to the sum" and "grace as the data for our calculations" clearly goes back to Kierkegaard, as he himself notes.[30]

Bonhoeffer wrote his *Nachfolge* (*The Cost of Discipleship* with its section on the Sermon on the Mount) apart from Barth. When it was nearly finished in 1936, he wrote to Barth: "The whole period was basically a constant, silent discussion with you, and so I had to keep silent for a while. The chief questions are those of the exposition of the Sermon on the Mount and the Pauline doctrine of justification and sanctification. I am engaged in a work on the subject and would have asked and learnt a very, very great deal from you. . . ." He adds that usually, "most of us who feel that they had to keep away from you for a while . . . seem to find that afterwards, in a personal conversation with you, they learn that once again they have seen the whole question in far too crude terms." At about the same time, Barth expressed his concern about the "odor of monastic eros and pathos" he thought he detected in Bethge's "Introduction to Daily Meditation" in Finkenwalde. Much later, in *Letters and Papers from Prison*, Bonhoeffer himself worried about similar concerns: "I thought I could learn to have

---

28. Pangritz, *Karl Barth in the Theology of Dietrich Bonhoeffer*, pp. 51-53.
29. Pangritz, *Karl Barth in the Theology of Dietrich Bonhoeffer*, p. 53.
30. Pangritz, *Karl Barth in the Theology of Dietrich Bonhoeffer*, p. 56.

faith by trying myself to live a holy life or something like it. I suppose I wrote *The Cost of Discipleship* as the end of that path. Today, I clearly see the dangers of that book, though I still stand by what I wrote."[31]

What Bonhoeffer wrote, based on lectures delivered at Finkenwalde from 1935 to 1937, included an extensive commentary on the Sermon on the Mount with little or no recourse to philology or the usual matters of historical criticism. Jesus speaks directly to every disciple, and perhaps to every moral agent in the Sermon with commands that are as unambiguous as they are non-negotiable. Bonhoeffer feared that interpreting the Sermon could become a substitute for doing it. "To deal with the word of Jesus otherwise than by doing it is to wrong him. It is to deny the Sermon on the Mount and to say No to his word. If we start asking questions, posing problems, and offering interpretations, we are not doing his word."[32]

In his chapter "Single-Minded Obedience," Bonhoeffer tells a parable:

When orders are issued in other spheres of life there is no doubt whatever of their meaning. If a father sends a child to bed, the boy knows at once what he has to do. But suppose he has picked up a smattering of pseudo-theology. In that case he would argue more or less like this: "Father tells me to go to bed, but he really means that I am tired, and he does not want me to be tired. I can overcome my tiredness just as well if I go out and play. Therefore though father tells me to go to bed, he really means: 'Go out and play.'" If a child tried such arguments on his father or a citizen on his government, they would both meet with a kind of language they could not fail to understand — in short they would be punished. Are we to treat the commandment of Jesus differently from other orders and exchange single-minded obedience for downright disobedience? How could that be possible![33]

In his *Ethics* Bonhoeffer writes, "The Sermon on the Mount is there for the purpose of being done (Matt. 7:24ff.). Only in doing can there be

31. Pangritz, *Karl Barth in the Theology of Dietrich Bonhoeffer*, pp. 56-57. See also Haddon Willmer's article, "Costly Discipleship," in *The Cambridge Companion to Dietrich Bonhoeffer*, ed. John W. deGruchy (Cambridge: Cambridge University Press, 1999), pp. 173-89.

32. Dietrich Bonhoeffer, *The Cost of Discipleship* (New York: Macmillan, 1949), p. 168.

33. Dietrich Bonhoeffer, *The Cost of Discipleship*, 2nd ed. (New York: Macmillan, 1959), p. 90. Karl Barth quotes this parable in IV/2, pp. 541-42; and at IV/2, p. 533, he comments on "The Call to Discipleship": "Easily the best that has been written on this subject is to be found in *The Cost of Discipleship*, by Dietrich Bonhoeffer."

submission to the will of God."[34] Bethge contends that prior to his studies in the United States in 1932, Bonhoeffer had read the Sermon in one of the traditional "Lutheran" ways, namely, that to understand it literally was to make it into a law, and that law was abolished in Christ. Afterwards, Bonhoeffer still read the Sermon christologically, but he had moved from a law/gospel hermeneutic to a theology of the cross. One must "follow Jesus" and must be in "fellowship with the Crucified." It is the cross that enables someone "to do" the Sermon on the Mount.[35] Of Jesus' prohibition of oath-taking, Bonhoeffer says: "The cross is God's truth about us, and therefore it is the only power which can make us truthful. When we know the cross, we are not afraid of the truth. We need no more oaths to confirm our utterances, for we live in the absolute truth of God." As for Jesus' words about nonresistance, the cross is the only justification for this precept, for it alone makes possible a faith in the victory over evil that will enable people to obey this command. Likewise, to love our enemies takes us along the way of the cross and into fellowship with the Crucified, where we are certain of the victory of love over the enemy's hatred.[36]

Bonhoeffer's commentary on the parable of the builders illustrates his approach: "Humanly speaking, we could understand and interpret the Sermon on the Mount in a thousand different ways. Jesus knows only one possibility: simple surrender and obedience, not interpreting it or applying it, but doing and obeying it. That is the only way to hear his word. But again he does not mean that it is to be discussed as an ideal, he means really putting it into practice."[37]

3. The Definiteness of the Divine Decision: Barth and the Sermon on the Mount

Barth lectured on the Sermon on the Mount at Göttingen in the summer of 1925 and again at Bonn during the winter of 1933-34.[38] But, unlike Bonhoeffer, he never wrote a treatise on it, although there are numerous references to the Sermon in his *Ethics* and especially in the *Church Dogmatics.*

---

34. Bonhoeffer, *Ethics* (New York: Macmillan, 1955), p. 166.
35. Kissinger, *The Sermon on the Mount*, pp. 84-86.
36. Kissinger, *The Sermon on the Mount*, pp. 120, 125, 129.
37. Kissinger, *The Sermon on the Mount*, p. 168.
38. Eberhard Busch, *Karl Barth: His Life from Letters and Autobiographical Texts* (Philadelphia: Fortress, 1976), pp. 155, 234.

The longest of these is about fifteen pages of small print in II/2 from 686 to 700. Under the heading in section 38, "The Command as the Decision of God," Barth deals first with "The Sovereignty of the Divine Decision," "The Definiteness of the Divine Decision," and finally, "The Goodness of the Divine Decision." It is within that second section, "The Definiteness of the Divine Decision," that we find Barth's discussion of the Sermon on the Mount, after a lengthy preliminary discussion that I shall summarize briefly.

Barth has been discussing God's graciousness to us in Jesus Christ as a total divine claim to our obedience and a total decision concerning good and evil in the choice of our decisions (God's sovereignty). He distinguishes the divine decision from "the idea of the good," from Kant's "categorical imperative," and from "conscience" (II/2, 665ff.). In its definiteness, the command is unconditional, leaving us no other choice than that between obedience and disobedience (II/2, 669). "Because God has given us himself and constituted himself our Lord, he has also given us his command" (II/2, 670). The objection that the divine will is not known to us or not sufficiently known in its definiteness is as futile as it is cunning and deceitful. Barth reminds us of Genesis 3:1, where this objection was first raised (by the serpent) and concludes that "we all are without excuse" (II/2, 671). Now Barth is ready to make some distinctions. We must distinguish between the following two facts: (1) that the divine law in the Bible is always a concrete command; and (2) that this concrete commanding to be found in the Bible must be understood as a divine command relevant to ourselves who are not directly addressed by it (II/2, 672).

Barth insists that the entire Bible is full of ethics, but we will fail to see the woods for the trees if we are looking for "universal rules," which are not to be found there (II/2, 672). We must divest ourselves of the fixed idea (fixed since Kant) that only a universally valid rule can be a command (II/2, 673) because God's commands belong directly to a specific history and must be left in all their historical particularity and uniqueness (II/2, 673). An excursus follows in which Barth demonstrates from both testaments the specific and personal character of God's commandments given to biblical persons. We have only to look to see commands everywhere. That God's commands are specific and contingently historical does not mean they are arbitrary, accidental, or meaningless (II/2, 676). Indeed, God is faithful and constant. God is the God who elects in grace (II/2, 677). Barth describes the community in the form of Israel and the church that God wills to bring into being, the history of God's covenant of grace (II/2, 677-78).

Nevertheless, Barth concedes that "there are some biblical contexts in which the command assumes the form of general rules which are valid for large numbers of people and are detached from any particular historical circumstances" (II/2, 679). This raises an important methodological question (Barth describes it as an exegetical question of the first importance): whether we have to interpret these special texts (he's going to be talking about the Ten Commandments and the Sermon on the Mount) in the light of their historical context or whether, conversely, we have to interpret their historical context in the light of a general ethical understanding of these texts, which is what the church and theology have mostly done, whether overtly or covertly (II/2, 680). The church has read these passages in isolation, as if their historical context were merely decorative, as if they stated ethical principles and definite norms that had their own autonomous significance (II/2, 680). It is obvious, says Barth, that this is not the case. The theme of the Bible is *not* the proclamation of ethical principles, whether *we* like it or not (680). In fact, what we have in the Ten Commandments and the Sermon on the Mount are summaries or collections of earlier specific divine commands.[39] These summaries or collections of commandments are not intended to blur the definiteness by which God gives specific concrete commands. Let us say instead that they present a concentrated form of the divine command, as when several beams of light are concentrated through a lens or several wires are combined to form a cable (II/2, 681-82).

Here Barth begins the extended excursus in small print, dealing with the Ten Commandments in the first few pages and turning to the Sermon on the Mount on pages 686ff. We can't possibly discuss everything Barth does in these fifteen pages of small print. What I hope to do instead is to give you a few examples of typically Barthian exegetical moves, some three or four of them, that occur in these pages on the Sermon on the Mount and effectively transform our reading of it from the set of general rules or principles we might have expected to the concentrated form of the divine command that he has just described.

A. Reading the Sermon on the Mount in Conversation with Other Biblical Texts This is not an unusual move for readers of the Sermon on the Mount. We've already seen several strategic instances of it. The Sermon

---

39. Here Barth is on solid ground exegetically, using the work of historical and literary criticism to shape his theological approach to these texts in opposition to Kant.

was read by Thomas Aquinas and others in conjunction with the story of the rich man and Jesus' word to him, "If you would be perfect . . ." in order to limit it to counsels of perfection for those with a special vocation. Abelard, Wilhelm Herrmann, and Martin Dibelius read the Sermon with Psalm 51:6, "you desire truth in the inward parts," or similar texts in order to see it as recommending attitudes instead of actions. Reinhold Niebuhr read the Sermon in conjunction with Romans 7:19, "I do not do the good I want but the evil I do not want is what I do," which provided reinforcement for the assumed impossibility of keeping its commandments. What other biblical texts does Barth bring alongside the Sermon on the Mount and why does he do so?

The most important intertextual move Barth makes with the Sermon on the Mount is to pair it with the Decalogue. Here Barth follows Matthew, who has already set up a Jesus/Moses typology earlier in the Gospel and continues it here by having Jesus as the new Moses going up the mountain and giving us the commandments of God. By placing Exodus 20 next to Matthew 5–7, Barth is attending to the question of their literary genre and theological purpose as collections or summaries of God's commands.

Barth had pointed out, with respect to the Decalogue, God's word to Moses in Exodus 23:20-21, "Behold I send an angel before you, to keep you in the way and to bring you to the place which I have prepared. Beware of him and obey his voice, provoke him not; for he will not pardon your transgressions, for my name is in him." Barth comments: the salvation or overthrow of Israel depends on whether it will hearken to the voice of this angel, of Moses, and later of the prophets, that is, to the living voice of God himself. That is the context in which the commandments are given (II/2, 686).

Similarly, in the Sermon on the Mount, Barth assumes an exegetical context: in this case, the consummation of the covenant of grace in Jesus Christ. Romans 10:4 seems to be in the background when Barth says: "Jesus himself is the kingdom of the new humanity. . . . Proclaiming this threefold unity, the Sermon on the Mount proclaims the consummation of the covenant of grace, and therefore the *telos* of the Law and the Ten Commandments" (II/2, 688). Not surprisingly, Barth uses an alternative scriptural passage to reframe the discussion christologically: it is Jesus Christ, the reign of God, the new humanity, all three, that is the point and final goal of the Law. At a later point, Barth imports a word from John 15 to underline another christological reality, "Without me you can do nothing," which serves to introduce the Sermon's discussion of prayer and the Lord's Prayer. There are several other texts that might be discussed,[40] but what is important to notice is that Barth does not bring other biblical texts into conversation with the Sermon in order to limit its authority or its scope, which is what many of his exegetical precursors do; instead, he uses other biblical texts to strengthen his christological reading of the passage.

B. "Like an Offered Checkmate": Reality and Illusion in Barth's Reading of the Sermon Barth insists that the Sermon on the Mount, like any other biblical text, must be read in the light of its context, that is, in a special connection with the theme of God's reign as it has come in the person of Jesus Christ in fulfillment of Old Testament prophecy. This is as true of the Sermon on the Mount as it is of the other great discourses in Matthew.[41] Now it is Jesus himself who defines the sphere in which he is present with those whom he calls. The order that constitutes the life of the people of God, for that is what the Sermon on the Mount is, as it repeats and confirms the Ten Commandments and the rest of the Law, is now fulfilled by God in Christ for human salvation (II/2, 687). So even if the Sermon seems to be concerned with problems of human life (marriage, swearing, enemies, almsgiving, praying, and fasting), this is incidental and by way of illustration — which is why it has always proved impossible to construct a picture of the Christian life from these directions. The picture they offer is the picture of the One who gives these directions and of the one who receives them. The picture shows God's reign, Jesus Christ, and the new human creature. They point, as the Ten Commandments point, to what God has done and is doing in Jesus Christ (II/2, 688).

So Barth can say: "If the Ten Commandments state where [humanity] may and should stand before and with God, the Sermon on the Mount declares that [it] really has been placed there by God's own deed. If the Ten Commandments are a preface, the Sermon on the Mount is in a sense a postscript" (II/2, 688). The only question now is whether the church will live or not live in the fullness of life already granted to it. The Sermon on the Mount declares: "God has irrevocably and indissolubly set up the kingdom of [God's] grace . . . which as such is superior to all other powers, to which, in spite of their resistance, they belong, and which they cannot help but serve" (688).

---

40. For example, Jeremiah 31 and "Thou art the man" from 2 Samuel.
41. Notice, again, that Barth is aware of and attentive to the literary design of the Gospel.

Barth offers an analogy: it is

> like an offered checkmate [in a chess game where one player has all but won] after which the defeated adversary, if . . . not sufficiently intelligent to give up the game, may wonder for yet a few minutes whether there is not the possibility of avoiding it. To the extent that this lack of understanding on the part of the defeated adversary is a fact, the conflict seems as if it would and could go on further. The reign of heaven seems not yet to have come, or merely to have drawn near, or merely to beckon . . . as a future possibility. The Sermon on the Mount reckons with this powerful and fatal appearance by saying of those that weep that they *shall* be comforted, of the meek that they *shall* possess the earth, of those who hunger and thirst after righteousness that they *shall* be filled. (II/2, 689)

But the Sermon attests that this is only an appearance by insisting of the poor in spirit that theirs *is* the kingdom of heaven, and again of those who are persecuted for righteousness' sake, that theirs *is* the kingdom of heaven. Because they hope for it, they already have it; because they know that it has come, they are already called to live as citizens within it.

It is striking what Barth has done here. Reality is defined as what God has already won in Jesus Christ while illusion is the temporary blindness or confusion whereby we humans and any other resisting powers fail to see that the chess game is actually already over. There are only one or two moves left and the outcome is determined in God's gracious covenant love. The Beatitudes, then, witness to this reality, and summon us to celebrate it by living into the reign of God.

Two other aspects of Barth's exegesis should be noticed under this heading. The first is that Barth has done his exegetical homework on the Beatitudes with care and thoroughness. His theological commentary shows that he has noticed the same pattern that other exegetes have also seen: although there are nine beatitudes, the ninth is set off by its length, its direct address to the disciples, and the mention of their reward. The remaining eight beatitudes describe in the third person a series of groups that are blessed (e.g., "blessed are the meek") and a warrant for the judgment that such a group is blessed by God, since in several cases, if not all, such a judgment is counterintuitive to human reasoning. These eight beatitudes are tightly framed by the first and eighth beatitudes, which use the present tense in conjunction with the reign of God (NRSV: "for theirs is the kingdom of heaven") while the middle six use the future tense (e.g., the meek "will inherit the earth"). Barth's exegetical study of the structure of the unit funds his theological reflection on the difference between the tenses, the dual witness of the Sermon about reality and illusion.

The other aspect of Barth's exegesis that is remarkable here is his personification of the Sermon on the Mount, almost as if it were a character in the story. The Sermon "declares" that God's gracious reign has begun; it "reckons" with the potency of the illusion that this reign has not yet arrived; and it "attests" that this appearance really is only an illusion. Although there is little warrant in Matthew's Gospel for this hermeneutical device, Barth may be consciously imitating the apostle Paul, who also personifies Scripture at key points in his argument and even invents a character called "the righteousness of faith" that is allowed to give its own interpretation of the Torah. Indeed, perhaps the link from Matthew to Paul in Barth's mind may have been the heavy concentrations of the word "righteousness" in Paul's letter to the Romans and in Matthew's Gospel.[42]

C. "Grace Itself Decides What Is Natural in Its Own Sphere": The "Strenuous Commands" of the Sermon on the Mount

Barth does not duck the hermeneutical issue that is responsible for so many attempts to honor the Sermon on the Mount in theory but to avoid it in practice: namely the apparent impossibility of fulfilling its commands in any ordinary life situation. What about those "strenuous commands" as Harvey called them, the rigorous requirements of giving to everyone who asks, not resisting evil, loving our enemies, abolishing unwelcome sexual thoughts? Barth comments:

> It has occasionally been said too loudly and confidently that in the examples formulated in 5:21-48 the radical deepening of the Old Testament Law is not meant to be understood in terms of Law, as so many precepts which we are literally to practice. And it is good that there have always been so-called fanatics[43] who have understood these require-

---

42. Sometimes I think Barth does this just to tease any modern and postmodern readers who are offended by the personification of the Bible. We all know, they tell us, that a text can't speak. It lies there inert and passive on the table while we perform some exegetical or hermeneutical operation on it. But for Barth, "the Word of God is active, sharper than any two-edged sword" (Heb. 4:12).

43. Like Tolstoy, who used the Sermon to argue for absolute nonviolence and nonresistance. See Barth's important note about Tolstoy and Gandhi in III/4, 429-30: "If Tolstoy and

ments, and all those of the Sermon on the Mount, as a Law which has to be fulfilled literally. For it is true enough that what we have here are only examples. But it is also true that these examples are intended to make clear that the grace of Jesus Christ, the grace of the kingdom which has dawned, has claimed the whole [person] absolutely. It is also true that the only One who really fulfils the Law as understood in this way is Jesus himself. . . . The uneasiness which this fact causes is very real and cannot be argued away. How can a [person] pray with Jesus [who] insulates himself against this uneasiness, or can handle it in such a way that it ceases to disturb? These sharpened requirements point — inevitably — to superhuman possibilities. It would be wrong to say that any of them are inapplicable to us — even the plucking out of the eye or the cutting off of the hand — on the plea that they have been fulfilled by Jesus, and therefore we do not need to fulfil them again, but have to learn from them how great is the sinfulness which separates Jesus from our sinfulness. Far too many things in the Sermon on the Mount and the rest of the Gospel would go by the board in this view.

These demands . . . claim us as sinners — but as those for whom Jesus prays and whom he summons to pray with him. They insist on the obedience of the disobedient and [those sinners] cannot elude this obedience by referring to the measure and limit of their capacity. The limit of their capacity becomes irrelevant when that which Jesus the Lord accomplishes for them occupies the center of the picture which is a norm for their own life's picture. We cannot play fast and loose with the grace of God, as if the supernatural life that it confers could suddenly have only what we judge to be natural consequences. Grace itself decides what is natural in its own sphere. And so we must accept the fact that — whether their fulfilment seems possible or impossible to us — these demands denote modes of conduct which can become possible and necessary even in their literal sense for those who hear and do the words of Jesus. (II/2, 696-97)

These words are sobering to anyone who has pondered the current preoccupation in exegetical and homiletical circles with the phenomena of "dif-

---

Gandhi were wrong, they were a hundred times nearer the truth with their teachings than are the primitive gospel of the mailed fist and all the doctrines which have tried to blunt the edge of these sayings by the sophistical distinction between a sphere in which they are valid and another in which they are not. And it would have been far better if history had known more of the exaggeration of Tolstoy and Gandhi than the opposite."

ficult texts" in the Bible. Of course, a text can be considered "difficult" in several ways, which are worth distinguishing: (1) It can be difficult to understand conceptually: What does it mean? (2) It can be difficult to understand as God's Word (apparently insensitive, factually incorrect or distorted, naïve or blind, perhaps even cruel). (3) It can be difficult to understand in the sense of counterintuitive, nonrational: Could this really be what the text intends? (4) It can be difficult to imagine living into or embodying: Is such a recommendation possible? Is it wise? And (5) it can be difficult to bear as a burden: the recommended action may be a costly, even frightening call to walk the way of the cross. Arguably, some of these heuristic distinctions may collapse into each other when applied practically, but it is already clear that examples of each of these occur in the Sermon on the Mount. Prayer will be important at every level of the discussion, as Barth indicates. There may be unexpected power available, both for understanding and for accomplishing what seems difficult or even impossible at first reading.

D. "Living Righteousness": A Difference Between the Christological Readings of Barth and Bonhoeffer

Both Bonhoeffer and Barth stubbornly refuse to eliminate the radical demands of the Sermon on the Mount. Barth insists that there is a place at the exegetical table for "so-called fanatics" like Tolstoy, the long stream of Anabaptist exegetes, and Mahatma Gandhi (III/4, 429-30). He asserts that Bonhoeffer got it right on the cost of discipleship, even if he is unwilling to follow Bonhoeffer's exegesis of the Sermon on the Mount. Both of these theologians "solve" the hermeneutical challenges of the Sermon christologically, but they do this differently: Bonhoeffer appeals to the Crucified One as the one who has the *exousia* "authority" not like that of the scribes (Matt. 7:29). While Barth also appeals to the "authority" of Jesus Christ, he grounds it in the Lordship of Christ. In another part of II/2 ("The Content of the Divine Claim"), Barth makes this grounding explicit:

> "And where I am, there will my servant be also." It is not possible to be with Jesus without necessarily being called and drawn into the occurrence indicated by these demands. . . . His servitude is his Lordship because in it he lives and proclaims the grace of God by his obedience. That is why he has "authority" *(exousia)*, why he does not speak as the scribes (Mt 7:29), why his doctrine is not a way of life or program for world betterment, or his life a pattern for its execution, but wholly and

utterly the event of God's dealing with [humanity]. We cannot, then, be with him merely to learn and accept this or that and leave on one side what we find inconvenient. (II/2, 570)

When Barth speaks of "living righteousness" he seems to have in mind the double meaning of the resurrection and vindicated righteousness of Jesus Christ and the righteousness required of those who live "in Christ" by virtue of their baptisms. On the one hand Barth can say: "Thus the righteousness which the Sermon exacts is inseparable from the One who exacts it. It is his righteousness. . . . He, this One, is the embodiment of the righteousness he demands" (II/2, 692, 693). "It is the Commander who embodies the command" (II/2, 690). On the other hand, he can also say, "The Sermon on the Mount tells us that the new [human] is called into life by the fact that there is addressed to him by Jesus the Word of the higher righteousness, the righteousness of the kingdom, the Word of the grace of God directed to him" (II/2, 693). "Thus the grace of this Word is itself the righteousness which comes to [human beings] and is to be exercised by [them] . . . and it is the righteousness of the kingdom (6:33) because it consists directly in the deed and gift of the Lawgiver and Judge, because it is powerfully created and imparted by him, because it is the living righteousness of those to whom he utters it" (II/2, 691).

"His Word Is Truth": A Brief Rhetorical Comment on Barth's Reading of the Sermon on the Mount

Twice in the fifteen pages of small print on the Sermon on the Mount that occasion these reflections, Barth refers to the "Word of Truth." "[Humanity] does not look only to the future as such, but to Jesus as [its] only and real future. And this future is not a mere future without present actuality, or a mere promise without present fulfillment. His Word is the truth — not tomorrow only but already today — for his kingdom, the kingdom of heaven proclaimed by his Word, is the kingdom of the eternal God himself, and this God is faithful" (II/2, 690). And again: "As it is said to a man by Jesus, and he allows it to be said: Thou art the man!, as he accepts the Word of Jesus and dares to live in the strength of it, righteousness is imparted to him, the unrighteousness that Satan and he himself have brought upon himself is dispelled, and he becomes a righteous man. The grace of this Word, the Word of truth, makes him this" (II/2, 691).

In one of his last books, *Divine Rhetoric*,[44] Jaroslav Pelikan returned to three earlier works on the preaching of Augustine, Chrysostom, and Luther on the Sermon on the Mount. In *Divine Rhetoric*, Pelikan explores the hermeneutical challenges of the Sermon, as reflected in its troubled history of interpretation, and shows how Aristotle's categories of *ethos, pathos,* and *logos* are useful for showing the differences among these three interpreters of the Sermon. If *ethos* has to do with the character and authority of the speaker, all three preachers understood Jesus Christ as the speaker of the Sermon, but in different ways: Augustine saw Christ as "Wisdom" and "Practical Wisdom" incarnate; Chrysostom's Christ the speaker was "Virtue" personified; Luther's Christ spoke as God's "Good Will" made manifest. For Aristotle, *pathos* had to do with the audience's frame of mind. Augustine saw the audience as "soldiers for God" while Chrysostom envisioned reaching all people through those who heard him, and Luther interpreted the audience as "Christians living in society." Finally, the *logos* of Aristotle concerned the content of the message itself and what sort of change was hoped for in the hearers. Augustine sought to communicate "the Perfect Measure of the Christian Life," and Chrysostom wanted to urge his hearers to "Become like God," while Luther wanted his audience to live into "God's Two Kingdoms."

It would be useful to attempt to apply Aristotle's rhetorical categories to the long history of interpreters of the Sermon on the Mount, but present constraints of space and time forbid anything more than attempting to apply them very briefly to Barth. Given Aristotle's categories as applied by Pelikan to Augustine, Chrysostom, and Luther, three earlier homiletical interpreters of the Sermon on the Mount, what should we say about Karl Barth on matters of *ethos, pathos,* and *logos*?

It seems clear that the most important thing to say is that Barth would *not* understand Jesus Christ to be the speaker of the Sermon on the Mount in quite the same way that Augustine, Chrysostom, Luther, Bonhoeffer, and perhaps Hauerwas would. On one level, of course, the narrative framework around the Sermon clearly ascribes it to Jesus. At 5:1, Matthew's Gospel describes Jesus going up the mountain, sitting down, and beginning to speak and teach: what follows is the Sermon on the Mount. At its conclusion in 7:28-29, it is Jesus who astonishes the crowds, teaches with authority, and descends the mountain, followed by great crowds. But the name "Jesus" does not appear in between, even at places where we might expect it: there is no narrative setting interposed at the start of the closing

44. *Supra* n. 12.

parable, such as "Jesus told this parable" although the authority of Jesus clearly stands behind it (cf. the "Lord, Lord" of 7:21-22 and "these words of mine" in 7:24 and 7:26). Matthew, or the tradition he reports, brackets the unit between these two narrative sections with discourse that could be lifted out as a separate unit. That is exactly what Barth does in this section of the *Church Dogmatics*, following Augustine and the Western Christian reading tradition, and perhaps following signals already present within the text of the Gospel itself.

To the extent that it makes sense to isolate the Sermon as a unit at all, Barth describes it, along with the Decalogue, as a witness to the Word of God who is properly Jesus Christ. These words of Scripture, whether we see them as words of Matthew's collection and composition or words of early Jesus tradition drawn into a single unit, have a witnessing function to the coming of God's reign, Jesus Christ, and the new human creature. It is not so much Jesus Christ as Author, though admittedly the Sermon is his in some sense, but it is Jesus Christ as Subject of the Sermon — the One to whom it points — who has the character and authority *(ethos)* that in Aristotle's view is the most important part of rhetoric. From Barth's rhetorical point of view, while Jesus may be the speaker of the Sermon on the Mount as it is narratively framed, the contents of the Sermon understood as a unit testify to his *ethos* as its Subject. Indeed, perhaps he is as much the *logos* as the *ethos*, for the rhetorical change desired (the awareness of the arrival of the reign of God, Jesus Christ, and the new humanity) is the subject of the Sermon's witness. As to the element of *pathos*, the frame of mind of the audience, as Barth conceives it, is that of the chess player who either does or does not realize the reality of the situation that God in Christ has defeated every power and principality. The game is over, even if it appears otherwise temporarily.

Conclusion: "On Christ the Solid Rock I Stand. All Other Ground Is Sinking Sand"[45]

The Sermon on the Mount ends with the parable that frames the issue of obedience or disobedience dramatically: whoever hears "these words of

---

45. Barth would not mind, I think, the interpolation of this hymn (words by Edward Mote, 1797-1874) here at the end. Hymn texts appear in the *Church Dogmatics* regularly, frequently aiding and abetting his own christological interpretation of biblical texts.

mine" and does them will be like the wise person who built on rock; that rock stands amid the floods and winds; but whoever hears "these words of mine" without doing them will be like the fool who built a house on sand and, in the time of turbulence, great was its destruction. This parable is the logical stepping-off place for closing observations about why Barth's theological exegesis, including historical, linguistic, and literary analysis, remains important for contemporary studies of the Sermon on the Mount.

I have called attention in this paper to several distinctive aspects of Karl Barth's theological exegesis of the Sermon on the Mount, using his own language to characterize them wherever possible. For Barth, "the definiteness of the divine decision" consists not only in its historical and personal specificity ("universal rules" are not to be found in the Bible but rather specific commands to particular persons in the peculiar circumstances of their histories) but also in its unmistakability and concreteness, not only to those who first heard the command but to us as well, who are not directly addressed by it. There are, however, some biblical contexts in which the command assumes the form of general rules, such as the Ten Commandments and the Sermon on the Mount. Barth's decision to read these biblical passages together not only follows Matthew's Jesus/Moses typology but also pays attention to the literary genre of the texts themselves. They are concentrated forms of the divine command, as when several beams of light are concentrated through a lens or several wires are combined to form a cable. Unlike many of his exegetical precursors, Barth does not yoke the Sermon on the Mount to another biblical text to subvert its claims, but to strengthen his christological reading of the passage.

Barth describes the rhetorical situation of the Sermon as being "like an offered checkmate" where discernment is needed by the hearers to recognize that the game is in fact over: the reign of God is at hand. Barth's decision to frame the situation in terms of reality or illusion matches the witness of the concluding parable: build your house on solid reality rather than on self-deception. The Beatitudes, which together with the parable frame the Sermon, testify both to the fatal attraction of the illusion and to its destiny of destruction: the truly fortunate are the ones who seem to be wasting their energy driving those piles into the hard rock when the soft sand would be so much easier to work with. Where is Wisdom to be found? Barth's christological reading of the Sermon matches Matthew's own description of the easiness of this yoke and the lightness of the burden. And if the "strenuous commands" and the "difficult texts" seem unrealistic or even impossible, Barth warns us against deciding in advance that

the supernatural life that grace confers could have only natural consequences. Since "grace itself decides what is natural in its own sphere," the
perceived limit of our capacity to obey becomes irrelevant and prayer becomes mandatory.

Yet the summons to obedience is not warranted by the authority of
"the Crucified One" as it is for Bonhoeffer. For Barth, the authority of the
command is grounded in the "Lordship of Christ," the Commander who
embodies the command, the "living righteousness" of the Word of God
("he lives!"). Finally, then, the decision upon what to build our lives is a
decision for God's own righteousness, demonstrated in the dawning of
God's gracious reign — in the death and resurrection of Jesus Christ, in
the renovation of the human creature. Or, to paraphrase Barth, "Left to
ourselves, we would certainly give that which is holy to the dogs in favor of
a system of law or lawlessness. Our gratitude would immediately be turned
into ingratitude. The goodness of our works would disappear at once. [As
our Lord says,] 'Without me, you can do nothing.'"

7. The Same Only Different: Karl Barth's Interpretation of Hebrews 13:8

George Hunsinger

For Karl Barth some biblical passages were of exceptional importance. Not only did they shape the New Testament message as a whole, but they were decisive in the construction of theological judgments. Marking such key passages can help to anchor Barth's difficult trains of thought and throw light on them. They illustrate how theological exegesis functioned for him within the larger framework of church dogmatics.

Barth learned to appreciate certain texts from the Reformers. Like Luther and Calvin, for example, he placed great emphasis on 1 Corinthians 1:30, which states that Christ has been made our wisdom, righteousness, sanctification, and redemption. For Barth as for the Reformers, this verse was seminal, because it meant that Christ's saving benefits were inseparable from his person.

Christ was not the source of some benefits — some wisdom, righteousness, sanctification, and redemption — other than himself. They were not detachable from him, as if external to his person, but could be received and enjoyed only in union with him. The grammar that governed Christ and his benefits was set by a pattern of unity-in-distinction. Only through union with the person of Christ could his saving benefits be received, for Christ and his benefits were one. His benefits were received only as he himself was received by faith.

To this insight, on which the Reformation entirely hinged, Barth added a characteristic note of his own. Christ's saving benefits, like righteousness and sanctification, were first of all worked out, Barth urged, apart from us. Their present-tense availability depended on, so to speak, their perfect-tense actualization — that is, on Christ's personal historical achievement of them — for our sakes. In other words, Christ's saving benefits were entirely a function of his active and passive obedience (Rom. 5:19). They were predicates of his person, which in turn was inseparable from his work. We receive the benefits or predicates of his person as accomplished by his work only through our life in fellowship with him, "whom God made our wisdom, our righteousness and sanctification and redemption" (1 Cor. 1:30 RSV).

Another verse that Barth learned to appreciate from the Reformers was Colossians 3:3: "You have died and your life is hid with Christ in God." Barth commented:

> In Christian doctrine . . . we have always to take in blind seriousness the basic Pauline perception of Colossians 3:3 which is that of all Scripture — that our life is our life hid with Christ in God. With Christ: never at all apart from him, never at all independently of him, never at all in and for itself. Human beings never exist at all in themselves. . . . The being and nature of human beings in and for themselves as independent bearers of an independent predicate, have, by the revelation of Jesus Christ, become an abstraction which can be destined only to disappear. (II/1, 149)

The central message of the Reformation was that Christ himself, and Christ alone, is our righteousness and our life. To the Reformers, Colossians 3:3 meant that this righteousness and life were fully real for us in Christ even now, although as such they remained hidden from us and were also yet to come. Barth shared this complex view.

> Is not our life hid with Christ in God (Col. 3:3)? Yet its concealment, and the fact that we cannot "see" in this concealment, does not alter in the very least the fact that in this concealment (with Christ in God), in which we can know it only by faith, it really is our own life, fully and radically renewed on the basis of and in correspondence with the reconciliation accomplished in him. (IV/3, 318)

What Barth perceived in Colossians 3:3, and what made it so seminal for him, was that he saw it as implying a christocentric eschatology of participation, a theme that we will have to leave for another day. Yet, to say at least this much, it meant that contrary to all appearances, all humankind and indeed the whole cosmos were already objectively included by grace as participants in the person and work of Jesus Christ, whose significance for human beings would be fulfilled only as they acknowledged him, and were received into fellowship with him, by faith, so that at last they might be glorified with him in eternal life.

Finally, as one last example of a key text, consider Barth's assessment of 2 Corinthians 5:19. "Dogmatics has no more exalted or profound word," he wrote, " — indeed it has no other word — than this: that *God was in Christ reconciling the world to himself*" (II/2, 88). For Barth God's reconciling work in Christ was the pivot on which all things turned. Reconciliation was in fact the central content of revelation. It determined all the ways and works of God with the world. Redemption was Barth's term for the absolute future of reconciliation, election was its pretemporal ground, creation and fall were its indispensable presuppositions, and revelation was its only means of being known.

Barth saw reconciliation, again with the Reformation, as a "self-contained and completed event":

> Reconciliation in itself and as such is not a process which has to be kept in motion toward some goal which is still far distant. It does not need to be repeated or extended or perfected. It is a unique history, but as such — because God in Christ was its subject — it is present in all its fullness in every age. It is also the immediate future in every age. And finally, it is the future which brings every age to an end. It rules and controls all the dimensions of time in whose limits the world and the human race exist. (IV/1, 76)

The three key verses we have mentioned — 1 Corinthians 1:30, Colossians 3:3, and 2 Corinthians 5:19 — were profoundly interconnected in Barth's mind.

- The first of them (1 Cor. 1:30) suggested various patterns of coinherence: Christ was coinherent with his saving benefits, even as his person was coinherent with his saving work, so that his benefits had to be conceived as predicates of his very person. As such they were achieved through his history of obedience as carried out for our sakes and in our place.
- The second verse (Col. 3:3) picked up on another pattern of coinherence, namely, that between Christ and the church. Our righteousness and our life are hid with Christ in God. Being directly present in eternity to God, the risen Christ is present to us in time only indirectly. He mediates his presence to us, for the time being, through

the earthly forms of Word and Sacrament. But through those earthly forms he unites himself with us and us with himself. Indeed through them we are made coinherent with him and he with us, by a pattern of mutual indwelling, so that we belong to him in the *totus Christus*. We therefore partake fully of his saving predicates even now — his righteousness and life — despite their being hid from us on earth apart from faith.

• Finally, the third verse (2 Cor. 5:19) suggested yet another pattern of coinherent relations. This time, however, the relations were largely temporal. Reconciliation as accomplished in Christ stood somehow at the center not only of creation and fall, but also of election and redemption. It therefore formed the essential content of revelation. The various moments of God's ways and works toward the world — including election, creation, and redemption, and all as oriented to reconciliation — could not be conceived, Barth argued, as merely external to one another. In some sense, as Barth saw it, they interpenetrated one another yet without losing their essential distinctions.

These three instances of coinherence — the indivisibility of Christ and his saving significance, the indivisibility of Christ in heaven and the earthly church, and the inseparability of reconciliation at the center from all God's other mighty acts — came to bear in various ways on Barth's interpretation of Hebrews 13:8: "Jesus Christ is the same, yesterday and today and forever."

Here Barth departed significantly from Luther and Calvin. Where the Reformers tended to focus on the sameness of Jesus Christ across the ages, Barth focused more pointedly, we might say, on the idea of difference in the midst of sameness, and sameness in the midst of difference. By devoting more attention to the actual differences between yesterday, today, and forever, he was in a position to reflect more explicitly on how these various times might be interrelated. Barth was intrigued by how the different temporal forms of one and the same Jesus Christ might be captured by a pattern of unity-in-distinction.

Barth regarded Hebrews 13:8 as seminal rather than merely incidental. He thus took it as a clue to unlocking the perplexing time-consciousness of the New Testament. This verse suggested a way to think not only about the apocalyptic turning of the ages as effected in Christ, but also about how that mysterious transition might be related to the eternity of God.

Barth estimated that, read in context, the emphasis in Hebrews 13:8 fell on the term "yesterday" and therefore on how the past was related to the present (I/1, 54). "Jesus Christ will not be, nor is he today, different from what he was yesterday. He is the same yesterday and today" (IV/3, 817). Christ's identity was not determined by his presence here and now but rather by the narrative of his life history. Christ was present to us here and now precisely as the one that he was for us there and then, as the one who had died for our sins and been raised again from the dead.

His presence, however, represented the fullness of time. It led to "an extremely accentuated consciousness" not only of the experienced present but also of "the past as past" and of "the future as future" (I/1, 54). Past and future no longer represented merely different times but indeed different "aeons," for the turning of the ages had occurred with the resurrection of Christ. The two aeons were "utterly opposed," yet both lived on in the present as "extremely real" — the one as essentially past and defeated, the other as essentially future and triumphant (I/1, 54). Therefore, despite this perplexing complexity, Jesus Christ was not now, nor would he ever be, different from the person he was for us in his life and his death. His absolute future could be proclaimed only in the form of recollecting his resurrection from the dead (I/1, 54).

Revelation was itself reconciliation, Barth argued; and conversely, reconciliation, by which fellowship with God was restored, took the mysterious form of revelation (I/1, 409). With these definitions in the background, Barth turned to discussing the being of God (II/1, 257-72). He stressed that God's revelation was God's act, and that as such it was "an event which is in no sense to be transcended" (II/1, 262).

Revelation was not an event that just happened at one point in time and then receded ever more remotely into the past. God's act in Christ was of course a past event. But, Barth suggested, it continued to happen here and now precisely as something that had occurred there and then. Revelation was therefore "also an event happening in the present" (II/1, 262).

Nor did revelation exhaust itself "in the momentary movement" by which it reached us from the past. Even as it occurred again today, revelation was still an event that had taken place once for all, and so was an accomplished fact (II/1, 262).

Furthermore, Barth continued, revelation was "also future." It was "the event which lies completely and wholly in front of us, which has not yet happened, but which simply comes upon us." God's act of revelation occurred as something completely future, Barth proposed, "without detriment to its historical completedness and its full contemporaneity. On the contrary," Barth stated, "it is in its historical completedness and its full contemporaneity that it is truly future" (II/1, 262).

Barth would seal this extraordinary argument by appealing to Hebrews 13:8. God's act of revelation, precisely because it was *God's* act, could neither be transcended, nor dispensed with, nor surpassed. In its very particularity it was all-encompassing. Revelation was at once historically complete, and yet fully contemporaneous, and yet also absolutely future. *Jesus Christ is the same yesterday and today and for ever.* Barth commented:

> What is concerned is always the birth, death and resurrection of Jesus Christ, always his justification of us through faith, always his governance of the church, always his coming again, and therefore himself as our hope. We can only abandon God's revelation, and with it God's Word, if we take up an external standpoint. With it we stand, or rather we move, necessarily in the circle of its occurrence. (II/1, 262 rev.)

These are difficult ideas. How could an event be fully contemporaneous if it was a once-for-all occurrence in the past? And how could it be both of these and yet completely future as well? In his highly intuitive and almost ecstatic discourse, Barth did not pause to sort all this out. His focus was on the being of God in act. His purpose was to indicate that since God's being was in God's act, God's act could not be transcended or surpassed. God's act was an act of revelation, and what was revealed was Jesus Christ, or more specifically, the narrative of his life, death, and resurrection as the narrative of our salvation. The name of Christ was inseparable from his narrative; his person, inseparable from his work. Barth's citation of Hebrews 13:8 in this context was at once cryptic and yet also luminous. What I think he wanted to suggest was that we are not saved by the work of Christ, but by the person of Christ in his work.

In the early volumes of *Church Dogmatics,* Barth may or may not have had the implications of his insight into Hebrews 13:8 fully worked out in his own mind. In any case, he did not provide anything like a developed account until near the end of his project, in IV/3. Along the way, however, were some scattered remarks. Three comments in particular are noteworthy, though they still remain fragmentary. One occurred in the section on "Jesus, Lord of Time," another in the section on "The Verdict of the Father," and finally another in the section on "The True Church."

In III/2, when discussing "Jesus, Lord of Time," Barth had occasion to remark on Hebrews 13:8. The time of Jesus, he argued, was "a time like all other times" (III/2, 463) and yet it was also identical with "the time of God: eternal time" (III/2, 462). Chalcedon was clearly in the back of Barth's mind here. If the mystery of the incarnation meant that Jesus was at once fully God and yet also fully human, it followed that this assertion could be, and at some point needed to be, transposed into temporal terms. That would make Jesus Christ at once fully eternal and yet also fully temporal.

Barth would make two points about Hebrews 13:8 in this context. First, because the time of the human Jesus was a time like all other times, he lived like anyone else in an ordinary sequence from yesterday through today to tomorrow. Supposing otherwise would make Christology out to be docetic. Nevertheless, secondly, Hebrews 13:8 also had, Barth stated, "deeper implications" (III/2, 463). What they may have been, however, were not developed in this place.

Then when discussing Christ's resurrection in IV/1, under the heading "The Verdict of the Father," Barth returned to this verse. The purpose of this section was to explain the risen Christ as "the living Savior." As such, Jesus Christ was "the same here and now as he was there and then: the Mediator between God and us human beings" (IV/1, 314). Barth then cited Hebrews 13:8. In the New Testament, he continued, the "today" of Jesus Christ was always seen from the standpoint of Easter. In the fullness of this present, the crucified Christ and risen Christ were one. They remained distinct and yet were joined together in an "eternal unity" or "temporal togetherness" (IV/1, 314).

Barth concluded that there was no moment in which Jesus Christ's work of reconciliation was not being accomplished. What Christ had accomplished once for all, he continued to accomplish here and now. "There is no moment," stated Barth, "in which this perfect tense is not a present" (IV/1, 315). "The eternal action of Jesus Christ," he continued, "grounded in his resurrection is itself the true and direct bridge from once to always, from himself in his time to us in our time. . . . [T]he fact of his death on the cross can never be past, it can never cease to be his action" (IV/1, 315). Christ's work, Barth was suggesting, could not be dissociated from his person. That work in some sense continued in his presence as the living Savior. The cross would never cease to plead for us. Its power lived on in the living presence of the One who had endured it. Barth did not comment, however, on how to understand the continuing occurrence of Christ's saving work in relation to its finished character.

Finally, in discussing "The True Church," Barth made this remark about what was revealed on Easter Day:

In its totality, in its movement to his final manifestation, it has the power of that which was once for all accomplished by him at Calvary. It is essential, and therefore necessary, to him (Heb. 13:8), to be not merely yesterday and forever, but today — in the intervening time which is our time. . . . It [the Easter revelation] would not be God's and therefore it would not be our salvation if it did not create and maintain and continually renew the provisional representation in which it is today. (IV/2, 622)

The Easter revelation, Barth maintained, had to be understood in its "totality," which meant that it involved the three temporal tenses. Only the past and the present tenses were elucidated here. The past was again the tense of the once-for-all occurrence, the tense of a finished and perfect work. What is interesting is what Barth now said about the present. What takes place in the present was now described as "provisional." The power of what had been accomplished at Calvary broke into the present in the form of a "provisional representation," namely, the church. The power of the cross as a finished and perfect work created, maintained, and continually renewed a provisional representation of itself in and as the church. The church became a provisional form today of the Christ who was present from yesterday, the same Jesus Christ who had revealed himself at Easter and who by his return in glory would come to make all things new.

In discussing "The Glory of the Mediator" in IV/3, and specifically in the section on "The Promise of the Spirit," Barth's explanation of Hebrews 13:8 at last took a quantum leap. Here Barth would introduce his profound idea of Christ's "threefold parousia," by which he meant Easter, Pentecost (with its aftereffects), and Christ's return in glory. By way of introducing the idea of the threefold *parousia*, Barth turned first to Hebrews 13:8. He began with this particular verse in order to establish the larger context. The threefold parousia of Easter, Pentecost, and Second Advent had to be understood within the larger context of Jesus Christ being the same yesterday, today, and forever.

We might diagram this ordering arrangement as a kind of tree where Barth began with the greater branchwork — Hebrews 13:8 — and then moved on out to a lesser form of the same pattern. Yet it was only with respect to the lesser form that Barth finally made explicit the inner logic of the whole. The same grammar that would govern the threefold parousia, in other words, also governed Hebrews 13:8 as Barth understood it. I will therefore apply Barth's remarks about the formal structure of the threefold parousia to his understanding of Hebrews 13:8.

What was at stake in Hebrews 13:8 for Barth was "one continuous event" in three different forms. The idea that different forms could be assumed by a single continuous event brought clarity to Barth's interpretation.

> In all these forms it is one event. Nothing different takes place in any of them. It is not more in one case or less in another. It is the one thing taking place in different ways, in a difference of form corresponding to the willing and fulfillment of the action of its one Subject, the living Jesus Christ. Always and in all three forms it is a matter of the fresh coming of the One who came before. (IV/3, 293)

We may take "Jesus Christ yesterday" as the first form of this event. In this form he acted, and suffered, and was finally crucified. He was temporally limited by his birth and death. Yet the reconciliation accomplished in him had power, range, and significance for all humankind and the entire created order (IV/3, 291). This form is therefore basic and constitutive. "From the standpoint of its substance, scope and content, it is identical with its occurrence in the forms which follow" (IV/3, 293). In other words, the subsequent forms have no other substance, scope, or power than that which was accomplished there and then in this basic past-tense form.

We may then take "Jesus Christ forever" as pointing to the final form of this event. In this form there occurs the redemption of all things. Jesus Christ no longer remains hidden, but is universally revealed in all his once-concealed glory. He is now openly manifested for what he had always been in himself, the only Mediator between heaven and earth, between God and humankind, the Lamb of God who took away our sin and the Lion of Judah who put an end to death. In this universal, glorious manifestation of his lordship, all things are made new.

This is the final and unsurpassable form of the one continuous event. It does not bring a new substance, scope, or power, but a new and glorious form to that one substance, scope, and power as accomplished in Christ there and then and inseparable from his person here and now. What was hidden is at last revealed in a marvelous, ultimate, and unsurpassable form. Yet is it only revealed for what it always had been, and disclosed in its intrinsic perfection. It still is what it had always been, namely, the absolute future of all things, the eternal life made possible by Christ's death and inaugurated by his resurrection. Jesus now reigns as the Lamb upon the throne, to whom all glory and honor and majesty are ascribed forever.

There is then the matter of "Jesus Christ today." This is the intermediate form of the one Jesus Christ, and it must be described in two aspects. In one sense it is secondary and dependent, while in the other it is provisional and anticipatory. It is a secondary and dependent form of the reconciliation he accomplished there and then. Yet at the same time it is a provisional and anticipatory form of the redemption that is promised to all persons and all things. Again, it is no different in substance, range, and power from the other two, but is different only in form, as it were, in its outward "character, colors and accents" (IV/3, 294), visible only to faith, but to faith really made known.

Jesus Christ today is Jesus Christ "in all his being and action of yesterday, and its whole power for the world" (IV/3, 291). His death and empty tomb are behind him, while his glorious return stands before him. Risen from the dead, he moves out from "the inoperativeness of his power" in his ignominious death. In appearing to his disciples, he appears "potentially to all human beings and the whole cosmos" (IV/3, 291). He declares himself to them, making known his presence and what he has accomplished, putting it provisionally and proleptically into effect. For what has come to them in him, and what will come into being through them, in the form of the new community, is destined to come to all.

The astonishing thing about Barth's account of this one continuous event in three forms, or three forms of one continuous event, is that he went on to elucidate it in terms of what I have elsewhere called "the trinitarian pattern." The three forms of the one Jesus Christ — yesterday, today, and forever — are governed, Barth suggested, by nothing less than the grammar of the doctrine of the Trinity.

> If we allow the New Testament to say what it has to say, we shall be led in this matter to a thinking which is differentiated even in its incontestable unity, formally corresponding to that which is required for an understanding of the three modes of being of God in relation to this one essence in triunity: *una substantia in tribus personis, tres personae in una substantia.* (IV/3, 294)

Not only do we have one indivisible event assuming three distinct forms, and not only do these three forms in some sense coexist simultaneously, but they also interpenetrate one another. Barth went so far as to invoke the trinitarian idea of perichoresis to account for how these three forms fell into a coinherent pattern of unity-in-distinction. He wrote:

> When we treat the unity of the three forms or stages of the one event . . . , it is perhaps worth considering and exegetically helpful, again in analogy to the doctrine of the Trinity, to think of their mutual relationship as a kind of perichoresis. . . . It is not merely that these three forms are interconnected in the totality of the action presented in them all, or in each of them in its unity and totality, but that they are mutually related as forms of this one action by the fact that each of them also contains the other two by way of anticipation or recapitulation, so that without losing their individuality or destroying that of the others, they participate and are active and revealed in them. (IV/3, 296)

Jesus Christ is the same, yesterday and today and forever. One and the same Jesus Christ — whose person was inseparable from his work, and whose name was inseparable from his narrative — would assume, and had to assume, three different temporal forms: yesterday, today, and forever.

The perfect tense of his yesterday made itself present in his today, and made itself present without ceasing to be what it was: a once-for-all occurrence in substance, range, and power.

The present-tense form of this event here and now was a secondary and dependent form of what had taken place there and then. Christ's work was made present as a living reality, because that work was present in his person, even as his person was present in his work, so that his work was always present in and with his personal presence to faith.

At the same time, and from another perspective, the present-tense form of Christ's person and work was provisional and anticipatory. It was filled not only with the substance, range, and power of the perfect tense but also as such with that of the absolute future. What was concealed in the present tense — hid with Christ in God — was destined to be revealed and come to all. It was destined to be unveiled in a way that would make all things radically new.

We might say that the perfect tense was the ground and that the absolute future was the consequence, or we might turn that around and say that the absolute future was the goal for which the perfect tense supplied the precondition. Either way, the three temporal forms were not external to one another. They were mutually related as forms of the eternal God's one action in Jesus Christ. Each of the forms also contained the other two by way of anticipation or recapitulation. Without losing their individuality or destroying that of the others, each one participated in the other two and was active and revealed in them.

This is a magnificent vision, at once carefully reticent and yet also obviously very bold. Barth did not want to turn the trinitarian pattern of mutual coinherence and inclusion into a systematic principle. Yet he offered it as a way of unlocking the mystery of the New Testament's peculiar sense of time, with its habit of scrambling ordinary temporal sequences, its dizzying apocalyptic reversals and upheavals of the already and the not yet. Its apparent contradictions and temporal puzzles could in some measure be explained on the assumption of such a perichoretic view. "This is not a key to open every lock," stated Barth. "But it is one which we do well not to despise" (IV/3, 296).

We may turn in conclusion to a disagreement that Karl Barth once had with Emil Brunner. Brunner had objected that it was inconceivable that all human beings, even those who had lived thousands of years before Jesus, should have their being in the history of Jesus, and that Jesus' history should be the source and ground of all other human existence. Barth vigorously denied Brunner's objection. The history of Jesus, he argued, was the history of the world's reconciliation. Because God himself had become human in order to be the Subject of this event, reconciliation was real and effective. In its Easter revelation, reconciliation had irresistibly called forth faith and obedience. Therefore in the history of Jesus, Barth suggested, "we have to do with the reality which underlies and precedes all other reality as the first and eternal Word of God" (IV/1, 53). "In this history," he added, "we have actually to do with the ground and sphere, the atmosphere of the being of every human being, whether they lived thousands of years before or after Jesus" (IV/1, 53 rev.).

As had been worked out in III/2, Jesus was the Lord of time. He was not, and could not possibly be, the Lord apart from his life history. But in and with his life history, he was the Lord of time. However, he was not, and could not possibly be time's Lord without partaking in the eternity of God. By virtue of his resurrection from the dead, Jesus had been elevated into eternity. In all the fullness of his historicity, finitude, and particularity, he himself was present to all history in the mode of God. As the one who had been eternally elevated and transfigured, he was present in his life history to all things, and he was present in many and various ways. Those ways were surely often hidden, not to say mysterious and incognito; nevertheless, his universal presence was always a differentiated and living presence, and it would be revealed universally for what it was on the last day.

Nothing fell outside the significance, scope, and power of the one Jesus, who was constituted by his own particular, and truly human, life history. He was present in his living historicity to all times and places, and to all persons and things, in what Barth once called an infinitely bewildering variety of ways. Absolutely nothing could fall outside the scope of his lordship, from the lifespan of the dayfly in the farthest reaches of primordial time on down to the final nanosecond of cosmic history. It was the lordship of the risen Jesus, the one Jesus, whose being, whether in time or in eternity, was identical with his life history. "Lo, I am with you always, even to the end of the age" (Matt. 28:20). "Jesus Christ is the same, yesterday and today and forever" (Heb. 13:8).

8. Barth's Lectures on the Gospel of John

John Webster

I

When Barth took up his post in Münster as Professor of Dogmatics and New Testament Exegesis in the autumn of 1925, his major teaching assignment in the Winter Semester 1925/26 was lecturing for four hours a week on the Gospel of John.[1] The series ran from early November 1925 to late February 1926. In the same semester, Barth also completed the cycle of dogmatics lectures that he had begun in Göttingen in the Summer Semester 1924 with a treatment of eschatology, under the title of "The Doctrine of Redemption."[2] Alongside the two-lecture series he also ran a seminar on Calvin, trying, as he reported to Thurneysen, to make the subject matter clear as much to himself as to his students "with a lot of stammering and hand-waving."[3] As usual with Barth's lecture courses from the 1920s, his ambitions far exceeded the available time, and by the close of the semester he had only reached the end of chapter 8. "Torso: 3/7 of the Gospel" he noted at the end of the manuscript (398). In a lightly revised form, the lectures were repeated in Bonn in the heady summer of 1933, when

---

1. Published in the Barth *Gesamtausgabe* as K. Barth, *Erklärung des Johannesevangeliums (Kapitel 1-8): Vorlesung Münster Wintersemester 1925/1926, wiederholt in Bonn, Sommersemester 1933*, 2nd ed. (Zürich: TVZ, 1999). Page numbers in the body of the article are to this text; all translations of the lectures are my own.

2. The lectures have recently been published as *Unterricht in der christlichen Religion 3: Die Lehre von der Versöhnung/ Die Lehre von der Erlösung (Eschatologie) 1925/1926* (Zürich: TVZ, 2003).

3. K. Barth and E. Thurneysen, *Briefwechsel II. 1921-30*, 2nd ed. (Zürich: TVZ, 1987), p. 396.

Barth was called upon at the last moment to offer a New Testament lecture course as a stand-in for his colleague Karl Ludwig Schmidt, who had just been suspended from teaching.[4] The second outing of the lectures was during a particularly heavy semester for Barth: he was also lecturing on the history of Protestant theology, running two seminars in systematics, and teaching a homiletics class, thus managing to turn his hand to four theological disciplines.

Barth prepared for his Münster course with characteristic intensity, veering as was his wont between elation and anxiety about the task. "Ich bin tief im Johannestunnel," he confessed to Thurneysen at the beginning of December (he was in the midst of explaining John 1:14).[5] Yet a little later, as he was working through chapter 8, he wrote to his philosopher brother Heinrich Barth: "This winter I'm also lecturing on the Gospel of John, and won't finish by a long way. . . . What a *remarkable* book! Often the entire room seems to go round me when I ponder the connections within the chapter and between the other chapters (and of course when I see everywhere something astonishing not noticed by previous exegetes). We theologians are better off than you philosophers in that our inquiries are undertaken with such *texts* of canonical authority" (cited on p. viii). Barth was certainly no stranger to lecturing on the interpretation of New Testament texts. In his first professorship in Göttingen from 1921, he had lectured on Ephesians, James, 1 Corinthians 15, Philippians, Colossians, and the Sermon on the Mount, all in the *lectio continua* format which is also adopted in the lectures on John's Gospel, and all attempting a dense theological exposition of a biblical text by which Barth finds himself seized and shaken.

In spite of the fact that they constituted a considerable share of his teaching in the 1920s, Barth's exegetical lectures have had remarkably little impact on the interpretation of his work. In part this can be explained by the fact that only the cycles on 1 Corinthians 15,[6] Philippians,[7] and John

---

4. The basis of the edition of the lectures in the *Gesamtausgabe* is the typescript of the 1933 version (Text B), which ends on p. 336 of the printed edition, near the beginning of Barth's account of John 7; from here the edition returns to the 1925/26 version (Text A). The changes between the two texts are mostly stylistic.

5. K. Barth and E. Thurneysen, *Briefwechsel II*, p. 390.

6. K. Barth, *Die Auferstehung der Toten. Eine akademische Vorlesung über 1 Kor. 15* (Munich: Kaiser, 1924); ET *The Resurrection of the Dead* (London: Hodder & Stoughton, 1933).

7. K. Barth, *Erklärung des Philipperbriefes* (Munich: Kaiser, 1928); ET *The Epistle to the Philippians* (Louisville: Westminster/John Knox, 2002).

have been published. But a number of other factors need to be borne in mind, all of which have encouraged a misperception of Barth's earlier theological work. One is the assumption that all that needs to be known about Barth's exegetical work can be found in *The Epistle to the Romans;* another is a concentration on Barth's supposed general hermeneutical principles or on his attitude to historical criticism, particularly in the prefaces to the various editions of *Romans,* to the neglect of detailed attention either to his doctrine of Scripture or to his exegetical practice. And there are other factors: selective reading of Barth without reference to his lecture cycles on the historical theology of the Reformed tradition; a correspondingly hazy picture of Barth's development in the 1920s between, say, *Romans* and *Fides Quaerens Intellectum,* in which only a few occasional writings feature; and the persuasive assumption that — especially in the 1920s — Barth's theology is dominated by a cluster of abstract themes. That Barth spent much of the 1920s in intense study of the biblical and theological canons of Christianity, and so came to learn what is involved in undertaking church dogmatics, still remains on the periphery of much of what is written about him.

The lectures on the Gospel of John suffer from this general neglect. The whole cycle has been available in published form for thirty years, and a (not wholly satisfactory) English translation of a portion of it appeared twenty years ago.[8] But the lectures have been almost universally ignored in a quarter century of Barth scholarship, despite their obvious relevance to such matters as the development of Barth's thought in Göttingen and Münster prior to the *Church Dogmatics,* or the content of his thinking about Scripture, the person of Christ, and the relation of God to history.[9] Their impor-

---

8. K. Barth, *Witness to the Word: A Commentary on John 1* (Grand Rapids: Eerdmans, 1986).

9. To cite only two very recent examples: Jörg Lauster's chapter on Barth in *Prinzip und Methode. Die Transformation des protestantischen Schriftprinzips durch die historische Kritik von Schleiermacher bis zur Gegenwart* (Tübingen: Mohr, 2004), pp. 258-76, does not treat the John lectures in his account of Barth's "renewal of the Reformation Scripture principle"; had he done so, the undifferentiated account of Barth as proposing "a kind of hermeneutical immediacy" (p. 261) would have had to be abandoned. Similarly, B. Bourgine's survey of the earlier Barth in *L'herméneutique théologique de Karl Barth. Exégèse et dogmatique dans le quatrième volume de la Kirchliche Dogmatik* (Leuven: Leuven University Press, 2003) pays no attention to any exegetical lectures by Barth. On the biographical side, W. H. Neuser's account of *Karl Barth in Münster 1925-30* (Zürich: Theologischer Verlag, 1985) makes no mention of the lectures. H. Kirchstein offers a very brief account of Barth's Introduction to the cycle in *Der souveräne Gott und die heilige Schrift. Einführung in die Biblische Hermeneutik*

tance is considerable, on at least three counts. First, they offer one of the fullest examples of Barth's labors in New Testament interpretation, and from them a good deal can be gleaned about the varieties of his exegetical practices and about his conception of the task of theological *Erklärung*. In the latter regard, Barth's introduction offers a much more extended treatment than can be found in the *Romans* prefaces or the remarks on theological interpretation in the brief foreword to *Die Auferstehung der Toten*.[10] Second, the lectures amplify the picture of Barth's Christology. His reading of the Johannine prologue, in particular, shows the extent to which Barth had schooled himself in the Calvinist divines over whose writings he pored in Göttingen. Third, what Barth makes of the Gospel of John — what catches his eye, how he goes about the task of explaining it to his audience — is an important register of his overall theological commitments and character as he is making preparations for the *Christliche Dogmatik* of 1927.

Behind these first lectures in Münster lie four years of extraordinarily accelerated theological development on Barth's part. He arrived in Göttingen ill-prepared for his task as Professor of Reformed Theology, full of instincts but lacking in the systematic and historical rigor required for their full articulation. By the time he left for Münster, Barth had more than made good many of these deficiencies, having taught (and fought) his way

---

Karl Barths (Aachen: Shaker, 1998), pp. 153-58. There is a perceptive review of Barth's text from the standpoint of New Testament scholarship by J. P. Martin in *Verkündigung und Forschung* 30 (1985): 50-57. J. Denker's *Das Wort wurde messianischer Mensch. Die Theologie Karl Barths und die Theologie des Johannesprologs* (Neukirchen: Neukirchener Verlag, 2002) considers Barth's *Erklärung* in the context of a study of the place of John 1:1-18 in Barth's theology, though he tends to force the material into an interpretative mold of what he calls the "Israeldimension" (p. 3) of the Johannine prologue, and so misses most of what Barth has to say. There is a detailed account of Barth's interpretation of the Johannine σημεῖα by K. Wengst, "Der Zeichenbegriff in Barths Kommentar zum Johannesevangelium," *Zeitschrift für dialektische Theologie* 16 (2000): 30-42, and a fuller account of the cycle as a whole by D. Boer, "'Bedrängnis muß groß sein . . .': Einführung in Karl Barths 'Erklärung des Johannesevangeliums,'" *Zeitschrift für dialektische Theologie* 16 (2000): 8-29, though the presentation is too schematic, and has little to say about Barth's exegesis. The best study so far is that by G. Plasger, "Wort vom Wort. Systematisch-theologische Überlegungen zur Bedeutung des Verhältnißes von Dogmatik und Schriftauslegung anhand von Karl Barths Erklärung des Johannesevangeliums," *Zeitschrift für dialektische Theologie* 16 (2000): 43-58. Plasger's account is thoroughly grounded in a consideration of Barth's writings from the 1920s, especially in the field of Reformed theology, though he probably overplays the significance of the church as the location of the reading of Scripture.

10. K. Barth, *Die Auferstehung der Toten*, pp. v and following (this material is not included in the ET).

through large tracts of exegetical and historical theology, gathering the results together in a remarkably ambitious cycle of lectures on dogmatics. When he came to lecture on the Fourth Gospel, he had seven New Testament courses behind him; as a result, he had developed some strategies in integrating detailed textual comment with classical Reformed theology, something that had at times eluded him in earlier courses. Further, his work on classical Reformed theology, both in historical theological lectures on the Heidelberg Catechism, Calvin, Zwingli, and the Reformed Confessions, and in the so-called Göttingen Dogmatics, gave him a set of theological questions, categories, and patterns of thought that resonated with the Johannine text. From this, Barth brought to his reading of John three concerns that both shaped and were shaped by what he had found. First, Barth had come to think of the Scripture principle as a cardinal piece of Reformed doctrine, both because it indicates the normativity of revelation in the life of the church and because it enjoins an attentiveness to Scripture as revelation's medium. This, in turn, shapes exegetical practice and requires a discriminating (though not unqualifiedly hostile) relation between theological interpretation and literary-historical enquiries. Second, Barth had come to have a deep appreciation for the emphasis in Reformed Christology upon the *unio personalis* (rather than the *unio naturarum* of Lutheran Christology), and upon the freedom of the Logos in the *assumptio carnis*. Having acquainted himself with the historical materials, Barth offered his own dogmatic account of the matter in his first dogmatic lectures — most fully in the treatment of the person of Christ, on which he lectured in May 1925, his final semester in Göttingen.[11] Third, in pondering issues concerning Christology, sacramental theology, and the theology of revelation, Barth had begun to map for himself the relation of God's perfect being and action and the being and action of creatures. All this informs the way in which he conceives of the task of theological *Erklärung*, and also the way in which he understands the material content of John's Gospel.

II

Barth's lectures on John are one of the most mature and considered products of the theological-exegetical work to which he had committed himself

---

11. *Unterricht in der christlichen Religion 3*, pp. 26-74; see also §6 of *The Göttingen Dogmatics* (Grand Rapids: Eerdmans, 1991), pp. 131-67.

in the middle of the First World War. As he distanced himself from the theological world of Protestant liberalism, he came to think that the reorientation of theology and church he considered necessary must include a reconception of the nature of Scripture and its interpretation, a reconception that could, of course, only be achieved in the closest possible connection to actual exegetical work. After the early lecture on "The New World of the Bible" from February 1917,[12] the most substantial exercise in this reconceiving of the exegetical task is *Romans* (it is an oddly neglected fact that *Romans* is intended by Barth neither as an onslaught on historical criticism nor as a statement of his own theology, but as a commentary on a Pauline epistle[13]). *Romans,* however, with its polemical prefaces to the first, second, and third editions, is only part of a larger project in which Barth rethinks Scripture and scriptural exegesis in the context of a renewed theology of revelation.

One commonly neglected factor in this rethinking is Barth's discovery of the "Scripture principle." He treated the topic in some detail in his 1923 lectures on *The Theology of the Reformed Confessions,*[14] and a year later in his first dogmatics cycle.[15] These lectures generated two substantial articles that touch on the theme: "The Doctrinal Task of the Reformed Churches"[16] and "Das Schriftprinzip der reformierten Kirche."[17] Barth's interest in the Scripture principle was as much material as it was formal. He found in it, on the one hand, a way of speaking of God's communicative presence (God's "Word") to the church through the testimony of the prophets and apostles, and, on the other hand, a pointer to the kinds of activities, including exegetical activities, that are fitting responses to that testimony. At the heart of the Scripture principle lie two axioms.

---

12. K. Barth, "The Strange New World Within the Bible," *The Word of God and the Word of Man* (London: Hodder & Stoughton, 1928), pp. 28-50 (the ET adds the word "strange" to the title).

13. See J. Webster, "Karl Barth," in *Reading Romans through the Centuries: From the Early Church to Karl Barth,* ed. J. P. Greenman and T. Larsen (Grand Rapids: Brazos, 2005), pp. 205-23.

14. K. Barth, *The Theology of the Reformed Confessions* (Louisville: Westminster/John Knox, 2002), pp. 38-64.

15. Barth, *The Göttingen Dogmatics,* pp. 201-26.

16. K. Barth, "Reformierte Lehre, ihr Wesen und ihre Aufgabe," in *Vorträge und kleinere Arbeiten 1922-1925* (Zürich: TVZ, 1990), pp. 202-47; ET "The Doctrinal Task of the Reformed Churches," in *The Word of God and the Word of Man,* pp. 218-71.

17. K. Barth, "Das Schriftprinzip der reformierten Kirche," originally in *Zwischen den Zeiten* 3 (1925): 215-45; reprinted in *Vorträge und kleinere Arbeiten 1922-1925,* pp. 500-544.

First, "God can only be known through God."[18] Knowledge of God is God's gift ("revelation"), borne to us through Holy Scripture, in such a way that to encounter Scripture is to stand before a witness to something that is not simply part of the immanent historical world. "The knowledge of God is not mediated but is only unmediated, that is, God is known through God himself. The expression for that immediacy, for the absolute *facticity*, for the paradox of revelation, is the Scripture principle, precisely *by virtue of* its offensiveness."[19] This does not entail, Barth insisted, a simple identity between God's Word and Scripture; any such suggestion would transform revelation as "sovereign act"[20] into a material textual condition. What it does mean is that for Barth, Scripture hovers on the border between the historical life of the church and the transcendent reality of God — a point he had sought to communicate in *Romans* and elsewhere, but which he only now was able to name in doctrinal terms. The second axiom is: "Speaking of God can only mean letting God himself speak."[21] The Scripture principle, in other words, is a determination of the situation of the interpreter who must say something about the Bible, and so it is a hermeneutical directive in which primacy is accorded to divine communicative acts over the interpretative undertakings of human agents. One way of putting Barth's point would be to say that he is radicalizing the notion of *Scriptura sui interpres* by pressing it back into the doctrine of God. As revealer, God is self-interpreting, and so to explicate the biblical auxiliaries of this divine communication is not to bestow meaning upon an inert text but to attend to the antecedent divine Word that Scripture indicates. For Barth, this meant that the interpreter is wholly referred to that which the text presents; the interpreter is hearer rather than conversation partner, and must struggle (as he believed Calvin did) "to stay close to the text, to focus with tense attention on what is actually there."[22]

Over the course of his stay in Göttingen, Barth came to believe that "the one serious necessity for Reformed theology is to study towards a new conception of the 'Scripture principle,'"[23] as a result of which "we shall need to think through the category of *revelation* again, and learn again to

18. Barth, "Das Schriftprinzip," p. 508.
19. Barth, *The Theology of the Reformed Confessions*, p. 48 (ET altered).
20. Barth, *The Theology of the Reformed Confessions*, p. 63.
21. Barth, "Das Schriftprinzip," p. 508.
22. K. Barth, *The Theology of John Calvin* (Grand Rapids: Eerdmans, 1995), p. 389.
23. Barth, "The Doctrinal Task of the Reformed Churches," p. 249 (ET altered).

read the Bible . . . from that standpoint."[24] It is precisely this — reading under the tutelage of revelation — that Barth attempted in the Münster lectures on John.[25]

In this connection, Barth's opening lecture is especially instructive. He began the cycle with a reflection on the first of Augustine's *Tractates on John*, intending to sketch "the fundamental elements of an overall biblical hermeneutics" (12). The lecture is a dense and demanding statement, packed with ideas, cross-grained in its conception of the nature of the Fourth Gospel and of the way in which it is to be read. The idiom is rather different from earlier statements about the nature of Scripture: the conversation partner is a church father, not a confessional Reformed theologian, and the tone is calmer and more assured than that of the combative early *Romans* prefaces. Looking back in February 1926 (the month in which he was lecturing on John 6–8), Barth noted in the preface to the fifth edition of *Romans* that in writing that commentary "I had set out to please none but the very few, to swim against the current, to beat upon doors which I thought were firmly bolted."[26] The introduction to the John lectures is more stately; but it is no less radical in its conception of the task of biblical interpretation. As he reflects on Augustine's complex arrangement of interrelations between God, the apostle, the preacher, and the hearer, Barth suggests that the question that must guide any understanding of biblical interpretation is: "Was ist das für eine Situation?" (4). Barth tries to subvert a conventional (and largely invisible) account of biblical interpretation as a transaction between a passive text from the past and an interpreter armed with a set of literary-historical questions and interests. The subversion is achieved by offering a description of the given situation of the interpreter: *this* person acting *thus* in response to *this* text as the herald of *this* God. In doing this, Barth struggles to be free from one of the primary commitments of hermeneutics after Spinoza, namely the association of textual inquiry with indeterminacy on the part of the reader. Placed in a particular situation by God's revealing presence, the reader of Scripture must ask for and exercise a different set of graces from those that restrict their inquiries to the *historia scripturae*. This conviction, which undergirds

---

24. Barth, "The Doctrinal Task of the Reformed Churches," p. 250.

25. Plasger is thus correct to note that "the Scripture principle" is "the fundamental methodological principle . . . which is worked out in the exposition of the Gospel of John" ("Wort vom Wort," p. 47).

26. K. Barth, *The Epistle to the Romans* (Oxford: Oxford University Press, 1933), p. 22.

all of Barth's work on Scripture from the middle of World War I onwards, is explored in three ways in the opening sections of the *Erklärung*.

1. The reader of John's Gospel is determined by the fact that in this text she finds herself addressed, and that this address is constitutive of, not accidental to, both the text and the reader's situation. "We cannot open and read the Gospel without being clear from the beginning that it comes to us as 'good news' . . . that the word of wisdom which the evangelist hands on . . . is spoken to us" (4). And so "we hear (and even more: we understand) the Gospel only when from the very first we do not set aside the relation between it and us, or ignore the actuality, that is, the reality, in which it does not so much stand over against us as face us. . . . We cannot ignore that relation" (4). If this relation of being addressed is fundamental to the reader's situation, then to adopt a stance of *wissenschaftlich* reserve, handling the Gospel as if it were not, in fact, divine address, is to take up a false position vis-à-vis the text. "In [this relation] and only in it the Gospel is what it is, and therefore in this relation seeks to be studied to the degree that it is an object of scholarly inquiry. Were we to ignore this relation, then with the same reasonableness or unreasonableness we might investigate wooden iron or frozen fire" (4f.).[27] Barth's point here is that the Fourth Gospel is precisely that: "gospel," a text bearing a divine communicative act to its readers, and only rationally accessible as what it is. "What could we say of a gospel, a Gospel of John, not directed to us in God's name, not presupposing and demanding our faith, except that it is a product of fantasy, however real it may appear really to stand before us under this name, in printed form according to its most probable early text?" (5). Barth found in Augustine a different ontology of the biblical text, one in which the text's relation to revelation is primary, taking precedence over determinations of the text's character in terms of genre, setting, or authorship. This enables Barth to challenge what he took to be the historical naturalism of mainstream biblical scholarship, according to which the text is the record of antique religious communication the reader is called upon to investigate and, perhaps, subsequently overhear for religious or moral guidance. For Barth, the Fourth Gospel *is* Scripture, and has to be read as what it is.

John's Gospel presents to the reader "something new over against the totality of his previous subjective knowledge" (5). It has its place in a do-

---

27. This point is expanded at some length in K. Barth, *Church Dogmatics* I/2 (Edinburgh: T. & T. Clark, 1956), pp. 458-70.

main that precedes and encloses the reader and from which the reader cannot extract himself without making it impossible to read the text fittingly. This is the domain of baptism, church, and canon. "If we wish to be truly objective *(sachlich)* readers and expositors of the Gospel of John, . . . we cannot and may not free ourselves from the fact that we are baptised, that therefore the Gospel of John does not exist for us as other than a part of the canonical Scripture of the Christian church" (5). Baptism, church, and canon precede inquiry, in that they are not simply the secondary context or subjective evaluations of Scripture but the real objective domain in which it exists, and which the reader cannot legitimately bypass. Baptism, canon, and church are more *sachlich,* and a surer guide to the reading of the biblical texts whose domain they are, than literary and religious history. "Canonical Scripture means a Scripture to which we stand in that relation from the very beginning, a Word spoken to us from the very beginning in the name of God and therefore claiming to say something fundamentally new to us, directed to us, a Word that, even before we could hear it, has opened a dialogue with us, a dialogue from which we cannot escape because it is conducted in the name of God" (5f.).

As in ethics, so in hermeneutics: what Barth resists is an artificial stance in which we consider ourselves capable of positioning ourselves behind the divine address, as if we preceded it rather than it comprehending us. Through baptism the Christian reader *has been* placed in the sphere of church and canon; far from guaranteeing freedom from prejudice, to extract oneself from that sphere undermines interpretative objectivity. "What do church, baptism, God mean if we have the possibility or can even reckon with the possibility of abstracting from it, of suspending our life in this context . . . ?" (6f.).

2. To promote an interpretation of the Fourth Gospel as Word, canonical Scripture, address, claim, and so forth may appear to neglect the text's human historical character. Barth takes this anxiety seriously, and his response to it is highly informative. What is most telling is that he does not rest content with simply laying "theological" and "historical" definitions of the text alongside one another, but attempts an integrated account in which the historical character of the text is *theologically* grounded, and only as such comprehensible. The text's human historical attributes are what they are only in relation to the divine Word of which they are a witness. Part of the "concrete specificity" (7) of the reader's situation is that "the Evangelist who in the Gospel addresses us in God's name is a human being" (7), and so "a phenomenon to which we must hold has a place and therefore a limit in

time. It shares in the relativity, the determinateness, the questionableness of all historical phenomena" (7). But what is to be made of this historical character? Rather than allowing that the historicity of the Evangelist and his text means that they are a matter for unconditional historical inquiry, Barth argues, in effect, that these historical properties only are what they are by virtue of the divine Word they serve, and are therefore only discernible in their historicity in relation to the Word. The Evangelist is "receiver" (8), not simply religious genius; he is, above all, apostle, and thus "not on the level of the historical phenomenon to which we are referred" (8). The Evangelist's humanity is not something anterior to or more comprehensive than his being an apostle, but identical with it; his apostolic character, and therefore his human historical reality, requires direct language about God for its description. "He does not proclaim God without God, and without God he cannot be recognised as one who proclaims God" (8).

Attending to the humanity of the text entails for Barth breaking free from historical naturalism. But categories such as "apostle" are not purely supernatural. That the Evangelist and his text are historical entities is beyond dispute. But the key questions concern the *conditions* under which they are such, and the *kind* of historical character they have as features in the economy of revelation. John's Gospel *is* "Anrede" (8), and sober investigation of its historical character can only begin from here. This historical character is not an absolute fact in itself, for whose explication the categories of natural causality are entirely adequate. Scripture is a historical product that serves the divine disclosure. And so: "as medium the *historical*, the *human* word of witness to revelation demands our total, concentrated and serious attentiveness. But only as medium, not for its own sake and not as understandable out of itself, but as witness which itself needs and expects witness — the witness that its object gives to it. And this giving is an event, an action, the action of God in the strictest sense of the term. The meaning of our action as hearers and expositors of the Gospel stands or falls with God's action through the instrument with which we have to do" (9).

3. So far Barth has described the situation of the reader of the Gospel in terms of its domain — the reality of revelation and church from which we may not abstract ourselves — and in terms of its textual component — a historical text as an *apostolic* reality having reference to or bearing witness to revelation. This situation, however, faces the reader with "a particular demand" (9). Augustine spoke in quasi-Platonic terms of the need to lift the mind to the invisible realm, there to perceive the reality indicated by the Evangelist. Barth — to whom this kind of Platonism was not with-

out its attractions at this period[28] — speaks of "readiness for faith or for the understanding of what faith and its object are about" (10). More concretely, what is required of the reader is a perception of what really is the case in the sphere in which she finds herself, a setting aside of the ruinous abstraction from the event of revelation. We need "a readiness to understand that only in the sphere denoted by the terms church, sacrament and canon can the Gospel of John be read and understood logically and objectively as a word of an apostle, that is, as the word of a witness not to himself but to a revelation imparted and entrusted to him — a readiness to follow the direction indicated. . . . There is an openness to the necessity of understanding this object in terms of its own logic and ethic. And there is a willingness to fall into line with this necessity because one desires to understand. Instead of readiness, then, one might also simply say objectivity" (10f.). It is this objectivity — openness to the *Sache* — that Barth prizes as the primary exegetical virtue, since it is on that basis that we approach the Gospel "not as teachers but as pupils, not as those who already know but as those who do not know" (11).

For Barth, then, theological *Erklärung* involves not only attention to the text's theological context but also the deployment of theological categories concerning God and God's action to describe the nature of the text and the task of its interpretation. Such theological categories are not ancillary but basic and irreducible. A key term here is "witness." Here, as throughout his work, Barth uses "witness" as a shorthand term to denote the ways in which creaturely persons, actions, and products serve revelation by a ministry of indication. Early on in the exposition of John, the term makes its appearance in the course of comments on John the Baptist in John 1:6-8, where, taking up a suggestion from Overbeck, Barth notes an (intentional) confusion between the Baptist and the Evangelist. The confusion indicates "an inner affinity of calling between the two Johns" (17). Of both the Evangelist and the Baptist it can be said: "Er bezeugt" (14). The Baptist is the paradigmatic witness, and in what he says about him, the Gospel writer is speaking about "the situation which arises . . . when someone other than Christ himself, a human person, but an authorised human person . . . speaks of Christ" (20). Through the figure of the Baptist, the Evangelist articulates "the existence and function" of "the human witness who stands between revelation and humankind" (19).

There are implications here for how Barth understands the nature of

---

28. See Barth, *The Theology of the Reformed Confessions,* pp. 45f.

the text he is seeking to explicate. Applied to the Evangelist and his text, the category of "witness" functions in a similar way to that of "apostle": it indicates that the communicative act by which the interpreter is encountered is not only a historical quantity, but also as such an element in an economy of communication whose primary agent is God. Where the historian of biblical literature might naturally deploy the category of "author" to describe John, and devote attention to that person's identity, community setting, and so forth, Barth's use of "witness" serves to show that the Evangelist is not the originator of a communicative act of which the text is the deposit, but rather one who writes in order to testify to a process of revelation anterior to his authorship. And this, in turn, suggests "what the Bible is: witness to revelation, in relation to but also in distinction from, revelation" (21). The entailed expository directive is thus "the great Yes! and But! with which these books call us to themselves, in order to point us to the Lord in the way in which the Baptist pointed his disciples" (21).

Barth's ordering of the practice of biblical exposition to revelation shapes his attitude towards historical methods in his exegetical work on the Fourth Gospel. He is generally relaxed about the matter, entering the lists on a few occasions, but not anxious either to defend himself with a historical arsenal or to renounce its possession. This continues the trend in *Romans* and *The Resurrection of the Dead* in allowing a necessary instrumental use of historical inquiries but retaining a sense of their "relativity."[29] There are passing references to history of religions topics such as Reitzenstein's suggestions about a possible Mandean cult of John the Baptist (19),[30] or to historico-genetic discussions of terms like λόγος or ζωή (27-29; 43f.); and Barth interacts quite frequently with his contemporary critical commentator Walter Bauer. But on the whole he is little interested in *religionsgeschichtliche* background, or in considering the origin, setting, and audience of the text in order to explain its treatment of (say) John the Baptist, Jesus' disputes with the Jewish leaders, or the Eucharist. This is partly because for Barth the material definitions of John's text as gospel and testimony carry a good deal more weight in deciding among exegetical options than do definitions derived from literary-historical study. Priority is given to *what* and *where* the Gospel is: apostolic address in the sphere of revelation, church, and faith; it is on this basis that Barth reaches judg-

---

29. K. Barth, *Die Auferstehung der Toten*, p. v.

30. Barth corresponded with Bultmann over this: see K. Barth, R. Bultmann, *Brief-wechsel 1911-1966* (Zürich: TVZ, 1992), p. 53.

ments about the suitability and limits of historical considerations. But, further, the *Sache* that is indicated by the text's testimony is only indirectly a matter for historical observation. The history of which John speaks is the history of the Word made flesh, and as such it is not comprehensible without immediate reference to the Word who is its subject and agent. As we shall come to see, the Word's "becoming" flesh does not mean the Word's collapse into historical availability or transparency, and so the historian quickly runs up against a limit to historical inquiry. The history of revelation eludes comprehensive historical description. A good instance of this is Barth's treatment of *die Wunderfrage* in his lecture on the Wedding at Cana (197-200). The key to the story, and the deciding factor in determining the scope of historical inquiry, is in the statement ἐφανέρωσεν τὴν δόξαν αὐτοῦ (John 2:11). Barth comments: "He [Jesus] shows himself as he is. He reveals his identity. Not directly, admittedly, but indirectly. He did indeed become flesh, and therefore in an earthly event, in a human action. But in an action which, in the midst of everything else that he and others do and everything else which takes place on earth, is pure, absolute miracle" (198). "Miracle" is on Barth's account "*beyond* the antithesis of history and myth" (199); it is "a *third, special* category or order of event" (199), namely the disclosure of the divine glory in the flesh. "Revelation *in the flesh.* Only in this way does revelation really occur. But 'in the flesh' also means: in ambiguity" (199). If Barth is troubled about historical inquiry, it is not because he wants to remove the matter of the Gospel from historical contingency *tout court* (hence his rejection of the category of myth). Rather, it is because of his understanding of the *kind* of contingent events with which the Gospel deals, namely, contingent events whose ground and substance is the divine Logos (hence their "ambiguity" and their resistance to the explanations of the historian of religion or literature).

Before moving to look more directly at the christological affirmations that underlie this interpretative strategy, we may pause to identify some specific characteristics of the kind of *Erklärung* that Barth undertakes.

His use of the *lectio continua* format allows him freedom to make substantial theological comment without losing the discipline of following the sequence of the text and attending to its linguistic detail. He is not attempting a commentary proper, which would commit him to having something to say about everything in the text; nor is he making a thematic or topical study, a "theology of John"; he is offering an *Erklärung*, an exposition or theologically interested reading. Throughout, the text takes the lead as Barth tries to respect his own principle of *Sachlichkeit*, straining to listen to what is there and repeat in his own words what he hears. There is a good deal by way of detailed textual, philological, and syntactical observation,[31] often in relation to recent and especially older commentators: Augustine and Calvin from the classics, Bauer, Holtzmann, Schlatter, and Zahn from the moderns. In assigning meaning to terms, Barth gives much greater priority to their immediate context in John's text than to the larger *Umwelt:* the meaning of λόγος, for example, is to be understood "exclusively from John itself" (29). A text with such a theologically resonant vocabulary as the Fourth Gospel might tempt a dogmatician to abstract exposition of some of its key terms. Though Barth does talk at length about such words as φῶς, λόγος, ζωή, τὰ ἴδια, or κόσμος, he does not simply fill them with dogmatic content but keeps his dictionary and concordance close to hand. This is particularly true in the lengthy account of the prologue, where Barth is able to hold together theological restatement and exegetical detail. If in *Romans* and *The Resurrection of the Dead* theological paraphrase threatened on occasion to overwhelm the Pauline text, the exposition of John is generally less cluttered, and the relation of Barth's own text to that on which he comments is more transparent.

There are certainly passages where Barth drifts into thematic restatement. He often uses a thematic summary to introduce or close detailed examination of a pericope,[32] but sometimes a presentation of themes replaces running exegesis, as in his accounts of 1:35-51 or 4:1-42. Overall, Barth is — as might be expected — less secure with the narrative portions of the text. He is not without a sense for the larger narrative structure of the Gospel (as in his discussion of the narrative context of 4:43-54, pp. 254f.) and has an eye for the operation of character. But he tends more naturally to gravitate towards the discursive rather than the dramatic. Only rarely, however, does he allow himself to be tugged away from the text into discussion of more general issues, as in the oddly detached comments on religious pluralism in the treatment of the woman of Samaria (243-50).

What Barth offered his hearers, then, was theological exposition, anchored in textual observation, attentive to recent and older commentators, and emerging from a conviction that questions about the nature and interpretation of Scripture have to be answered by appeal to the notion of divine revelation. The Fourth Gospel must be read as words about the Word.

---

31. See, for example, pp. 33f. (on οὗτος); p. 36 (on the punctuation of John 1:13); 73f. (on the grammatical subject of John 1:19); pp. 348f. (on the exegetical crux John 7:38).

32. See, for example, pp. 210f., 333f., 357f.

III

Much of Barth's intellectual energy in his first years as a theological professor was devoted to trying to think through the relation of God to creatures. In his judgment, his teachers had ordered that relation around a center in human religious and moral history, and this troubled him because he considered it threatened by a fatal exchange of subjects in which the divine term became a function of the human. Barth's response was not to eliminate the human term: theomonism was never on his agenda as an admirer of Calvin's theocentric humanism. Rather, through a series of breathtaking descriptions of God's freedom and perfection, he sought to restore a theology of divine prevenience as the ground of the encounter of God and creatures. The idiom of his various attempts at the matter was in large part drawn from classical Calvinist divinity; the topics that called for his attention were those in which the relation of God and creatures is pivotal: revelation, the sacraments, the Christian life and, above all and as the clue to the others, the person of Christ.

At the same time, Barth was engaged in New Testament exposition, and what he found there shaped and was shaped by the problems he was trying to solve in his historical and dogmatic studies. The treatment of christological materials in the Gospel of John lectures, notably the Prologue, is an especially vivid example. Here we can watch Barth in the midst of trying to get some purchase on the issues and to submit his instincts and preferences to close exegetical scrutiny. Barth does not simply plunder the Prologue for raw material: what he has to say is exegesis first and foremost and only then conceptual paraphrase. Nor does he extract the Prologue from the rest of the Gospel and make it into a freestanding unit. Rather, it functions for him as the entrée to the Gospel as a whole. It is a statement of the identity of the one who is subject and agent of the history that follows as the Gospel unfolds. What Barth finds in John — namely, that it is only in the setting of the mystery of his divine-human person that the history of Jesus is comprehensible — is materially and formally fundamental to his Christology; and the exegesis of John 1:1-18 afforded him an opportunity to attain a clarity in his thinking on the matter, which he was not subsequently to abandon.[33]

---

33. This can be seen from subsequent expositions of incarnational teaching such as those in *Die Christliche Dogmatik im Entwurf I. Die Lehre vom Worte Gottes, Prolegomena zur christlichen Dogmatik* (Zürich: TVZ, 1982), pp. 289-308; *Church Dogmatics* I/2, pp. 132-71, or *Church Dogmatics* IV/2 (Edinburgh: T. & T. Clark, 1958), pp. 36-106.

What attracts his attention from the beginning of the Prologue is the free majesty of the Logos by which he utterly surpasses created reality. *In the beginning* was the Word, Barth stresses. "The Logos was in, with, before and above the totality of the created world! No space in the world which is not limited by it. No possibility of evading or escaping it! No more than escaping from God himself!" (23). Ἐν ἀρχῇ means, in effect, "as God" (23). "His being as such is not . . . one which becomes. It is not a temporal being but the eternal being which in principle precedes, encloses and releases all time" (23). Barth moves very swiftly to explicitly Nicene and Athanasian categories: "the nature of the Logos in our statement [John 1:1] is identified with the nature of that reality called ὁ θεός. To him there is ascribed that reality's θεότης'" (25) — and this is explicable only in terms of the eternal distinctions between Father and Son (24-26). And as Barth views the Prologue from the vantage point of its opening assertion, he sees the ontological affirmation about the status of the Logos extending in two directions.

The first concerns the relation of the Logos' relation to creation, which is not only redemptive but also original. "The revealer is so great that in him there becomes visible not merely a subsequent, ad hoc fellowship between God and the world established for the purpose of redemption, but the original fellowship" (38). *Theologia revelata*, because it concerns the eternal deity of the revealing Logos, is necessarily *theologia naturalis*, an account of the Word as the world's origin. Barth makes much of this in his exegesis of John 1:3: "All things were made through him, and without him was not anything made that was made." There is, he takes John to be saying, "no reality whose coming into being is independent of the Logos, which flows from itself and is as it were immediate to God" (41). But Barth finds this emphasis on the aseity and transcendence of the Logos throughout. In 1:4, ζωή is defined as "thoroughly supernatural *new* life" (47), a life that is "not the life which comes from creation" but life that "in contrast to all our past breaks into the present" (50f.). Barth fastens particularly on verses 10-13 in this regard. He understands the verses to refer to the Logos' relation to the world prior to the incarnation, not to the Word made flesh, and is especially drawn to what they affirm about the transcendence of the Logos even in his "immanence . . . in the world" (78). ἐν τῷ κόσμῳ is *Ereignis* (78), not state, condition, or continuous relation: "it is act, it is action" (78). Though the Logos is "in the world" and not "remote from humankind" (79), he nevertheless "stands over against the human world with all the superiority of the creator" (80). Similarly, in verse 11, the Logos' relation to τὰ ἴδια is not such that the world is the Logos' home and its occupants his compatriots: τὰ ἴδια refers not to the Logos' determination by creatures but to their ordering to him. It is thus only because "[t]he world is not by nature the home of the Logos" (82) that we may say that "the human world created and determined by the Word and belonging to him, is the Word's own" (84). Further, the relation of the Word and creatures is not serenely constant but broken by human rejection: his own received him not, "as though his claim were not natural, legitimate, proper and self-evident" (83). If this reality of rejection is to be overcome, if there are to be "children of God," then this possibility can arise not from the "strength and deed" of creatures, but "wholly and directly in God himself and not otherwise" (85). The authority by which creatures receive the Word is given by the Logos, "who has it himself in an original way" (91) as the Son of God. "Can one fail to recognize that here revelation is presented as a closed circle into which no-one can leap from outside? . . . *He*, the Word, convinces, *he* convicts, *he* compels, *he* decides. He is subject and not object in this action" (92).

There is much more here in what Barth has to say — about "believing in his name," for example, or about being born of God. But as Barth reads John, the heart of the Prologue is a theology of the Word and of creatures' relation to the Word whose leading motifs are θεὸς ἦν ὁ λόγος and ἐκ θεοῦ. Whatever else must be said about the Word's becoming flesh is said as a necessary derivative, extension, and completion of his antecedent deity and sovereign liberty.

This leads, second, to what Barth has to say of the incarnation. In his reading of the Gospel he identifies a certain reserve, both in the Prologue and elsewhere, a reluctance to consider that the Word's becoming flesh entails any kind of relaxation of the strict demarcation between God and creatures. This is not because Barth thinks John holds back from the full reality of the Word's incarnation by making the assumption of flesh a mere episode. Far from it: in looking at John 1:1, for example, he argues that the term "Logos" is a *Platzhalter*, "the provisional designation of a place which will later be filled by something or someone wholly other" (27). That is, "already in the Prologue, ὁ λόγος is unmistakeably substituted for *Jesus Christ*. It is *his* place which is at one and the same time cleared, secured and demarcated by the predicates ascribed to the Logos and the history narrated about him" (27). So also in verse 2: οὗτος refers forward to Jesus Christ and his history, rather than backward to the Logos, so that the Logos is by definition *incarnandus*. But as Barth unfolds John's incarnational teaching, above all in John 1:14, it becomes clear that any such affirmation must not compromise the integrity of the Logos, whose entire perfection is retained in the act of *Menschwerdung*.

Incarnation means: "The divine, creative, redeeming and revealing Word whose sovereign being and action have been portrayed in verses 1-13, leaves his throne, steps down to the level of creatures, of the witness, of those who are called, joins their ranks, as it were losing himself among everything and everyone who could only be the *objects* of his action, himself becoming an object. He, the Logos, is there, in the way that something else is there" (106). It is just this which constitutes the incarnational "paradox": "ὁ λόγος ἐγένετο, the Word became, it was there," sharing "concreteness, contingency, historical particularity" (107). But here Barth introduces a crucial christological rule: making sense of John's affirmation entails that "we must not take away anything from either side" (107). There can be no "*single* concept" or "*single* word" that can comprehend Logos and flesh.[34] In effect, Barth finds in the Johannine material a basis and confirmation of the Christology to which he was also being led in his study of Reformed theology: resisting any unified, comprehensive statement of the metaphysics of the incarnate one, resisting also any generalization of the specific event of union of the Word and Jesus into an overall relation of God and humanity, the emphasis of this Christology is upon the particular, personal *unitio* and *unio*.

This means, initially, that according to Barth John's accent is upon the "coincidence" *(Zugleichsein)* of Word and flesh (107). This rather unhappy term is not meant to signal a drawing back from the Chalcedonian "without division," but to alert the reader to the fact that John's ἐγένετο does not entirely abolish the distinction of Word and creature. Further, Barth assigns priority to the single subject — *this* one, acting *thus* — of whom deity and humanity are predicated, since only in this way can "without confusion" be maintained. For John, what matters is "one and the same subject" (107) — in effect, *unio hypostatica* rather than *unio naturarum*. This is not (perhaps not *quite*) the Nestorian co-presence of deity and humanity, but rather what Barth, in his previous semester's lectures on the hypostatic union, spoke of as the emphasis on "dissimilarity" in a Re-

34. From this perspective Denker's concern (*Das Wort wurde messianischer Mensch*, pp. 27f.) that Barth "de-historicizes" John's Christology is misplaced. He misreads Barth by placing all the emphasis on only one side of the incarnational paradox, and so fails to see that Barth is not denying the concreteness of Jesus' history but affirming that Jesus is the historical figure that he is solely by virtue of the divine Word. Denker is also incorrect to see Barth as in the tradition of Luther rather than Calvin.

formed doctrine of the two natures,[35] in which there can be no *Aufhebung* or *Indifferenzierung* of the unlikeness of God and creaturely being.[36]

Some of this is spelled out in Barth's interpretation of ἐγένετο, where he draws attention to three resonances of the term to demarcate incarnation from μέθεξις. The becoming of which John speaks is, first, an "equals sign" between Logos and σάρξ, but one in which the equation is "irreversible" (112). Put differently: "We have to hold fast to the fact that ὁ λόγος is the subject and σάρξ is the predicate. . . . The Logos is the person who here is a human person" (112). There is an asymmetrical relation between Word and flesh in which priority is to be assigned to the Word. "The *Word* speaks, the *Word* acts, the *Word* reveals, the *Word* redeems. The *Word* is Jesus, is the I which afterwards in the Gospel will speak alone. Certainly the *incarnate* Word and therefore not without the flesh, but in the flesh, through the flesh, as flesh — yet the *Word*!" (112f.).[37]

Second, the Word does not cease to be the Word in becoming flesh. "The equation [of Word and flesh] cannot cease to be an equating of the unequal, a paradox. No change occurs, no transubstantiation, no replacing of one mode of the Word's being by another, no dissolution of λόγος into σάρξ, and also no emergence of the product of a mixture of both, but a full uniting of the Logos to flesh, in which nothing is subtracted from the divine determination of the Logos and nothing added to the creaturely and sinful determination of the σάρξ" (113).

Third, "revelation" (that is, the communicative and saving divine action undertaken in the incarnation) is not "a condition or quality of the flesh" (113). This is a point of especial importance, and Barth expends some labor over it, because it touches on the problem of the relation of revelation and history for whose solution Barth was finding the Reformed doctrine of the hypostatic union so resourceful. Taking John seriously certainly entails an affirmation that "revelation is historical" (114); what it does not entail, however, is that "history is itself revelation" (114). Jesus' history is not simply revelation *tout court,* but rather history that has its being only under a specific determination, namely its relation to the antecedent Word. "The so-called 'historical Jesus,' abstracted from the action

35. *Unterricht in der christlichen Religion 3*, p. 42.
36. *Unterricht in der christlichen Religion 3*, p. 44.
37. Barth's interpretation of later chapters of John bears this out, when he draws attention to Jesus' detachment and his incommensurability with his surroundings; see p. 256 (on John 4:43-54), pp. 335f. (on the conflicts of John 7), or pp. 267f. (on Jesus as judge).

of the Word, is *not* revelation! The revelatory power and effect of the predicate σάρξ stands and falls with the action of the subject ὁ λόγος" (114).

Many of the same patterns of thought could be traced in what Barth says elsewhere — his interpretation of "dwelt among us" in terms of "provisionality" rather than complete fulfillment of the divine presence; his emphasis upon the glory and antecedent Sonship of the incarnate one; his definition of the grace and truth of the only-begotten Son as the "inner divine ground" (126) of what takes place in Jesus' history. Barth does not take to his reading of John a strong sense of the *communication* between the divine and human natures, still less a sense of the participation of creatures in God. Instead, schooled in the strict demarcations of Zwingli and others, he finds in John a theology of incarnation that cannot be pressed beyond the particularities of person, event, and act, undergirded by an immensely powerful theology of God's perfection. Yet it ought not to go unrecorded that three years earlier Barth was already troubled by Zwingli's failure to move beyond the Nestorian negative and go on to positive interest in *Gottmenschheit*.[38] By the time he comes to address himself to the Johannine Prologue, Barth is able to resolve Zwingli's negations in a larger structure, in a way that points towards his later christological affirmation that God's freedom includes his freedom to be God with us. "ὁ λόγος σάρξ ἐγένετο means that . . . the antithesis, the distance, the abstraction created by the fact of the darkness . . . is . . . overcome by a third inconceivable thing: the Word is precisely where humankind is, in the midst of darkness . . . the Word is not only the divine Word, the Word of the beginning, the superior Word, the quintessence of creation and redemption, but also flesh — *as* all this, *as* all that we are, in the way that we are, and the way to us and accessible to us" (110f.). Incarnation is a "third" reality beyond the antithesis of God and sinful flesh, which Zwingli's metaphysical dualism could scarcely allow him to acknowledge. Yet even this reality is, on Barth's reading of John, "inconceivable, that is, conceivable only in the event of its occurrence and not on the basis of a general principle of *unio*. The Word *became* flesh."

IV

Barth's lectures are neither a hermeneutical nor a christological treatise but a reading of the Fourth Gospel, intended to lead his students into the same

---

38. See K. Barth, *Die Theologie Zwinglis 1922/1923* (Zürich: TVZ, 2004), p. 496.

wonder by which he himself was overcome as he listened to the testimony of John. Students of the Gospel with an ear for its theology cannot fail to be moved by what Barth has to say, even though it lacks a treatment of so much on which we might wish to have heard him speak: the farewell discourses, the passion and the resurrection narratives. In the end, however, the lectures are probably more important for what they say about Barth. They indicate, first, that for Barth questions about exegetical or interpretative practice have to be answered in terms of a broader theological description of the situation in which revelation places its hearers. That situation is a set of prior realities and relations, given in advance of exegetical and interpretative labor, and conditioning the ways in which that labor may fittingly be undertaken. Above all, the situation is one in which the reader is preceded by that fact that "a Word, no *the* Word, has been spoken, original, as the creative Word preceding and surpassing all that is" (13). Exegesis and interpretation are second, responsive moves: what comes first is the fact that this Word has been spoken and reverberates in the testimony of the prophets and apostles. Because of this, the reader of the Gospel is its "prisoner" (13): "the dice have been cast" (14). Barth thinks of exegetical and interpretative work as an exercise *in,* not just *about,* the economy of God's revelatory grace. Second, Barth's lectures on John occur at a point in his theological development when he is struggling to give a biblical and dogmatic account of the relation of the self-sufficiency of God and the contingent realities of existence in time. Barth sought in the 1920s (and beyond) to portray that relation as irreversible and asymmetrical but also as one in which creaturely substance is not evacuated but established, and he sought to do so without recourse either to an abstractly monistic conception of God or to a theology of participation of creatures in the divine. He took to his reading in the Reformed tradition a strong interest in the theology of mediation, and the same interest often guided his reading of John. He found there the elements of a theological metaphysic centered on the freedom with which the self-revealing Word relates to ὁ γέγονεν as its origin and redeemer. Even in the Word's becoming flesh and dwelling among us, there is no mixture or elision of the difference between creator and creature that is the founding condition of their relation. This means that analyzing Barth's Christology only in terms of supposed Alexandrian and Antiochene elements is less than adequate, for his idiom is driven by biblical categories, as well as by classical Reformed dogmatics of the incarnation.[39]

39. See, for example, G. Hunsinger, "Karl Barth's Christology: Its Basic Chalcedonian

At the end of the "torso," Barth noted: "A first attempt at understanding. Sphinx. Offensive because of the persistence of the *one* note. Take note: the one between God and humankind. Audible only as one hears it itself. There must be great affliction, if it is to be heard. And there must be great grace. In this sense, the beginning of an exegesis" (398). This says much about Barth. Whether he was doing dogmatic, historical, or exegetical work, he always found the matter of theology utterly overwhelming, always reserving itself ("Sphinx") against comprehension, demanding intellectual and spiritual "affliction" in order to be known in its integrity. Even the most technical exegetical tasks involve dispossession. Moreover, there is Barth's characteristic singularity: the *one* reality between God and humankind, the *one* note that must be heard. For all his prolixity and spaciousness, Barth is an intensive — almost at times compulsive — thinker, nowhere more so than when explicating a biblical text by which he is entirely overwhelmed.

Character," in *The Cambridge Companion to Karl Barth*, ed. J. Webster (Cambridge: Cambridge University Press, 2000), pp. 127-42; C. T. Waldrop, *Karl Barth's Christology: Its Basic Alexandrian Character* (Berlin: Mouton, 1984); R. Prenter, "Karl Barths Umbildung der traditionellen Zweinaturlehre in lutherischer Beleuchtung," *Studia Theologica* 11 (1958): 1-88.

III. Application

9. "Thy Word Is Truth": The Role of Faith in Reading Scripture Theologically with Karl Barth

Paul D. Molnar

For Karl Barth, four vital words are indissolubly connected: *faith, grace, revelation*, and *truth*. It is only through God's self-revelation that we can speak truly of faith. Otherwise we would be speaking primarily of ourselves in place of God. Grace alone is the objective and subjective possibility of faith. For Barth, humanity's greatest need is for the righteousness of God — a righteousness without which we cannot live but that we cannot grasp at or control either — because it can only come to us as an act of revelation and reconciliation on God's part that itself establishes and maintains us in fellowship with God. This is ultimately an act of divine election that cannot be systematized by identifying it with any absolute decree or any result visible to historical, philosophical, psychological, or even theological inquiry. Just as there is a *creatio continua* there is an *electio continua*, which Barth says is better described as "God's faithfulness and patience" (I/2, 349).

In 1916 Barth identified the "Strange New World Within the Bible" as "the world of God"[1] which consists in the truth of the biblical witness and which we do not read about "either in the daily papers or in other books" (*W*, 29). For Barth "the Bible gives to . . . every era such answers to their questions as they deserve" (*W*, 32), and so it can be disconcerting to discover that we are challenged to wonder exactly what it is that we are looking for in the Bible. For Barth the Bible gives us no rest at all and drives us "out beyond ourselves and invites us . . . to reach for the last highest answer" (*W*, 33-34). Moreover, the Bible will interpret itself to us "in spite of

---

1. Karl Barth, *The Word of God and the Word of Man* (hereafter: *W*), trans. and foreword by Douglas Horton (Gloucester, MA: Peter Smith, 1978), p. 33.

also p 31 foot notes.

151

all our human limitations" if only we dare to move through the Spirit of God beyond ourselves and into this new world. What is it that constitutes this daring? It

> is *faith;* and we read the Bible rightly . . . when we read it in faith. And the invitation to dare and to reach toward the highest, even though we do not deserve it, is the expression of *grace* in the Bible: the Bible unfolds to us as we are met, guided, drawn on, and made to grow by the grace of God. (*W,* 34)

Even though Barth's emphasis here is on the world of God coming to us as an act arriving from outside of history, it is a divine act that includes us in a genuine relationship with God in faith. That is God's grace. Without being obligated to us God places himself under obligation to us in his Son Jesus Christ (II/1, 101). Hence, "Where grace is revealed and operative, God Himself is always revealed and operative. It is not necessary for us to strive after a higher, better, more helpful revelation" (II/1, 356).

Because this is God establishing his kingdom on earth in Jesus Christ, Barth insists: "One can only believe — can only hold the ground whither he has been led. Or not believe. There is no third way" (*W,* 41). Knowledge of the truth that takes place in faith is a knowledge that is obedient to the call of God in Jesus Christ himself. And obedience for Barth is a free human act ratifying the divine action in our favor that has taken place in Jesus' life, death, and resurrection (see III/3, 264ff.). The kind of faith Barth has in mind "cannot be compromised" because it is "a victory of grace towards and in ourselves which corresponds to the death and resurrection of Jesus Christ and is like the divine certainty of Jesus Christ" (II/1, 155). Since we are enemies of grace apart from Christ, Barth seeks a "true and certain faith," that is, a faith that is not the continuation of our self-knowledge because "the New Testament witnesses tell us how their unbelief, not their knowledge, was changed into faith" (I/1, 404 rev.).[2] Faith's meaning therefore must "not start from the believing person but from Jesus Christ as the object and foundation of faith" (II/1, 156). The Holy Spirit creates the relation between God and us without which we cannot exist (I/1, 450). "He is the Spirit of truth because in Him it is none other than the living God, i.e., the trinitarian God, who is present and revealed and active. He is the Spirit of the Father and the Son" (IV/2, 350). For that reason

---

2. "The genuine believer will not say that he came to faith from faith, but — from unbelief" (I/2, p. 302).

[the Church] puts to itself the question of truth . . . [which] is the question as to the agreement of the Church's distinctive talk about God with the being of the Church . . . namely, Jesus Christ, God in His gracious revealing and reconciling address to man. Does Christian utterance derive from Him? Does it lead to Him? Is it conformable to Him? (I/1, 4)

In this light "what is required is [the Church's] criticism and correction in the light of the being of the Church, of Jesus Christ as its basis, goal and content" (I/1, 6). That is what is witnessed to in the whole of the Bible beginning with the story of Abraham and ending with Pentecost and beyond.

The Bible and Religion

Barth also stated that true religion, i.e., "what we are to think concerning God, how we are to find him, and how we are to conduct ourselves in his presence — all that is included in . . . 'worship and service'" (W, 41), is revealed in the Bible. But he immediately insists "there is something greater in the Bible than religion and 'worship,'" noting that Catholics and Protestants each appeal "with the same earnestness and zeal to the Bible," each insisting that it is the "religion revealed in the Bible, or at least its most legitimate successor" (W, 41-42). Yet Barth will not enter the dispute about which group is right or wrong because he sees that as an unending conflict about "religion"; nor will he say that everyone is right either. Arguing over the truth of religion leaves us "in the midst of a vast human controversy and far, far away from reality, or what might become reality in our lives." Here Barth turns his definition of religion upside down by reversing the whole enterprise:

> It is not the right human thoughts about God which form the content of the Bible, but the right divine thoughts about men. The Bible tells us not how we should talk with God but what he says to us; not how we find the way to him, but how he has sought and found the way to us; not the right relation in which we must place ourselves to him, but the covenant which he has made with all who are Abraham's spiritual children and which he has sealed once and for all in Jesus Christ. (W, 43)

While religion concerns our inquiry about what we are to think about God and how we are to reach him, Barth claims that if we read the Bible in faith we discover that this is entirely the wrong question. It only leads to conflict and controversy; it represents a form of self-justification and thereby illustrates why religion is so problematic and can never in itself lead to the truth revealed in the Bible. Without faith we will always assume that we actually can find the proper way to speak about God by means of our religious quest. But faith alone will allow us to recognize that God has already sought and found us in Jesus Christ. Consequently, we not only do not have to put ourselves into right relation with God through some religious practice; we cannot. We only have to believe and accept the Word of God, which binds us and enables us to worship God in Spirit and in truth and also to know him with a certainty that is impossible to achieve without relying on the grace of his own self-revelation in Jesus Christ. In this sense "to speak God's Word, and cause it to be heard, is and remains God's concern" (I/2, 763). Right religious practice then will follow from faith and not otherwise, since the Word "claims ourselves as doers of the work which corresponds to its content" (I/2, 365; see also I/1, 457).

The Righteousness of God

In another 1916 lecture Barth observed that "the really tragic, the most fundamental, error of mankind" is that "[w]e long for the righteousness of God, and yet we do not let it enter our lives and our world" (*W*, 14-15), because we are concerned primarily with *our* seeking God. Therefore we place ourselves and our various moral, religious, and political ideals at the center in a way that changes the righteousness of God, which is the "surest of facts," into "the highest among various high ideals" and thus something that is "our very own affair," instead of something that can be realized only by God himself (*W*, 16). Recognized or not, this taking God's righteousness under our management is the pride from which only God can rescue us. But this is impossible as long as we do not believe — as long as we cling to the deception that we can rely on ourselves at least in part to become righteous with the righteousness that comes only from God. Clinging to this deception represents the failure to believe, the failure to accept the grace of God's election and revelation itself as the truth of our lives and activities. As Barth explained in 1920:

> When we ask the Bible what it has to offer, it answers by putting to us the fact of *election*. What we call religion and culture may be available to

everybody, but the belief . . . which is offered in the Bible, is not available to everybody: not at any time nor in any respect can any who will, reach out and take it. (*W,* 58)[3]

The Bible offers true knowledge of God, which is not "one supposed truth among other truths." Responding to "the fact of election" we discover the meaning of both our own existence and of history. Whereas Augustine and the Reformers unfortunately shaped the doctrine according to the "*psychological* unity of the individual" and then stamped the "rigid laws of nature . . . once and for all . . . upon each man's salvation or damnation," Barth insists that the doctrine of election is indeed "well adapted to the requirements of individual *freedom*" because "our responses cannot be determined once and for all: they are constantly to be made anew" (*W,* 58-59). Here the Bible tells us that "the knowledge of God is the eternal problem of our profoundest personal existence, that it is the starting point at which we begin and yet do not begin, from which we are separated and yet are not separated" (*W,* 59). In other words we are sinners whose unbelief and belief leave us in perplexity and fear so that we are led to the point where we realize that religion, culture, history, and psychology cannot provide an answer.

But God himself can and does. God's truth is the secret meaning of history, piety, and experience; yet the moment we focus on these in themselves we ignore the truth of God's electing grace attested in Scripture — we ignore the very reality that alone gives meaning to our lives. Within this perspective the "Messiahship of Jesus must be kept secret," Barth says, because "[i]t is not a possibility of the old order: it is not a *religious* possibility. Jesus will be understood wholly or not at all" (*W,* 82). Flesh and blood did not reveal to Peter that Jesus was the Christ but the Father in heaven did. And it is upon this rock that the church is built. Thus when Peter began to question Christ's going to the cross, he no longer spoke from revelation but humanly "in the rôle of Satan" (*W,* 83). The knowledge of *the truth* comes only from beyond the grave because "in the sacrifice of Christ the sacrifice demanded of us is *made* once and for all." Because we ourselves are sacrificed with Christ, we have nothing to bring. Barth asks: Does life really come from death? Perhaps "it is possible to remain standing before the secret of the cross in perplexity, terror, and despair" (*W,* 84). Death really is a "closed wall" before which we all stand, and the resurrection can-

---

3. Cf. IV/2, p. 380; I/2, p. 103; and IV/3, pp. 44f.

not simply be presupposed, because it is an act of God. *We* really may find the cross a stumbling block and foolishness (*W*, 85). But Barth insists

> Resurrection — the Easter message — means the *sovereignty of God.* Resurrection, the sovereignty of God, is the purport of the life of Jesus from the first day of his coming. . . . He is . . . the champion of the divine honor, the authoritative bearer of divine power. Jesus simply had nothing to do with religion. The significance of his life lies in its possessing an actuality which no religion possesses. . . . "Behold, *I* make all things new." (*W*, 88)[4]

And the secret of Jesus' life is that he is the Son of the living God. This act of God opposes "Religion's blind and vicious habit of asserting eternally that it possesses something, feasts upon it, and distributes it" (*W*, 86-87). Hence:

> The believer knows that he lives. . . . We are first known by the One whom we may know, and it is only then that we may know and believe and confess. The fact that Jesus lives is true and real in itself. It precedes with sovereign majesty all knowledge and therefore all faith and confession that it is so. (IV/3, 45)

Yet this secret "belongs neither to history nor to psychology; for what is historical and psychological is as such corruptible." In this sense Christ's resurrection and second coming, which Barth says is the same thing, "is not a historical event"; as the only real happening *in* history this event is "not a real happening *of* history" (*W*, 90; see also II/1, 200). Because Christ's power comes into history from outside in order to completely re-create it, his divinity and power cannot be read off history. Consequently, "The Logos, if misunderstood, will stand in shame in the corner, as a myth" (*W*, 90). Better this, according to Barth, than attempting to explain who Jesus was historically. Since the resurrection means a wholly new creation, a new world, a world of an entirely different quality and kind, we cannot discover the genuine meaning of our world except in the power of the resurrection itself. That meaning "is not a continuation of anything that has been or is, either in the spiritual or the natural realm, but [it] comes to our mind spontaneously as a new creation" (*W*, 91). This is why

---

4. This is the central statement of the biblical witness for Barth: "If there is any Christian and theological axiom, it is that Jesus Christ is risen, that he is truly risen" (IV/3, p. 44).

Barth says that the truth of dogmatic inquiry which is known in faith "is in no sense assumed to be to hand. The truth comes, i.e., in the faith in which we begin to know, and cease, and begin again . . . [theological work] always takes place on the narrow way which leads from the enacted revelation to the promised revelation" (I/1, 14). And for Barth

> revelation denotes the Word of God itself in the act of its being spoken in time. . . . It is the condition which conditions all things without itself being conditioned . . . [it] means the unveiling of what is veiled. . . . Revelation in fact does not differ from the person of Jesus Christ nor from the reconciliation accomplished in him. To say revelation is to say "The Word became flesh." (I/1, 118-19)

Furthermore, the Holy Spirit who alone makes us participants in revelation is the Spirit of Jesus Christ and "is not to be regarded . . . as a revelation of independent content, as a new instruction . . . that goes beyond Christ; beyond the Word . . ." (I/1, 452-53).

Faith and Unbelief

The stark disparity that Barth perceives between faith and unbelief applies to all aspects of theology, including biblical theology. For Barth if we read the Bible carefully, it "makes straight for the point where one must decide to accept or to reject the sovereignty of God. This is the new world within the Bible" (W, 41). But again, since this new world of God himself comes from beyond the scope of history, morality, and religion, it often contradicts what these pursuits present as truth. For instance, Barth notes that in light of God's morality and his kingdom, "David is a great man in spite of his adultery and bloody sword: blessed is the man unto whom the Lord imputeth not iniquity!" And in this world "the publicans and the harlots will go before your impeccably elegant and righteous folk of good society!" Indeed in this world Barth explains that "the true hero is the lost son, who is absolutely lost and feeding swine — and not his moral elder brother" (W, 40). God's morality, the kingdom of God for which we pray, "Our Father . . ." is not a kingdom that we must create by our acts of good will.[5] It is not the unfolding of love as we may know it and practice it at all but "the

---

5. See IV/3, p. 670, for how this applies to Christianity and other religions.

existence and outpouring of the eternal love, of love as God understands it" (W, 40). And that love confounds our ordinary sense of morality because God's love takes place in accordance with his own sovereign decision to be for us in his own way. Because it also confounds our ordinary view of religion and of history Barth insists upon seeking the truth of revelation and not just religion in the Bible (W, 44).

Perhaps the disparity between faith and unbelief can be most clearly seen when contrasted with a view that has become rather widespread today. For example, Sallie McFague writes that Jesus is "special to us as our foundational figure: he is our historical choice as the premier paradigm of God's love."[6] Since Jesus' significance for faith rests on the community's choice, she claims "Jesus is not ontologically different from other paradigmatic figures" who manifest God's love for the world.[7] In reality, however, Jesus' uniqueness is not at all defined by the decisions of the community but by who he is as the only begotten Son of the Father from all eternity. His true divinity can never be seen or acknowledged unless it is accepted on its own terms (I/1, 400, 422) as the starting point for all theological reflection, since Jesus himself is the way, the truth, and the life (I/2, 105; II/1, 319-20; III/3, 179-80). In other words, in a dogmatic theology that is biblically grounded, one literally cannot speak of truth in abstraction from God's grace, faith, and revelation (I/1, 461). It is revelation as a sovereign act of God hidden in the cross and revealed in his resurrection that makes faith objectively true precisely because such faith is tied exclusively to the person and work of Jesus Christ himself as *the* true Son of God by nature. And faith itself is not under our control because "[t]he Spirit guarantees man what he cannot guarantee himself, his personal participation in revelation" (I/1, 453). As such the Spirit is in us but never becomes identical with us since the Spirit remains the Lord (I/1, 454). And it is indeed only by the Holy Spirit that anyone can confess Jesus himself as the Lord (IV/2, 328). Consequently, there literally can be no circumventing Jesus Christ if there is to be genuine knowledge of God, revelation, and grace. In McFague's perspective, faith is no longer tied to the object of faith presented by the Bible but is tethered to our own attempts to construct theological meaning by relying on our own self-chosen agenda. Hence, she believes we should remythologize the incarnation to recognize that we now

---

6. Sallie McFague, *Models of God: Theology for an Ecological, Nuclear Age* (hereafter: *Models*) (Philadelphia: Fortress Press, 1987), p. 136.

7. McFague, *Models*, p. 136.

have the power to kill God in the body of the world rather than in the particular man Jesus in order to help us preserve the earth.[8] This thinking, however, represents a form of self-justification; it is docetic in orientation and design and thus fails to allow the man Jesus from Nazareth in his unity with the divine Word to be the starting point and determining factor for its reflections.

This is why Barth firmly asserted that "sin is always unbelief. And unbelief is always man's faith in himself" (I/2, 314). By contrast, McFague speaks for many when she redefines sin:

> sin is the turning-away not from a transcendent power but from interdependence with all other beings, including the matrix of being from whom all life comes. It is not pride or unbelief but the refusal of relationship. . . . It is a horizontal refusal to be part of the body of God rather than a vertical refusal to be inferior to God.[9]

By reconceiving God as "mother, lover, and friend" instead of recognizing God through his self-revelation as Father, Son, and Holy Spirit, McFague has difficulty in properly distinguishing God from the world.[10] For her the word "God" has become a "myth," a term that describes our relationship with the world and a vague belief in a God who is on the side of life and its fulfillment.[11] Sin becomes merely a horizontal relation between us and the world imagined as God's body. It can no longer be understood as a vertical relation of opposition to the God who is above. Barth's thinking about God's righteousness, as already noted, was not only profound but prophetic. When God's sovereignty is ignored or called into question, as in McFague's analysis, the problem of sin and unbelief arises. For Barth, any refusal to allow God to be God for us in the way he has freely chosen, that is, in his Word and Spirit, would be a form of pride.[12]

Many today argue that sin should no longer be understood as pride and thus espouse some form of religious self-reliance. This subverts the biblical

8. McFague, *Models,* pp. 72-73.

9. McFague, *Models,* pp. 139-40.

10. See my "Myth and Reality: Analysis and Critique of Gordon Kaufman and Sallie McFague on God, Christ, and Salvation," *Cultural Encounters: A Journal for the Theology of Culture* 1 (2005): 23-48; at pp. 38-48.

11. McFague, *Models,* p. 192.

12. See II/2, pp. 579-83. Even after our reconciliation with God in Christ, the resisting element in us continues especially when we create worldviews in order to avoid the truth of God's action in Christ on our behalf (IV/3, pp. 254ff.).

meaning of faith as faith in Christ himself and not at all in ourselves. Faith in Christ means precisely surrendering to him alone as the source of all freedom and truth (IV/2, 407). In Barth's words, "To become obedient to Jesus is actually to become obedient to God, not a conceived and imaginary God, but to God as He is in His inmost essence, the gracious God, the God in whom we may believe" (II/2, 568-69). "He is the truth. . . . To be of the truth means to hear His voice in encounter and confrontation with Him. . . . To be of the truth means first to believe in Him" (IV/1, 252). Hence Barth insists that "if the Son therefore shall make you free, you shall be freed indeed" (I/1, 456; cf. II/1, 208), and that "if in one sense or another the faith of the Christian is faith in himself . . . then we need not be surprised if it is not the victory which overcomes the world" (III/3, 249-50). Christ is the one who represents us by turning faithfully to God in our place. Conversion to God takes place in Christ alone so that in the power of the Holy Spirit "in Jesus Christ man is directed by God to awakening and life in the freedom for which he has made him free" (IV/1, 102; cf. IV/2, 503).

Barth rightly insists that when we encounter the triune God we renounce any attempt to bring about our own conversion because "[t]his is forbidden and prevented by the object of faith," since faith in Christ "absolutely excludes any other helpers or helps" (IV/1, 632). If we try to understand faith by looking at ourselves, what we see is a lie, and it may well lead us to question its possibility and to regard it as intolerable; yet we continually try to flee from this faith. Here, Barth insists, we must do the better thing, the needful thing: "We have to believe: not to believe in ourselves, but in Jesus Christ. In Him, along with our enmity against God's grace, our flight from faith too is limited, ended and destroyed" (II/1, 159; cf. II/1, 386).

Since faith means allowing God to speak to us through the biblical witness, it entails subordinating ourselves to the witness of Scripture. But this does not mean that we allow our thoughts, concepts, and convictions to be "supplanted" by those of the prophets and apostles. "In that case we should not have subordinated ourselves to them, but at most adorned ourselves with their feathers" (I/2, 718). It means accepting the true implication of their witness and acknowledging that God is right "instead of trying to prove ourselves right." That is what it means to believe — hence the new world of God's sovereignty, which meets us in the biblical witness, is his glory and his incomprehensible love. "Not the history of man but the history of God!" writes Barth. "Not the virtues of men but the virtues of him who hath called us out of darkness into his marvelous light! Not human standpoints but the standpoint of God!" (W, 45). Once again, this thinking is not meant to eliminate human being and action in face of God's action but to say that no human action can be allowed, even momentarily, to have the first and final word concerning our morality, history, and religion. Whenever that happens God is displaced, and certainty concerning the truth of all human activity becomes shrouded in obscurity and doubt once again. This is perhaps the greatest challenge for much contemporary theology since so many today, in spite of all their good intentions, do not actually allow the Word of God, namely, Jesus Christ himself, to be the first and final Word in all their reflections upon God, faith, grace, revelation, and truth itself. This is the problem of self-justification.

Faith and the Knowledge of God

At the close of his "Strange New World" lecture Barth notes that a whole new series of questions may arise about who God really is who meets us in the Bible and calls us to faith. While we might say that the content of the Bible is God himself, Barth asks, "What is the content of the contents?" (*W*, 46; cf. II/2, 580). And he lists a number of answers that, while true, are nonetheless inadequate because they may still represent the content of our wishes and not God himself as he comes to us, the Lord and Redeemer, the Savior and Comforter of all who turn to him. The new world is the world of "incomparable peace of such a life hid with Christ in God" (*W*, 46).[13] All of this and more Barth says is true. But it is not the whole truth because we must grow beyond the question "Who is God?"

Barth's thinking here is similar to the way he began *CD* II/1 concerning our knowledge of God, where he insisted that knowledge of the truth that takes place in faith never asks *whether* God is known (II/1, 4ff.), because

> [f]aith is the total positive relationship of man to the God who gives Himself to be known in His Word. It is man's act of turning to God, of opening up his life to Him and of surrendering to Him. It is the Yes which he pronounces in his heart when confronted by this God, because he knows himself to be bound and fully bound. (II/1, 12)

Accordingly, "Biblical faith excludes any faith of man in himself — that is, any desire for religious self-help, any religious self-satisfaction, any religious self-sufficiency. Biblical faith lives upon the objectivity of God" (II/1,

---

13. See also, e.g., I/1, p. 463; I/2, p. 240; II/1, p. 149; II/2, pp. 158, 580; and IV/1, p. 729.

13). And because God can only be known in faith and by his own gracious self-revelation, true knowledge of God is "an event enclosed in the bosom of the divine Trinity" (II/1, 205; cf. II/1, 181), so that we really know God himself in our views and concepts as God enables us to participate in his own self-knowledge.

In his "Strange New World" lecture Barth says that one who is led by God himself to "the gates of the new world, to the threshold of the kingdom of God . . . asks no longer. There one sees. There one hears. There one has. There one knows. There one no longer gives his petty, narrow little answers" (W, 47). Anyone who is still asking "Who is God?" has halted, refused to let the Bible speak and has "failed somewhere truly to desire — to believe. At the point of halt the truth again becomes unclear, confused, problematical — narrow, stupid, high-church, non-conformist, monotonous, or meaningless" (W, 48). It is because of our unbelief that we are so perplexed by the question "Who is God?" The answer the Bible gives is: "'He that hath *seen* me hath *seen* the Father.' . . . When we find God in the Bible, when we dare with Paul not to be disobedient to the heavenly vision, then God stands before us as he really is. 'Believing, ye *shall* receive!' God is *God*" (W, 48). Even when we believe, however, we must still pray "Lord, I believe; help thou mine unbelief." Yet in the midst of our unbelief we may really know God through his grace; and when we do know God, we know him as the heavenly Father. But we know him as "the heavenly Father even upon *earth*, and upon earth really the *heavenly* Father." This God does not allow his "life to be divided between a here and a beyond and he will not leave to death the task of freeing us from sin and sorrow. He will bless us, not with the power of the church, but with the power of life and resurrection. In Christ he caused his word to be made flesh." In Christ eternity has dawned upon time and he has in fact established a *new* world. Yet that is not the end of the story.

The Bible also tells us that God is God the Son who has become the Mediator for the entire world. He is the redeeming Word of God who existed in the beginning and is expected as the one who is coming again. He is the redeemer of humanity as it has gone astray, and indeed he is the redeemer of all creation. It is in this sense that "all the events of the Bible are the beginning, the glorious beginning of a new *world*" (W, 48-49). And the Bible tells us further that God is the "Spirit in his believers" who

> makes a new heaven and a new earth and, therefore, new men, new families, new relationships, new politics. It has no respect for old traditions

simply because they are traditions. . . . The *Holy* Spirit has respect only for truth, for itself. The Holy Spirit establishes the righteousness of heaven in the midst of the unrighteousness of earth and will not stop nor stay until all that is dead has been brought to life and a new *world* has come into being. (*W*, 49-50)

But it would be the greatest misunderstanding of Barth's intentions if one were to shift the weight of emphasis here away from the Spirit acting within us as the Lord and giver of life and onto our own new families and new relationships with the idea that wherever families are renewed and relationships change for the better there can be seen the kingdom of God.

Once again, any attempt to explore the meaning of our relationship with God by focusing on ourselves as those justified and sanctified by the Holy Spirit through grace alone means we have already ceased to live by grace and by faith.[14] Barth saw this critical point in a number of contexts with great clarity, and his vision is worth noting today especially when so many theologians seem to want to divide their loyalties between a strictly theological method that operates in faith by allowing the object of faith — the triune God — to determine what is thought and said, and a method that allows our human experiences and insights to set the questions that faith is then supposed to answer. Barth's dogmatic theology is an application of his understanding of biblical faith; dogmatics itself is an act of faith that has "its basis in the divine predestination, the free act of God on man and his work," which will enable dogmatic work but will always question it as well (I/1, 22). This questioning by the Word of God is not something that can be solved humanly speaking. That is why prayer is necessary. Prayer allows us to recognize that we can accomplish nothing by ourselves; it is not a means by which we can count on success in our work but an act of faith, trusting completely in the Lord to enable our work (I/1, 23-24).

Knowledge of God too must be prayed for because only God can make himself known; here too faith, grace, and revelation are indissolubly connected. Hence "[t]he position of grace cannot be taken up and held in any other way than by asking and praying for it" (II/1, 22-23).[15] This means that

14. See I/2, p. 358, where Barth insists that the Christian religion can never find its justification in itself either. We must simply live *by* grace and *for* grace, according to Barth (II/2, p. 576). Heidelberg Q1

15. See also III/3, p. 246, where Barth links faith, obedience, and prayer together in a manner similar to the way the three persons of the Trinity are perichoretically related.

knowledge of God takes place only as free obedience, i.e., as a human decision that corresponds with God's decision concerning us.[16] Hence,

> [t]he being of God is either known by grace or it is not known at all. If,
> however, it is known by grace, then we are already displaced from that
> secure position and put in a position where the consideration of God
> can consist and be fulfilled only in the act of our own decision of obedi-
> ence. (II/1, 27)

Here we pray to be relieved of the many temptations that would lead away
from clinging to grace alone for our knowledge of God. Interestingly, in his
doctrine of Providence, Barth links faith, obedience, and prayer in a similar way and concludes that when God guides creation he does so in the
eternally rich activity of his Word and Spirit, and "[t]he eternal riches of
God are the riches of His trinitarian life as Father, Son and Holy Spirit."
Because of this "it is necessarily the case that the omnipotent operation of
God not merely leaves the activity of the creature free, but continually
makes it free." It is because the triune God is eternally rich that in his works
in his Word and Spirit "there is no reason whatever why the activity of the
creature should be destroyed or suppressed by his omnipotent operation"
(III/3, 150). In what follows we shall explore some implications of such a
biblically grounded dogmatic theology for our knowledge of God, focusing on the relation of religion and revelation.

Religious Experience and Self-Justification: Paul Tillich

Contemporary theology often does not allow Jesus to have the first and final word. From Barth's point of view, those who believe they can know
God and thus also the truth of "religion" by exploring people's religious
experiences have fallen into some form of self-justification or self-
sanctification. Some believe that Barth went too far in his critique of religion in I/2. Yet it is worth asking whether and to what extent those who believe this have embraced a view of religion that has already domesticated
revelation in some subtle or overt way. T. F. Torrance accurately described
Barth's theology "as the application of justification to the whole realm of

---

16. "God's action is that he is gracious, and man in his action is committed to correspondence to this action. He is the image of God and his action when his own action reflects
and to that extent copies the grace of God" (II/2, p. 576).

man's life, to the realm of his knowing as well as the realm of his doing."[17] Let us compare some of what Barth says about the truth of religion and our knowledge of God with what Paul Tillich proposes when he sees faith as in some sense dictated by our "ultimate concern."

Barth insists that "[r]evelation is understood only where we expect from it, and from it alone, the first and the last word about religion" (I/2, 295) and that even the slightest concession to "religionism" in the attempt to understand religion theologically is fatal. What is the reason for this? It is the plain fact that Jesus alone is the Word of God incarnate. Hence

> [t]he Christian religion is simply the earthly-historical life of the Church and the children of God. As such we must think of it as an annexe to the human nature of Jesus Christ. And we must remember what we are told concerning his human nature in Jn. 1:14. There never was a man Jesus as such apart from the eternal reality of the Son of God. (I/2, 348)

Importantly, Jesus' humanity "has no hypostasis of its own" because "[i]t has it only in the Logos. The same is true, therefore, of the earthly-historical life of the Church and the children of God, and therefore of the Christian religion" (I/2, 348).

By contrast, relying on depth psychology and exploring experiences of depth to understand God, Tillich claims:

> The name of this infinite and inexhaustible depth and ground of all being is *God.* That depth is what the word *God* means. And if that word has not much meaning for you, translate it, and speak of the depths of your life, of the source of your being, of your ultimate concern, of what you take seriously without any reservation. Perhaps, in order to do so, you must forget everything traditional that you have learned about God. . . . For if you know that God means depth, you know much about Him. You cannot then call yourself an atheist or unbeliever. For you cannot think or say: Life has no depth! . . . If you could say this in complete seriousness, you would be an atheist; but otherwise you are not. He who knows about depth knows about God.[18]

---

17. T. F. Torrance, *Theology in Reconstruction* (London: SCM Press, 1965), p. 163. Barth's thinking confirms Torrance's judgment. See Barth, *CD* II/1, p. 213.

18. Paul Tillich, *The Shaking of the Foundations* (New York: Charles Scribner's Sons, 1948), p. 57. John A. T. Robinson, *Honest to God* (Philadelphia: Westminster, 1963), p. 22, and John Haught, *What Is God? How to Think about the Divine* (New York: Paulist Press, 1986), pp. 14-15, rely on this thinking for their approaches to God.

Tillich begins with religious experience and not with faith in Jesus Christ, and thus subverts the priority of revelation over religion.[19]

While Tillich assumes we can know the Christian God by exploring our experiences of depth, by equating our experience of depth with knowledge of God, and by concluding that we can change the word "God" as traditionally understood as long as we know that depth means "God," faith, as understood by Barth, knows God precisely as the eternal Father, Son, and Holy Spirit — as one who is hidden from any and all our experiences no matter how deep they may be. And when God is truly known in an encounter with his Word through his Spirit as attested in Scripture, one immediately knows that we cannot learn of God by exploring our experiences of depth. Such an approach is closed to us. Thus, any attempt to equate experiences of depth with knowledge of the triune God amounts to an overt reduction of theology to anthropology, and opens the door to a universalism that can claim knowledge of God without ever believing in God himself who is present to us in history in his Word and Spirit. As Barth insisted:

> We cannot say anything higher or better of the "inwardness of God" than that God is Father, Son and Holy Spirit, and therefore that he is love in himself without and before loving us, and without being forced to love us. And we can say this only in the light of the "outwardness" of God to us, the occurrence of his revelation. (I/2, 377)[20]

This is why grace, faith, revelation, and truth are inextricably connected in Barth's theology. Faith is not something we create or can control since, as we have already seen, it is a specific freedom that comes miraculously from the Holy Spirit in particular circumstances. And since this freedom comes to us and enables us to know God in truth and to act as those who have been liberated for service of the Word, this shows that there is no true knowledge of God outside of our relationship with God established and maintained by God himself in Christ and through the Holy Spirit. For Barth, "Christian experience . . . is true . . . to the extent that it lives entirely by Him and cannot curve in upon itself in self-sufficiency. It is true in and

19. For Barth "revelation does not link up with a human religion which is already present and practised. It contradicts it, just as religion previously contradicted revelation" (I/2, p. 303).

20. Cf. IV/2, pp. 345, 347. Barth observed: "If 'Immanuel, with us sinners' is true, then our own deepest ground of being, whatever we think concerning it, cannot be the past revelation of God" (I/1, p. 108).

by its source, in and by Jesus Christ as its basis, upon which it is dependent but which is not dependent upon it" (IV/1, 249).[21]

John Haught

One can see the problematic nature of Tillich's thinking when one sees what John Haught makes of it. Citing Tillich, Haught reasons that "God may be 'thought of' as the inexhaustible depth and ground out of which all of our experiences arise. We continually dwell in this depth without focusing upon it."[22] Hence, "religion may be understood as the search for depth,"[23] but "religion is more than a search. For religion is also a confident *naming* of the dimension of depth." And conversion means "a new turn and a new confidence in the unending journey to the depth of our lives."[24] In sum Haught says

> if God is the depth of existence, then religion is the confident search for this depth as well as the celebration of those events, persons or occasions where the depth has broken through the surface of our lives in an exceptional way. . . . It is the degree of seriousness whereby we ask ultimate questions, and not the degree of doctrinal certitude, that determines whether we are surrendering to the transcendent depth of our lives, that is, to God.[25]

Such thinking seems to confirm the accuracy of Barth's understanding of religion as our attempt to create the God we want instead of living by faith and accepting God as he has acted for us in his Word and Spirit.[26] Haught's idea that religion is our confident search for depth would seem to confirm Barth's view that "religion is . . . thoroughly self-centered" (I/2, 315) and cannot transcend the limit of experience; it thus reduces God to

---

21. This is why faith always means acknowledgment of God's Word and Spirit coming to us "absolutely from without." See I/1, pp. 90, 176, and 205-8.

22. Haught, *What Is God?* p. 20.

23. Haught, *What Is God?* p. 21.

24. Haught, *What Is God?* p. 22.

25. Haught, *What Is God?* p. 24.

26. For Barth, "man tries to grasp at truth of himself . . . *a priori*" and in that way demonstrates unbelief because "he does not do what he has to do when the truth comes to him. He does not believe. . . . If he did, he would accept a gift; but in religion he takes something for himself" (I/2, p. 302).

our knowledge of our own depth. In this sense a study of religion and religious experience leads directly to the conclusion that we can have a true knowledge of God without relying on the grace of God revealed in Christ.

John A. T. Robinson

John Robinson explicitly relies on Tillich's thinking and reaches the following questionable conclusions:

> The question of God is the question *whether this depth of being is a reality or an illusion,* not whether *a* Being exists beyond the bright blue sky, or anywhere else. Belief in God is a matter of "what you take seriously without any reservation," of what for you is *ultimate* reality.[27]

Consequently God "is to be found only in, with, *and under* the conditioned relationships of this life: for he *is* their depth and ultimate significance."[28] No wonder T. F. Torrance believed Robinson's thinking was "unable to distinguish God from [our] own swollen subjectivity"[29] and called him a "theological solipsist, who cannot see finally outside of himself or identify a God 'out there' in distinction from the ground of his own being."[30] By resorting to "pictorial images" for God, Robinson's thinking becomes unscientific because it is a "failure to understand things out of themselves in accordance with their natures."[31] Torrance concludes that Robinson and other so-called "new theologians"

> are out for *cheap grace,* i.e. the "God" *they* want, one to suit themselves and modern "secular" man, rather than the God of *costly grace* who calls for the renewing of our minds in which we are not schematized to the patterns of this world but are transformed in conformity with His own self-revelation in Jesus Christ.[32]

---

27. Robinson, *Honest to God,* p. 55.

28. Robinson, *Honest to God,* p. 60.

29. Thomas F. Torrance, *God and Rationality* (London: Oxford University Press, 1971; reissued Edinburgh: T. & T. Clark, 2001), p. 29.

30. Torrance, *God and Rationality,* p. 40; also p. 44. Torrance believes Robinson's thinking is merely mythological projection and as such is useless for any real understanding of God (p. 80).

31. Torrance, *God and Rationality,* p. 41.

32. Torrance, *God and Rationality,* p. 82.

Barth's view of Robinson's *Honest to God* was similar.[33] Both Torrance and Barth refused to allow grace to be detached from Jesus himself as the Word of God incarnate, and relocated in the wider sphere of religious experience, because they believed such universalism represented a gnosticizing of the gospel. The thinking offered by Tillich, Haught, and Robinson was excluded by the very nature of revelation as Barth understood it. Any such thinking would undermine the intent and content of various Christian doctrines, not least of which is the doctrine of Trinity; indeed even trinitarian theology can become very uncertain when placed within this Tillichian context.

S. Mark Heim

Let me illustrate this latter point very briefly with several remarks made by S. Mark Heim. *First,* he believes "The Trinity teaches us that Jesus Christ cannot be an exhaustive or exclusive source for knowledge of God nor the exhaustive and exclusive act of God to save us."[34] Compare this assertion to Barth's unequivocal remark that

> the true and essential distinction of the Christian religion from the non-Christian, and with it its character as the religion of truth over against the religions of error, can be demonstrated only in the fact, or event, that taught by Holy Scripture the Church listens to Jesus Christ and no one else as grace and truth, not being slack but always cheerful to proclaim and believe Him. (I/2, 344)[35]

Hence, the truth of the Christian religion is the fact that Christians may live by grace because "[i]t is of grace that the Church and the children of God live by His grace." Consequently, the church lives "through the name of Jesus Christ" (I/2, 345). This exclusivity is not meant to exclude other religions by way of competition, because it is the action of the one, true, and

33. *Karl Barth Letters 1961-1968,* ed. Jürgen Fangmeier and Hinrich Stoevesandt, trans. Geoffrey W. Bromiley (Grand Rapids: Eerdmans, 1981), pp. 102, 116.

34. S. Mark Heim, *The Depth of the Riches: A Trinitarian Theology of Religious Ends* (Grand Rapids: Eerdmans, 2001), p. 134.

35. Thus Barth insists that "[m]an never at all exists in himself [but] in Jesus Christ and in Him alone; as he also finds God in Jesus Christ and in Him alone" (II/1, p. 149). And "the Church must . . . see that it expects everything from *Jesus Christ* and from Jesus Christ *everything,* that he is unceasingly recognized as the way, the truth, and the life (Jn. 14.6)" (II/1, p. 320).

ever-living God on behalf of all people, whatever their religious commitments may be.[36] As a christological statement "[i]t looks away from non-Christian and Christian alike to the One who sovereignly confronts and precedes both" (IV/3, 91). Heim claims that Jesus cannot be the exclusive source of our knowledge of God and the exclusive saving act of God at work in history. He in effect denies the content and meaning of the doctrine of the Trinity in a way that undermines soteriology. He proposes a trinitarian theology of religions. At the crucial point, however, he exchanges the uniqueness of Jesus Christ as the one Word of God for a "religious" approach. He sees the doctrine of the Trinity merely as a way of affirming "communion" and "relationality." The Trinity is used to affirm the goodness of a plurality of religious ends.

Second, because his starting point for a theology of religions is not Jesus Christ and faith in him as the one Word of God and the unique savior of the world, Heim then argues that "[t]he communion Christ came to instigate is itself the fundamental instrument for understanding who Christ is."[37] It is not Christ who defines communion, but a general experience of "communion" that defines Christ. But if communion is the "instrument" for understanding who Christ is, then and to that extent it can no longer be Christ alone who is and remains the criterion of our thinking about communion, salvation, and the Trinity. In this way the instrument clearly becomes "religion" and a study of "religious ends" that receive their truth not from the Word of God incarnate in Jesus Christ but from the degree of communion thought to be perceived by the inquirer. Barth insisted that all religion (including the Christian religion) is inherently unbelief insofar as it refuses to allow Christ himself to be the starting point and norm for what is said about the truth of God and revelation. By contrast, Heim claims that religions

> demonstrate that every movement of human response to God's "Yes" to creation is met by God's further "Yes" as well. . . . Religions represent real relations to aspects of the triune life and aspects of God's economic activity. . . . God will in crucial measure conform God's relation with the person to the person's choice of terms on which to relate to God.[38]

36. In fact Barth believes the will of God is often done better outside the church than in it (II/2, p. 569). And we must apply the judgment of grace acutely to ourselves and others and see ourselves in solidarity with them as we anticipate them in repentance and hope and live by faith and grace (I/2, pp. 327-28).

37. Heim, *The Depth of the Riches*, p. 137.

38. Heim, *The Depth of the Riches*, p. 268.

For Barth, the triune God relates with us according to his free choice and not at all according to ours. He justifies the ungodly. Barth thus insisted that because God is "both gracious and holy: gracious as he is holy and holy as he is gracious, . . . the *freedom* of grace is revealed in the fact that it is always manifest in judgment. But it is the freedom of *grace* which is revealed in this way" (II/1, 367). Importantly, however, for Barth, God is always present to us as one who is in opposition to us as we are (II/1, 361). Only the believer speaks of this opposition of grace; thus the truth of religion can only be recognized through faith and not by incorporating revelation into the context of a conception of communion dictated by anything or anyone other than Jesus Christ. Heim asserts that "Trinitarian conviction rules out the view that among all the possible claimed manifestations of God, one narrow strand alone is authentic."[39] Here truth in its identity with Jesus Christ, who is the truth, has been undercut at its root. Instead, Heim proposes that the doctrine of the Trinity allows and commands us to recognize as valid a plurality of religious ends.

Heim contends that other religions with their very different ends place their members in contact with dimensions of the triune God. On the one hand he argues that Islam finds the Christian doctrine of the Trinity offensive because Muslims think it introduces division into God. On the other hand he claims that "the Muslim religious end focuses on the personal 'I' of the Trinity."[40] Yet if the Muslim idea of God's oneness excludes the oneness in being between the Son and Father, how can Muslims in any sense be said to have recognized the "I" of the Trinity? Whatever "I" they have conceptualized, as long as the *homoousion* between the Father and Son is denied, it is certainly not the divine subject confessed by Christians through faith in Jesus Christ and by the power of his Holy Spirit.

What Heim describes as dimensions of the triune God, then, would seem to represent little more than aspects of the dimension of depth articulated by Tillich, Robinson, and Haught. Accordingly, Heim's trinitarian theology of religions fails to allow God in Christ to determine his understanding of who God is. God is not just a "communion-nature" as Heim believes. As three persons, one being, God's being is in communion. But communion is not God. Failure to make this distinction leads Heim to say:

39. Heim, *The Depth of the Riches*, p. 127.
40. Heim, *The Depth of the Riches*, p. 233.

The very fact that our being is constituted in relation with others, relation with what is unlike (and this includes most basically of all the fact that we are different from God who made us), is the most fundamental way that we are like God. It is the deepest thing we have in common.[41]

But do we really have a life in common with God that is directly perceptible in this way without faith in Christ?

This is a relevant question when you consider Heim's statement that "I as a Christian do not deny that a Hindu may actually realize identity with the divine, with absolute *Brahman*. I regard this as in fact identity with the underlying immanence of the triune God."[42] Yet, the only way this could be true is if divine and human being and action are identified so that our relationality gives us something in common with God. Moreover, in light of biblical revelation and faith, this thinking fails to acknowledge that God's immanence is identical only with his immanence in his Word and Spirit. It is not an immanence that can be seen or described apart from faith in Christ himself — a faith that itself comes only from the Holy Spirit. In faith one discovers that "[i]f the freedom of divine immanence is sought and supposedly found apart from Jesus Christ, it can signify in practice only our enslavement to a false god" (II/1, 319).

For Barth the God we grasp at in religion is a sign of our unbelief, our sin, our sloth, and therefore our attempt to render innocuous the revelation of God in Jesus Christ. Christ causes offense because of his exclusive claim on us. The God of religion does not. So we are "basically illuminated and radically questioned and disturbed and therefore offended by the deity of God in the concrete phenomenon of the existence of this man."[43] And yet, as I have argued in this chapter, following Barth's thinking, faith, grace, revelation, and truth are so indissolubly connected according to the biblical witness that both religion and trinitarian theology itself are necessarily and always directed away from all self-chosen agendas, no matter how universally appealing, and toward faith in the Word of God incarnate in Jesus Christ who, as the grace of God manifested in history, alone is the truth who promises to give meaning to our thinking — but only on his terms and not at all on ours — no matter how offensive that may be.

41. Heim, *The Depth of the Riches,* pp. 126-27.
42. Heim, *The Depth of the Riches,* p. 229.
43. Barth, *CD* IV/2, p. 406.

10. The Heart of the Matter:
Karl Barth's Christological Exegesis

Paul Dafydd Jones

This essay expounds a single interpretive conviction: that Barth's interpretation of the New Testament plays a pivotal role in his mature christology. To appreciate fully Barth's actualistic understanding of the union of divinity and humanity in Christ's person, whereby the divine Son's prevenient determination to be the "Word become flesh" is matched by Jesus of Nazareth's human determination to be the flesh that the Word becomes, one must reckon with Barth's exegetical claims. Why? Because the biblical witness affects, decisively, key aspects of the dynamic theological ontology of the *Church Dogmatics;* because the twists and turns of the Gospels, in particular, shape Barth's description of Christ's person and work.

I develop this argument in three stages. My first section considers the prolegomenal doctrine of Scripture sketched in *Church Dogmatics* I/2. It aims to clarify what Barth means when he posits the "indirect identity" of the Word of God and the biblical witness. The second section examines the treatment of the prologue to John's Gospel in *Church Dogmatics* II/2. In parsing the exegetical moves that inform Barth's understanding of election, I venture a somewhat controversial interpretation. To wit: Barth believes that God *qua* Son transforms Godself by way of the incarnation — "transforms" in the sense that God freely wills that the incarnational action of the Son have an eternal bearing on God's own "heart." Refusing to drive a wedge between the *logos asarkos* and the *logos ensarkos*, though not dispensing entirely with the distinction, Barth contends that the Son is always becoming and being the concrete person of Jesus Christ, "electing God" and "elected human." My third section discusses Barth's treatment of a single Greek word used in Matthew 9:36: *esplanchnisthē.* This word, loosely translatable as "being moved with compassion," indicates that

God's elective self-determination *qua* Son is complemented by Christ's human elective self-determination. Just as God wills that God's own heart be touched and transformed in view of the incarnation, so too does Christ humanly will that his heart be touched and transformed. Indeed, just as God determines Godself to bear sin and misery, so too does Jesus humanly determine himself to bear sin and misery, thereby enacting an identity in which he lives (and dies) as the "flesh" that the Word assumes. In conclusion, I consider how Barth's insights might contribute to constructive theological work today.

I. Barth's Doctrine of Scripture

Barth's initial discussion of "Holy Scripture" (I/2, §§19-21) has negative and positive aspects. Negatively, Barth cautions against perspectives that make the Word of God directly identical with Scripture. He also protests reductionistic historical-critical stances[1] that ignore the (possible) relationship between the divine Word and the biblical witness, and thereby denude Scripture of revelatory import. The problem on both counts: Scripture is being subjected to undue human control. A predetermined "method" neglects both revelation's anterior condition and its content: the disclosure of God's freedom to relate graciously to human beings, here and now, on terms established by God Godself. Certainly, this problem manifests itself in different ways. There is a world of difference between an ossified biblicism that fixes doctrine through prooftexting and putatively "critical" investigations that seek only to discover "what really happened." But both stances betray the same dogmatic error. The task of theological *nachdenken*, undertaken in response to God's (past and present) action in Scripture, has been replaced by human religiosity. Instead of attending to

---

1. Though I do not have space to expand this point, note that historical-critical stances are not necessarily "reductionistic," even if some authors risk suggesting as much. Barth neither disregards nor treats historical-critical studies with disdain. Rather, he acknowledges their value both explicitly (thus the treatment of Genesis 1 and 2 in *Church Dogmatics* III/1) and implicitly (thus the differentiation of the synoptic gospels and John as they relate to christological reflection; see here I/2, §13, esp. p. 16), while insisting also that the conclusions of such inquiries subserve theology's primary task, *viz.*, articulating the "understanding" that attends Christian faith. Put in terms of a dogmatic rule: historical-critical insight may not control theological exegesis; historical-critical insight can only add texture to theological exegesis.

the divine Word that sounds in the biblical words, the theologian has exchanged divine speech for human chatter.

An acclamation of the "indirect identity" (I/2, 492) that obtains between the biblical witness and the divine Word announces Barth's positive agenda. The phrase aims to preserve the elements of truth in "orthodox" doctrines of inspiration and "modern" appreciations of Scripture's historical conditioned-ness. Barth wants, in other words, to avoid thinking either purely in terms of Scripture's "divinity" (a vulgar construal of inspiration) or purely in terms of Scripture's "humanity" (a risk run by some historical-critical scholars). He wants to affirm *both* that Scripture reveals God *and* that Scripture is a human affair, limited by the finitude of the authors who bore witness to the Word of God through poetry, prose, history-like narrative, etc.

Barth articulates this both/and with characteristic flair. On the one side, he insists on Scripture's unique standing — the fact that God establishes an "indirect *identity*" between Scripture and the divine Word. Though the biblical texts share the limitations of all human documents, God "assumes" (or "sanctifies")[2] them for the purpose of God's self-disclosure. God's action is such that it renders these texts uniquely revelatory of God's being and God's action. Thus:

> Holy Scripture attests to . . . the revelation of God, Jesus Christ, the Word of God. The power in which it does so is the power of the object to which it bears witness and which has also made and fashioned it as that witness. . . . In doing so it mediates revelation; it presents Jesus Christ; in the servant form of a human word it speaks the Word of God. (I/2, 538)

On the other side, Barth affirms the "creatureliness" of Scripture — the fact that there is an "*indirect* identity" between Scripture and the divine

---

2. I refer here to the excellent work of John Webster, *Holy Scripture: A Dogmatic Sketch* (Cambridge: Cambridge University Press, 2003). See esp. pp. 5-41, where Webster develops a stance congruous with Barth's. His argument *in nuce*: "[T]he notion of Scripture as 'sanctified' [distinguishes a] dogmatic ontology of the biblical texts that elides neither their creatureliness nor their relation to the free self-communication of God. At its most basic, the notion states that the biblical texts are creaturely realities set apart by the triune God to serve his self-presence . . . talk of sanctification moves discussion of the nature of Scripture out of the dualism . . . [that] force[s] a choice between either a divine or a human text, either inspiration or naturalism" (pp. 21-22). For additional elaborations of this standpoint, see also "The Dogmatic Location of the Canon" and "Hermeneutics in Modern Theology: Some Doctrinal Reflections," in John Webster, *Word and Church: Essays in Christian Dogmatics* (Edinburgh: T. & T. Clark, 2001), pp. 9-46 and 47-86 respectively.

Word. Though God's self-disclosure stimulates and superintends the discursive work of its witnesses, and though God acts, in ways that are appropriable to the operations of God *qua* Spirit, to shape the receptive "experience" of Scripture's readers, this divine economy maintains and respects the finitude of the documents in question. Thus:

> It is quite impossible that there should be a *direct* identity between the human word of Holy Scripture and the Word of God, and therefore between the creaturely reality in itself and as such and the reality of God the Creator. It is impossible that there should have been a transformation of the one into the other or an admixture of the one with the other. Such is not the case even in the person of Jesus Christ. Already here the identity between God and human, in all the originality and indissolubility in which it confronts us, is an assumed identity, one specially willed, created and effected by God, and to that extent indirect, i.e. depending neither on the essence of God nor on that of the human, but on a decision and act of God to the human. It is exactly the same, necessarily allowing for inherent differences, with the unity of the divine and human word in Holy Scripture. (I/2, 499 rev.)

Barth's point is this: while the biblical texts are "assumed" by God in a way that enables the theologian to claim that Scripture *is* the Word of God — both in the past, in the present, and in the future — at no point should it be thought that these texts become simply equivalent to the Word of God. The Reformed principle of *finitum non est capax infiniti,* initially formulated in response to putatively excessive construals of the *communicatio idiomatum* favored by some Lutheran scholars, has relevance for a doctrine of Holy Scripture.

I draw this christological comparison for good reason, for it is by employing terminology typically associated with christological reflection that Barth lends fascinating nuance to his position.[3] On one level, Barth establishes an intriguing analogy between the Son's "assumption" of humanity and God's accreditation of Scripture as the preeminent witness to God's Word. As with Christ's humanity, there is nothing inherently special about the creaturely texts that God commandeers. From a certain vantage point,

---

3. Barth's extensive use of christological terminology is of course not restricted to his account of Scripture. For excellent commentary on Barth's use of the "Chalcedonian" pattern, see George Hunsinger, *How to Read Karl Barth: The Shape of His Theology* (New York: Oxford University Press, 1991).

the Bible is simply a collection of ancient writings — nothing more, nothing less. But by way of God's gracious action, these texts mediate God's speech in the here-and-now. In the same way that Jesus *qua* human is assumed by the Word, capacitated as the "light of life" (IV/3, §69.2), so too does God's action confer upon the biblical texts a unique power to bear witness to divine speech. Such is the extent of God's generosity: allowing "the servant form of a human word" to "speak the Word of God." Indeed, the implication of this christologically framed claim is close at hand: each and every reading of Scripture points towards the fact that "God was in Christ, reconciling the world to himself" (2 Cor. 5:19).

On another level, Barth sets an upper limit on his doctrine of inspiration. Just as the theologian ought to recognize the primacy of God's act in Christ and thereby acknowledge that Christ's humanity has no revelatory value in and of itself,[4] so ought she to avoid overly inflated descriptions of Scripture. The revelatory power of biblical texts is derivative, not innate; it depends on the prevenient act of God, as and when God deigns to "assume" and "adopt" these texts for God's purposes. As such, the (potential) "indissolubility" of the union between the divine Word and human words ought not to be considered in terms of a permanent and/or necessary admixture, whereby the texts of Scripture are elevated beyond the status of finite witnesses. Certainly, the authority of Scripture ought not to be construed in terms of "inerrancy": such "bibliolatry" simply gives new life to the error of docetism by collapsing the distinction between divine and human. One ought rather to recognize and acclaim God's decision to reveal Godself through the texts of the Bible — *human* texts that, by the grace of God, retain their imperfections and limitations.

What does this dialectical acknowledgment of Scripture's "divinity" and "humanity" mean for the theological task? What does this acclamation of an "indirect identity" analogous to — or, more precisely, derivative of — the hypostatic union definitive of Christ's person portend for the Christian exegete? Barth's own writings suggest at least two responses. First, if the Word sounds in the words, then it does so in ways that reveal God to be a dynamic act of inexhaustible meaning. Think of God's "perfections," described in the second half of *Church Dogmatics* II/1. Following upon a suggestive identity-description of the divine in §28 (God as "the one who loves in freedom"), §§29, 30, and 31 show this description to be but a starting point for dogmatic reflection — thus the expositions of

---

4. See here I/1, p. 323.

God's grace and holiness, mercy and righteousness, patience and wisdom, and so on. A presentation that gains density thusly signals that the doctrine of God cannot be "closed," lest God be reduced to human standards. And just as Barth avoids "closure" in his account of God's being, so too ought the exegete to delight in the prospect of multiple interpretative claims. While God's self-revelation, witnessed in the Bible, has a definite shape — indeed, a triune shape — it does not carry with it noetically restrictive limits. Quite the opposite. It liberates human thought from "business as usual"; it enables and sponsors a wealth of ever-new exegetical reflections. Why is the *Dogmatics* so long? Why, more specifically, does the first index to each part-volume cite verses from nearly every chapter of every book in the Bible? Simply because the Bible bears witness to the fact that "even in our knowledge of the one perfect God, we stand before God's *richness*" (II/1, 322 rev.). A plurality of readings of the Bible, "limited" only by the particular shape of revelation, points towards God's being an infinitely provocative event that the theologian must seek neither to contain nor control through exegetical parsimony.[5]

Second, while Barth views the witness-like quality of the Bible as a gift graciously given (what could *we* have done to deserve it?), he insists also that this gift requires human response. Certainly, it is *God* who incepts this response. Only by way of the prevenient action of God *qua* Spirit does individual and communal awareness of God's triune self-revelation arise (Barth, one even might say, views the *filioque* as a doctrine with epistemological relevance — for after "proceeding" from God's second way of being, the Spirit involves the human in a movement back towards God's second way of being, adopting her as a participant in the reality and rationality of the divine life). Yet Barth also affirms the necessity of human interpretative work. The conjoint actions of the Word and the Spirit do not overpower the human; they elicit creative reflection. By dint of God's action, the Christian finds herself caught up in the fascinating richness of the divine life — "caught up" in the sense that as she is brought into "the strange new world"[6] of the Bible by God, she is also made a *citizen* of this

5. Immediately subsequent to his claim about God's richness, Barth writes: "To know Him means to know Him again and again, in ever new ways — to know only Him but to know Him as the perfect God, in the abundance, distinctiveness, and variety of His perfections" (II/1, p. 322).

6. See here, of course, Karl Barth, "The Strange New World Within the Bible," in *The Word of God and the Word of Man,* trans. Douglas Horton (Gloucester, MA: Peter Smith, 1978), pp. 28-50.

new world. The Christian is in fact tasked to inhabit this world purposefully, mapping its territory in ever-new ways, discovering unseen pathways and vistas, maybe even venturing towards forgotten continents. This means, once again, that precipitous attempts to effect interpretive "closure," at least when it comes to biblical texts, ought always to occasion protest. A broad range of interpretive options (*not* the same as interpretive anomie) reminds both church and world that God's being entails more than we will ever know; that, whatever riches we may amass on earth, true richness abides eternally in the triune life of God.

II. The Self-Determination of the Word:
John 1 in *Church Dogmatics* II/2

Barth had of course considered the prologue to John's Gospel prior to *Church Dogmatics* II/2. As well as remarks in earlier dogmatic cycles, he offered lectures on John in 1925 and 1926, revising them again in 1933.[7] He also organized the important preliminary christological statement of I/2 around John 1:14. However, it is the treatment of John 1:1-2 ("In the beginning was the Word, and the Word was with God, and the Word was God. He was in the beginning with God") in Barth's revolutionary doctrine of election that I wish to focus on in this section. Barth's remarks on these verses attest to the continued relevance of Eberhard Jüngel's description of God's "being in becoming"[8] in the *Dogmatics*. Considering Barth's exegesis in four steps shows, more specifically, that the Son's "being in becoming" — at least as presented in II/2 and thereafter — entails God's prevenient transformation of Godself.[9]

---

7. See here Karl Barth, *Witness to the Word: A Commentary on John 1*, ed. Walther Fürst, trans. G. W. Bromiley (Eugene, OR: Wipf & Stock, 2003). Barth in fact lifts sections from these lectures to pad the excursus in II/2, thereby ensuring a degree of continuity, even as his attitude towards the *logos asarkos* shifts. For an excellent treatment of these lectures, see the essay by John Webster in this volume.

8. Eberhard Jüngel, *God's Being Is in Becoming: The Trinitarian Being of God in the Theology of Karl Barth. A Paraphrase*, trans. John Webster (Edinburgh: T. & T. Clark, 2001).

9. Barth scholars will be aware that the position sketched in this section contributes to recent debates about Barth on election. While the interpretation offered is very much my own, it shares features with perspectives advanced by Hans Theodor Goebel, Thies Gundlach, Bruce McCormack, and Matthias Gockel, and others. For Goebel, see "Trinitätslehre und Erwählungslehre bei Karl Barth: Eine Problemanzeige," in *Wahrheit und Versöhnung. Theologische und philosophische Beiträge zur Gotteslehre*, ed. Dietrich Korsch

First, as might be expected, Barth insists on the divinity of the Word. Since the Gospel describes the Word as being "in the beginning with God," then this Word "belongs to God, because His being is as the being of God Himself . . . ὁ θεός is . . . ascribed to ὁ λόγος" (II/2, 96). The Word of God/ Son of God is God's second way of being, coessential with the Father. God's personal simplicity and unity go hand-in-hand with God's internal differentiation.

Why does the author of John's Gospel identify God's second way of being as *Word*? Barth's exegesis takes its second step at this point. The Son can be thusly named because he forms the leading edge of God's communication with humankind. "Jesus was the life which was light, the revelation of God," Barth writes. Then, exchanging an optical for an acoustic metaphor, he describes Christ as "the saying *(Spruch)*, the address *(Rede)*, the communication *(Mitteilung)* in which God declares Himself to us." Indeed, if "[w]ord or saying is the simple but genuine form in which person communicates with person," then the condition of possibility for this human event is God's action: the fact that through the divine "Word . . . God communicates *(mitteilt)* with man" (II/2, 97). The references to "commu-

and Hartmut Ruddies (Gütersloh: Gütersloher Verlagshaus Gerd Mohn, 1989), pp. 147-66; also the brilliant *Vom freien Wählen Gottes und des Menschen: Interpretationsübungen zur "Analogie" nach Karl Barths Lehre von der Erwählung und Bedenken ihrer Folgen für die Kirchlichen Dogmatik* (Frankfurt: Peter Lang, 1990). With respect to Thies Gundlach, see *Selbstgrenzung Gottes und die Autonomie des Menschen: Karl Barths Kirchliche Dogmatik als Modernisierungschritt evangelischer Theologie* (Frankfurt: Verlag Peter Lang, 1996), esp. p. 164. With respect to Bruce McCormack, see "Grace and Being: The Role of God's Gracious Election in Karl Barth's Theological Ontology," in *The Cambridge Companion to Karl Barth,* ed. John Webster (Cambridge: Cambridge University Press), pp. 92-110; "Barths grundsätz-licher Chalkedonismus," *Zeitschrift für dialektische Theologie* 18, no. 2 (2002): 138-73; and "Seek God Where He May Be Found: A Response to Edwin Chr. van Driel," *Scottish Journal of Theology* 60, no. 1 (2007): 62-79. For Matthias Gockel, see *Barth and Schleiermacher on the Doctrine of Election: A Systematic-Theological Work* (Oxford: Oxford University Press, 2006), esp. pp. 158-97. Given the proximity of my interpretation to the work of these authors, what follows is at odds with the interpretive stance adopted by Paul Molnar (see *Divine Freedom and the Doctrine of the Immanent Trinity* [London and New York: T. & T. Clark/Continuum, 2002], esp. pp. 61-64; also "The Trinity, Election, and God's Ontological Freedom: A Response to Kevin Hector," *International Journal of Systematic Theology* 8, no. 3 [July 2006]: 294-306) and the somewhat different position forwarded by Edwin Chr. van Driel (see here "Karl Barth on the Eternal Existence of Jesus Christ," *Scottish Journal of Theology* 60, no. 1 [2007]: 45-61). Despite my preference for the former interpretative trajectory, I hope the one outlined here can be read as something of a *via media*. Certainly, I have endeavored to learn from each of the scholars involved in the dispute.

nication" are of tremendous importance here, signaling that God *qua* Word does more than simply convey "information" about God. It is more that God *qua* Son wills to *impart* Godself; that God's second way of being forms the leading edge of God's decision to give Godself to humankind. To talk of God's second way of being as "Word" is, then, to identify God as outgoing in a quite radical sense. It identifies the Son as the divine "person" who will be (and will be known as) Emmanuel, God with us (Matt. 1:23).

Barth's third step considers what it means to claim that "the Word became flesh and dwelt among us" (John 1:14) in the person of Jesus Christ. From the vantage point of pretemporal eternity, the Word is of course "before and above all created realities, standing entirely and quite outside the series of created things" (II/2, 95 rev.). There is here a passing affirmation of the *logos asarkos*. However, instead of pausing to reflect on the so-called "immanent" Trinity, Barth quickly suggests that the Word must be understood as always readying itself for incarnation. Using language from his earlier lectures on John, he describes *ho logos* of John 1:1 as a *Platzhalter:* "a preliminary indication of the place where something or someone quite different will be disclosed" (II/2, 96). Something? Someone? Barth of course means the person of Jesus Christ. *This* is how God communicates Godself to humankind; thusly does the Prologue to the Fourth Gospel refer to an "eternal happening and to a temporal happening: to an eternal in the form *(Gestalt)* of time, and to a temporal with the content of eternity" (II/2, 97). Indeed, the eternal and temporal ought not to be held apart. The Son is always "on the way" to implementing God's incarnational intention. Or, to put it more boldly: the divine Word is always *in the process of being spoken* as Jesus Christ. As such, whatever function might be ascribed to the *logos asarkos* — say, an emphasis on the exclusively prevenient origin of Christ's person — this theologoumenon cannot take on a dominant role in dogmatic reflection. Such would focus undue attention on the condition of possibility for God's action, thereby neglecting the concrete fact of God's action in and as Jesus Christ. It would risk describing God's freedom without recognizing what God does with God's sovereign freedom. Thus Barth sounds a cautionary note regarding speculation over antique precedents for the threefold *ho logos* of John 1:1. This historical question has little relevance for dogmatics, since the "answer" to the question has already been given: "[T]here can be no point in attaching oneself to this or that signification of the concept. As an ideogram, it is there like the surely readable but not understandable inscription on the diadem of the Rider of the

Apocalypse, chapter 19; like the x in the mathematical equation, the value of which is only known when the equation is solved. Jn. 1:19" — the point at which the concrete narrative of John's Gospel commences — "is the beginning of this solution" (II/2, 97 rev.). In other words, the identity of God's second way of being can only be properly known when one connects the prologue to John with what follows; when one sees the structure of the Fourth Gospel as revealing the decision of God *qua* Word to become and be the *logos incarnatus*. God's act-in-being, with reference to the Son, is always moving towards the event of incarnation; always moving towards the moment at which the title "Son of God" cannot be separated from the name "Jesus of Nazareth." The theologian must take due account of this movement.

The fourth step shows how innovatively Barth handles the doctrine of election. Having offered an exegesis that acclaims (first) God's Word as divine, (second) the Word as the leading edge of God's relationship with humankind, and (third) the identity of the Word with Jesus Christ, Barth writes that "[i]t is he, Jesus, who is in the beginning with God" (II/2, 96); that "this one, Jesus, is the Word who is participant in the divine essence; who was in the beginning, because as this same divine Word he belongs legitimately to God" (II/2, 98 rev.). What do these claims mean? Some interpretive options can, I think, be excluded. Barth has not given up on the idea that "[t]he Word as such is before and above all created realities," in the sense that he remains committed to affirming God as the "prior" Subject who establishes and indwells Jesus Christ. Barth therefore does not retroject the human, Jesus of Nazareth, into the sphere of "Vor-zeitlichkeit," as Emil Brunner thought.[10] Equally, Barth does not collapse the distinction between God and humanity in Christ. As the next section shows, Barth follows Reformed precedents in preserving the integrity of Christ's divinity in distinction from Christ's humanity. Finally, Barth does not suggest that God is unavoidably conditioned by the incarnation — as if God has no option but to be ontologically qualified by God's economic activity. Rather, what Barth aims to describe is the manner in which the divine Son wills to be a "being in becoming." In that the divine Son is always (obediently) implementing his elective role in the incarnation, *God is always making the human, Jesus of Nazareth, a constitutive part of the identity of God* qua *Son.* As such, the prevenient "assumption" of the individual human essence, Jesus,

---

10. See here Brunner's excursus on "Die Erwählungslehre Karl Barths," in *Dogmatik I: Die christliche Lehre von Gott* (Zürich: Zwingli-Verlag, 1960), pp. 353-57.

by the Word, has ramifications for God's eternal being-in-act. Not only does God will that the Son's identity never be dissociated from the event of incarnation; God wills also that God's enactment of the event of incarnation have a bearing on God's life as such. So while Barth finds a role for the *logos asarkos* — specifically, in affirming divine prevenience — he is more vitally interested in what the *logos asarkos* makes of himself. He aims to show that God sovereignly effects the transformation of God in God's second way of being: "transformation" in the sense that God's free elective action lends God an identity, the form of which is more than that which God possesses pretemporally, and the content of which is more than the ontological simplicity (somewhat hypothetically) associable with God's pretemporal, human-less, triune interrelating. God can do this. God's freedom is a freedom to determine Godself thusly, to move towards and to draw the time and space of the human assumed by and set in union with the Son — namely, Jesus of Nazareth — into the time and space of the divine life, thereby making the concrete union of Christ's divinity and Christ's humanity abidingly constitutive of God's being. So while Barth begins his excursus by differentiating John 1:1 and Colossians 1:15 (Christ as the "firstborn of creation"), he ends by positing their indirect identity. With respect to the person of Jesus Christ, God Godself "in all his ways and works willed wholly *(schlechterdings)* to bear this name, and therefore actually bears it" (II/2, 99 rev.). By way of God's prevenient decision, the "end" of God's communication with humankind loops back to the beginning. God's being *qua* Son is bound, eternally, to the person that God wills to become. Thus: "[o]ver against all that is really outside God, Jesus Christ is God's eternal Word, God's eternal decree, and" — the last clause clinches it — "God's eternal beginning" (II/2, 99 rev.). The endpoint of God's "being in becoming" is that God *qua* Son becomes a being that God need not be, but truly is: the ontologically and agentially complex person of Jesus Christ.

Does this interpretation overreach? Am I here radicalizing Jüngel's interpretive stance problematically, forgetting Barth's initial remarks on the Trinity and the *logos asarkos/Extra Calvinisticum* in *Church Dogmatics* I?[11] I do believe that Barth's doctrine of God undergoes significant revision between *Church Dogmatics* I and *Church Dogmatics* II. With Hans Theodor Goebel, Bruce McCormack, and others, I consider Barth's initial account of the Trinity in I/1 to be valuably complicated by Barth's doctrine of election — "valuably" in that, while holding fast to an understanding of God's

11. See here esp. I/2, pp. 167-71.

independence and triune sovereignty in *Church Dogmatics* II/2, Barth has expanded his outlook to include the claim that God wills, freely, that the incarnation of the Word have an eternal bearing on the divine life. I would also concede that I am using the word "transformation" in a somewhat risky fashion. The risk is in suggesting an adventitious qualification of God's being: the possible insinuation being that God "changes" in light of the incarnation. But God's "changing" — in the sense that God's economic activity *qua* Son *inevitably* impinges on God's being, thereby compromising God's sovereignty — is not at issue here. At issue is the way in which God works out the free decision to be *pro nobis*. In realizing God's decision to relate graciously to humankind, God *elects* to give up the "inviolability" or "purity" of God's second way of being. And God does this freely, without any cause other than God's freedom to determine God's being in whatsoever way God chooses. The extent of God's love — God's love at its most *jealous* pitch, one might say — is that God wills to qualify Godself *qua* Son for all eternity. Again: this does not make for a diminution of divine freedom. Quite the opposite. To talk in terms of God's self-transformation is to affirm God's sovereignty over God's being. God's sovereignty is such that God wills to be *this* God — the God who is *never* human-less, given God's incarnational action.[12] And, crucially, it is the biblical record that pushes Barth to advance this claim. Read in terms of John 1:14, the pregnant triptych of John 1:1 and the bold declaration of John 1:2 propel Barth towards a doctrinal innovation that coordinates a passing but crucial glance at the *logos asarkos* with a powerful affirmation of the primacy of the *logos ensarkos* — the basic fact that God *qua* Son is always becoming and being the person of Jesus Christ, *vere deus vere homo*.

One final point, implicit in many of my preceding claims, forms a fitting close to this section. God's prevenient self-transformation *qua* Son has as its motivation God's free decision to *love* humankind. On occasion, Barth employs figurative language to articulate this point, suggesting that God's incarnational love means that God opens God's "heart" to humankind. Thus a key passage in §33: "The primal and basic decision of God with regard to humanity," Barth writes, "is his mercy: the engagement *(Beteiligung)* of his heart, and therefore his most intimate and most intensive engagement in humanity's existence and condition" (II/2, 211 rev.).

---

12. I borrow this phrasing from Eberhard Jüngel. See his ". . . keine Menschenlosigkeit Gottes . . . zur Theologie Karl Barths zwischen Theismus und Atheismus," in *Barth-studien* (Gütersloh: Gütersloher Verlagshaus Mohn, 1982), pp. 332-47.

Thus these words in IV/1: "If for us humans God himself has become human, then we can, then we must look into the heart of God — he himself has opened it to us — to accept his saying as a *first* as well as a *last* saying: 'I will be your God'" (IV/1, 38 rev.). My claim is that Barth's exegesis of the prologue to John helps one to understand such statements. For Barth, the opening of the Fourth Gospel bears witness to the fact that God puts God's heart on the line; that God wills that God live in utter solidarity with the humanity that God loves; that God, by making the humanity of Christ part of God's own life, grants humanity as such a reality commensurate with that definitive of God Godself. Thusly is God the one who loves us in freedom; thusly does God put God's freedom in the service of God's love.

III. Jesus' Compassion: Matthew 9:36

Thus far, I have outlined a reading of Barth's doctrine of Scripture and given an interpretation of Barth's treatment of the prologue of the Fourth Gospel. In so doing, I have in fact hinted at Barth's concern to effect some manner of rapprochement between the often-competing insights of his Reformed and Lutheran forebears.

Following the Reformed, Barth hopes to emphasize Christ's ontological complexity. Just as a clear distinction must be made between the divine Word as such and the biblical witness, so too must Christ's divinity and humanity be distinguished. Barth never relaxes his commitment to the "infinite qualitative difference" between Creator and creature. Thus, on one level, even though the *logos ensarkos* motif has a "strong" role in christological reflection, a "weak" version of the *logos asarkos* is maintained. Thus, on another level, even as Barth insists that the human, Jesus of Nazareth, does not exist apart from the divine Son, he reaffirms the "sharp distinction and even antithesis," indeed, the "infinitely qualitative" (IV/2, 61) differentiation, of Christ's divine and human essences. Indeed, it is for this reason that Barth insists on a Reformed construal of the *communio naturarum;* on a rejection of the Lutheran *genus maiestaticum;*[13] on the value of the *communicatio gratiarum* and the *communicatio*

---

13. Whether Barth fully understands what he is rejecting is an interesting question. See here Piotr Malaysz, "Storming Heaven with Karl Barth? Barth's Unwitting Appropriation of the *Genus Maiestaticum* and What Lutherans Can Learn from It," *International Journal of Systematic Theology* 9, no. 1 (2007): 73-92.

operationum. However, as Barth pays his Reformed dues, he also strives to do justice to Lutheran affirmations of Christ's personal simplicity. So much is evident in striking remarks about the concrete identity of the divine Son and the human, Jesus, in IV/1;[14] so much is evident in his discussion of the *unio hypostatica* in *Church Dogmatics* IV/2. Furthermore, Barth seeks to radicalize the Lutheran perspective in a novel way. He effectively redeploys the *inseparabiliter* and *indivise* adverbs of the "Definition" of Chalcedon, applying these adverbs to God's second way of being as such.[15] God's second way of being is never *not* becoming and being the *logos incarnatus.* Barth therefore offers no staunch defense of the *Extra Calvinisticum* in the later volumes of the *Dogmatics* and makes only passing reference to the *logos asarkos.* Were he to foreground either theologoumenon, he would be emphasizing the condition of possibility for the incarnation while forgetting about God's self-transformation by way of the incarnation. God in God's second way of being is always moving towards, and always wills to be defined in terms of the ontologically complex but personally simple person of Jesus Christ, "the Word become flesh."

My principal focus in this section, of course, is not Barth's relationship to post-Reformation dogmatics, as interesting an issue as that is. I want rather to consider a remarkable analogy that Barth proposes between the divine Son's self-transformation and the self-transformation effected by Christ *qua* human. In discerning this analogy, the continued importance of exegetical reasoning for the formation of Barth's christology will become evident. By way of a striking analysis of a single Greek word, Barth ventures a remarkable claim: just as God freely and lovingly transforms Godself, willing that God's own heart be touched by the (suffering) human other, so does Jesus, the human elected and assumed by God *qua* Son, act analogously.

My point of reference is an excursus in the second subsection of §64.3 in IV/2. This excursus is positioned within the second stage of Barth's creative treatment of the *munus triplex,* which considers Christ as "priest/judge" (IV/1), "king" (IV/2), and "prophet" (IV/3). Crisscrossing this gen-

14. See esp. IV/1, p. 199: "[T]he one true God . . . Himself [is] the subject of the act of atonement in such a way that His presence and action as the Reconciler of the world coincide and are indeed identical with the existence of the humiliated and lowly and obedient man Jesus of Nazareth."

15. As Jüngel puts it: "Gott sich in Jesus *vollständig* definiert . . . hat." See ". . . keine Menschenlosigkeit Gottes . . ." (p. 338).

eral structure is Barth's concern to complement a discussion of Christ's justifying exinanition (humiliation) with his sanctifying exaltation. So, having focused on the obedience of the divine Son in IV/1 — God's "way into the far country" being an instance of God laying God's heart on the line, even unto death — in IV/2 Barth considers the uplift of humanity in Jesus Christ. This exaltation has as one of its conditions of possibility Christ's human "correspondence" to God, carried out in seamless union with the Son before the Father — the fact that in Christ's "thinking and willing . . . actions and comportment, there occurs a correspondence (*Entsprechung*), a parallel in the creaturely world, that shows the plan and the purpose, the work and conduct of God" (IV/2, 166 rev.). By the time we reach the excursus in question, Barth has described this correspondence as (1) Jesus humanly paralleling the disregard of God in the world (for "[a]s the exalted Son of Man He did not deny the humiliation of the Son of God, but faithfully represented and reflected it even to the minutest of details" [IV/2, 167]); (2) Jesus' especial concern for the marginalized and downcast of society; (3) the "revolutionary character of [Jesus'] relationship to the order of life and value current in the world" (IV/2, 171); and (4) the fact that "Jesus, like God himself, is not against but for humanity — even humanity in the total impossibility of its Fall, in its form as the humanity of the old world of Adam," since Jesus humanly "reflects and represents . . . the love in which God has loved, loves, and will love the world; the faithfulness that God has sworn and will uphold; the solidarity with it into which God has entered and in which God persists" (IV/2, 180 rev.).

A key moment in this excursus comes with Barth's treatment of Matthew 9:36. The King James rendition of this verse, reproduced in the *Dogmatics*, is much preferable to that in the Revised Standard Version: it hews most closely to Barth's own blending of Luther and the Zürich Bible. It reads: "But when he saw the multitudes, he was moved with compassion on them, because they fainted, and were scattered abroad, as sheep having no shepherd." Here are Barth's remarks about a single Greek term, *esplanchnisthē*, which the KJV translates as "moved with compassion":

> The expression is untranslatably strong. Jesus was not only affected to the heart by the misery which surrounded him — "sympathy" in our sense of the word would not be right — but this misery went right into his heart, into himself, so that it was now entirely his misery, more his than that of those who suffered it. He took it from them and assumed it himself. . . . To the thoroughgoing, total and definitive saving mercy of

> God there now corresponded the help which Jesus brought to humans through his thoroughgoing, total, and definitive self-giving to and for their cause. In this self-giving, in the fact that his mercy led Jesus to see humans thusly, he was on earth as God is in heaven. In this self-giving he was the reign of God come on earth. (IV/2, 184 rev.)

As with so many excursive passages in the *Church Dogmatics,* the statements are almost too rich. There is a quiet jab at the superficial emotionalism of polite society in the late modern West; an anticipation of §65.3's discussion of "The Misery of Man"; a glance back to the discussion of "mercy" as a divine perfection (§30.2); a deft political hint with talk of "das . . . Reich Gottes." And surrounding the passage I have quoted, there are an association of the "crowds" with modern views of the "masses"; intriguing attention to a freighted word "solidarity"; and intrabiblical allusions to Jesus' own proclamation, "I am the good shepherd: the good shepherd giveth his life for the sheep" (John 10:11; see also Ezek. 34).

Consider specifically, though, the claim that the misery of Jesus' fellows "went right into his *heart,* into himself, so that it was now entirely his misery." Barth here establishes an analogy between God's self-determination, in terms of the sinful and miserable other, and Jesus' self-determination, as a human, in terms of this other. In an action that parallels God's incarnational self-determination — God's decision to transform Godself *qua* Son, drawing humanity into the time and space of the divine life — Jesus humanly identifies and enburdens himself with the suffering of those around him, drawing their travail into the time and space of his human being. Divine action and human action co-term in a remarkable way: just as God's heart is touched and transformed in face of the other, as God wills sovereignly that Christ's humanity be drawn into the divine life, so too is Jesus' human heart touched and transformed as he wills humanly to make others constitutive of his being. Jesus reiterates God's action in a thoroughgoing sense. God's gracious self-giving as Son is paralleled by Jesus' human self-giving. As with God's love — a love so extreme, so jealous, that God transforms God's being in face of the beloved, sinful as that beloved may be — so too with Jesus' human love: Jesus humanly determines himself in terms of "unity and solidarity" (IV/2, 185) with the suffering other; Jesus wills to become and be the "true royal man whose human compassion mirrored the compassion of the God who had sworn fidelity to man" (IV/2, 187 rev.). And the consequences that attend such sanctifying solidarity are close to hand: Jesus' self-giving is so extreme that the "misery of the common people that

[he] saw, which moved him to compassion, which he took away from them and took to himself" (IV/2, 186 rev.), eventually overcomes him.[16]

Two qualifying remarks are useful at this point. First, notice that Barth's actualist ontology "goes all the way down," applying both to Christ *qua* divine Son and Christ *qua* assumed human. It is not only that God Godself wills to embrace and "catch up" the life of the human, Jesus, in the space and time of the divine being. Jesus, as the "true human" who lives in correspondence with God, also wills to embrace and "catch up" the suffering of his fellows. Thus, in an analogous fashion, he too is a "being in becoming." Certainly, Jesus, as a human being, does not have God's untrammeled liberty of self-determination. Not only is his humanity defined in terms of its union with God *qua* Son (which means that his human essence does not amount to a "person" as such, for it lacks the property of self-individuated personality — God *qua* Son is the Subject of Jesus Christ),[17]

16. In the course of Matthias Gockel's excellent study of Barth and Schleiermacher on election, he discerns a "subtle ambiguity . . . regarding the relation between the human being Jesus and the Son of God." He asks: "Does the claim that the Son of God instead of the Son of Man suffered God's wrath contrast with the . . . claim that the elected human being Jesus is the target of 'offering' of God's wrath?" (*Barth and Schleiermacher on the Doctrine of Election*, pp. 182 and 183). I would counter with a question of my own: Why must Christ's (divine) suffering as the Son of God stand at odds with his (human) suffering as the Son of Man? Because Barth's actualistic christology views Christ's person as constituted by two agencies, albeit agencies related in an asymmetrical fashion, Jesus Christ is not only the "electing God" who also takes the "rejection" that humankind deserves — though he is certainly that. He is also the "elected human" who enacts an identity that, by the grace of God, endures reprobation in unity with the divine Son. Thus the *whole* person of Christ — divine *and* human — suffers God's justificatory wrath. Put a bit differently: it is true that the "Word became flesh" and suffered the (righteous) judgment of God for sin. But it is *also* true that the "flesh" that the Word assumed constitutes itself as a target for God's (righteous) judgment — even though an anterior condition of possibility for this human self-constitution is the prevenient superintendence of God *qua* Son. Thus it is that "it is in the unity of this steadfastness *both divine and human* that we shall find the peculiar secret of the election of the man Jesus" (II/2, p. 125, my emphasis). Thus it is that "[t]he man Jesus is not a mere puppet moved this way and that by God. He is not a mere reed used by God as the instrument of His Word. . . . He thinks of himself as the Messiah, as the Son of God. He allows himself to be called *Kyrios*, and, in fact, conducts Himself as such. He speaks of His suffering, not as a necessity laid upon Him from without, *but as something as He Himself wills*" (II/2, p. 179, my emphasis). For more on this issue, see my essay "Karl Barth on Gethsemane," *International Journal of Systematic Theology* 9, no. 2 (2007): 148-71.

17. The absence of a human personhood in Christ need not put into question an affirmation of the integrity of Christ's humanity. It is theologically (and philosophically) cogent to view personhood as a non-necessary property of human being — even if this "non-

but the anterior condition of possibility for Christ's human action is the sovereign action of God *qua* Son. The *communicatio operationum* is asymmetrically defined; it is God's action that enables Jesus humanly to constitute himself in terms analogous to the divine Son. Nevertheless, while Jesus' human action is of a derivative sort, it has as much reality as any human action can have. As the divine Son determines himself on behalf of the other — the *sinful* other, since God wills to become "flesh" — so too does Jesus humanly act to determine himself on behalf of this other. Indeed, it is Jesus' human self-constituting activity that grounds Barth's extensive understanding of human agency, the nuances of which George Hunsinger and John Webster have emphasized in recent years[18] — human agency not understood in a crudely autarchic form, as if each has the freedom to do whatsoever he or she might choose, but human action as an event elicited by and carried out under the auspices of God's gracious call for companionship, partnership, and collaboration. Because Jesus humanly acts on behalf of God, enacting an intention and determining his humanity in accordance to the will of the Father, human agency becomes a genuine potentiality that awaits realization.

Second, notice again that it is attention to the biblical record that stimulates Barth's formulation of finely grained doctrinal claims. With John 1:1-18, exegesis threw new light on the difficult question of the identity of the divine Son. By way of close attention to the scriptural record, Barth found some role for the *logos asarkos* while, at the same time, trumping this potentially problematic theologoumenon with an emphatic affirmation of the *logos ensarkos*. With Matthew 9:36, exegesis plays a part in Barth's resolution of an age-old conundrum: how to balance an affirmation of Christ's ontological complexity with an affirmation of Christ's personal simplicity. This issue, of course, has been a battleground throughout

---

necessary" property is present in the vast majority of human beings. Some recent articulations of this viewpoint: Thomas Morris, *The Logic of God Incarnate* (Eugene, OR: Wipf & Stock, 2001), pp. 62ff.; Brian Leftow, "A Timeless God Incarnate," in *The Incarnation: An Interdisciplinary Symposium on the Incarnation of the Son of God,* ed. Stephen T. Davis, Daniel Kendall, S.J., and Gerald O'Collins, S.J. (Oxford: Oxford University Press, 2002), pp. 273-99, esp. 277-87; and Oliver D. Crisp, *Divinity and Humanity: The Incarnation Reconsidered* (Cambridge: Cambridge University Press, 2007), pp. 61ff. Behind many of these perspectives stands Thomas Aquinas; see here esp. *Summa Theologica,* III.2.2, III.2.5, III.4.1-6.

18. See here George Hunsinger, *How to Read Karl Barth,* pp. 185-224; John Webster, *Barth's Ethics of Reconciliation* (Cambridge: Cambridge University Press, 1995) and *Barth's Moral Theology: Human Action in Barth's Thought* (Grand Rapids: Eerdmans, 1998).

much Christian history. Not only did it plunge the so-called schools of Alexandria and Antioch into acrimonious dispute, but it was also a point of contention during and after the Reformation. Barth's genius is to carve out a standpoint that refuses to pit Cyril's "hypostatic" union against Nestorius's preference for "conjunction."[19] The integrity and clarity of Christ's person is accomplished by two agencies, one divine, the other human, that determine themselves in terms of the same end. Christ's person is of course dominated by the Son, who forms the defining subject of this individual. But contributing to Christ's simple identity and securing, in part, the coherence and simplicity of this person is the determination of Jesus of Nazareth to be the assumed human. Christ is "one," in part, because Jesus *qua* assumed human has mercy with, loves, and relieves misery in union with God *qua* Son. Barth's actualist ontology therefore circumvents the problem of how two different realities, separated by an "infinite qualitative difference," can be effective of a unified person. And it does so exactly because Barth allows his ontology to be controlled by the particulars of the biblical record. God is what God wills to be — in this case, the Word become flesh, the Son who determines to be Jesus Christ. And the human essence that God assumes corresponds itself seamlessly to God's action. Guided by the Son, but genuinely nevertheless, the flesh that the Word assumes plays its part in the "drama of the covenant,"[20] thereby helping to bring about reconciliation.

IV. Conclusion

The concern of my first section was Barth's doctrine of Scripture, considered in light of programmatic statements in *Church Dogmatics* I/2. I focused on the "indirect identity" of the Word and the biblical witness, showing how Barth attends to both the "divinity" and "humanity" of Scripture. Scripture can be associated with the divine Word — indeed, in some sense it *is* the divine Word — given that God Godself "assumes" it, rendering it revelatory of God's being and action. Granted, in and of themselves the biblical texts have no especial merit. Scripture is an indefea-

19. See George Hunsinger, "Karl Barth's Christology: Its Basic Chalcedonian Character," in *The Cambridge Companion to Karl Barth*, ed. John Webster (Cambridge: Cambridge University Press, 2000), pp. 127-42.

20. I borrow here from Hans-Wilhelm Pietz, *Das Drama des Bundes* (Neukirchen-Vluyn: Neukirchener Verlag, 1998).

sibly human document; it therefore can never be crudely equated with revelation as such. But God commandeers the texts of the Hebrew Bible and New Testament as witnesses, sanctifying them as media that bear unique witness to revelation. The task for the Christian (theologian or not) is therefore to hear God's speech in the here-and-now, to participate in the action of God's Word and the Spirit as it draws her into the unendingly rich life of God Godself. Indeed, because, as Calvin suggests, "by a kind of mutual bond the Lord has joined together the certainty of his Word and of his Spirit so that the perfect religion of the Word may abide in our minds,"[21] the Christian may cheerfully go about the task of reading and reflecting on the Bible, delighting in a broad range of interpretive options.

My second section examined Barth's treatment of John 1 in *Church Dogmatics* II/2. I argued that Barth's doctrine of election entails an intriguing claim, routed through the straits of careful exegesis — that God transforms Godself by way of the incarnation. While Barth makes some fairly unsurprising claims about the Word as God's second way of being, God's decision to be *pro nobis,* with the Word as the leading edge of God's gracious advance, and the identity of the Word with the person of Christ, his more startling suggestion is that God renders the person of Christ, in all of his ontological and agential complexity, eternally determinative of the identity of God *qua* Son. By dint of God's gracious decision, the economic "end" of a narrative that begins with the *logos asarkos* becomes an immanent "beginning." Thus it is that any dogmatic acclamation of the *logos asarkos* must be trumped by a stronger emphasis on the *logos ensarkos.* God *qua* Son wills to be a being that is always becoming the ontologically and agentially complex person of Jesus Christ. Such is the extent of God's love, realized in freedom.

In my third section, I took a close look at Barth's treatment of Matthew 9:36, focusing on a single Greek word: *esplanchnisthē.* I suggested that the Son's being in becoming is matched by a correspondent being in becoming of the human, Jesus of Nazareth. This is a condition of possibility for Christ's personal simplicity as the "Word become flesh." While the union of divinity and humanity definitive of Christ's person is established by God alone, it is in part maintained by the perfectly coincident actions of Christ's divine *and* human essences. Just as God lovingly self-determines in view of the human other, so too does Jesus *qua* human self-determine in

---

21. John Calvin, *Institutes of the Christian Religion,* vol. 1, trans. Ford Lewis Battles, ed. John T. McNeill (Philadelphia: Westminster Press, 1960), p. 95.

view of the human other. Indeed — and this point should not be forgotten, even though I have not given it much emphasis in this essay — just as the active self-determination of God *qua* Son leads Christ to the cross, so too does Christ's human self-determination lead to the cross. Barth puts it plainly: "Jesus saw their misery, and . . . given his *compassion* for them, stepped simply into the breach. Exactly here was the place he belonged. Thus he did not take their misery only to heart, but rather into his heart, into himself. 'I am the good shepherd; the good shepherd gives his life for the sheep'" (IV/2, 187 rev.).

Finally, two comments about what Barth's reading of Scripture, especially as it pertains to his christology, means for Christian theology today. The first comment has to do with "theological method" as it relates to the biblical witness. As should be evident from my remarks on I/2, I am interested in gaining clarity about Barth's doctrine of Scripture. This issue has relevance both for understanding what the *Dogmatics* is about and, more generally, for Christian thought in the current moment — buffeted, as it so often is, between facile (and politically dubious) forms of prooftexting and theologically lackluster historical-critical work. But my more urgent interest is not the methodological "how" of Barth's exegesis. It is rather its dogmatic "*what.*" That Barth ultimately made questions of method secondary to the task of thinking clearly and imaginatively about Scripture provides a salutary lesson for academic theologians, scholars of religion, and ministers alike. We ought not to worry so much about how to read and respond to Scripture; we ought simply to get on with the business of reading and responding to Scripture. The vitality of the Word requires nothing less.

My second comment has a more constructive import. Generally, it is fair to say that Barth believed exegesis has relevance beyond the merely "systematic." This is evident in both editions of *The Epistle to the Romans:* Barth's challenge to the European theological establishment is inseparable from his challenge to bourgeois morality. It is also possible to discern a political edge to Barth's comments on Jesus' compassion in *Church Dogmatics* IV/2. Barth no longer wishes to lift his readers out of the "anthroposophical chaos"[22] of belligerent Wilhelmian nationalism and self-serving religiosity; rather, he now hopes to show how the task of rebuilding relationships in postwar Europe has its index in the person of Christ. Not only does Christ constitute himself in terms of the misery of the other, but

---

22. Karl Barth, *The Epistle to the Romans,* trans. Edwyn C. Hoskyns (Oxford: Oxford University Press, 1968), p. 11.

"obedience to Jesus Christ necessarily leads us to believe, without any res-
ervations, that our fellow-men belong to God."[23] The Christian's basic de-
meanor must reflect exactly this belief.

Perhaps, in addition, there is a more contemporary lesson buried in
Barth's reflections on the prologue to the Fourth Gospel and Matthew
9:36. Might Barth be pointing the way beyond a pernicious dichotomy that
juxtaposes immobile forms of essentialism and overinflated construals of
the self's elasticity? On the one hand, Christian theology, if it learns from
Barth, rightly attributes an "essential" stability to each human. This stability has to do with God's loving approach, which encloses all of humankind
in Christ. At its best, Christian theology conveys a plain truth to each human being: despite your unflagging and atrocious sinfulness, God has
brought you back from the brink. You are, in a word, *saved*. Accordingly,
any attempts to replace this axiomatic claim with other criteria, presump-
tively definitive of the human — gender, sexual orientation, race, even the
attribute of "evil" or its new opposite, "freedom-loving" — ought to be re-
sisted, lest it be forgotten that Christ's reconciling life and death have an
abiding impact on human being as such. On the other hand, Barth can be
read in ways that suggest each human being lives in the process of becoming — that our beings, by the grace of God and by virtue of the fact that we
live "in Christ," are always being "set in motion," always being propelled
towards God in constantly surprising ways. The *Dogmatics* has something
in common, in fact, with perspectives that value positively the "mobility"
of the self.[24] As such, even granted Barth's failings with respect to issues of

---

23. I take these words from "The Christian Message in Europe Today," a lecture that
Barth gave in 1946. The text can be found in *Against the Stream: Shorter Post-War Writings
1946-52,* ed. Ronald Gregor Smith (New York: Philosophical Library, 1954), pp. 165-91, with
the quotation on p. 179. The passage from which the words hail merits fuller quotation: "Have
we learnt that obedience to Jesus Christ necessarily leads us to believe, without any reserva-
tions, that our fellow-men belong to God, not only those who think as we do, and who are recognisable as fellow-Christians, but our fellow-men whoever and whatever they may be,
whatever their names? That means in effect that in obedience to Jesus Christ we must not first
think the worst of every one of those frightened, miserable, erring, misled and perhaps really
godless creatures around us, but rather the best, just as we like to think well of ourselves. We
must impute to them good, not any good, but the good which consists in the fact that Jesus
died and rose again for us all, including those who are outside the fold, those who no longer
acknowledge him or who do not yet know him." For more on Barth's activities immediately
after World War II, see Eberhard Busch, *Karl Barth: His Life from Letters and Autobiographical
Texts,* trans. John Bowden (Philadelphia: Fortress Press, 1976), esp. pp. 322-31.

24. An obvious *locus classicus* for thinking about the "mobility" of the self is Judith But-

gender, sexual orientation, familial relationships, and the like (for they are legion), his thought might usefully fund theological anthropologies that refuse to fix human identity, and that delight in the fluid possibilities of self-formation and self-reformation. The human is always becoming — exactly because of the grace that impels the grateful and responsible action of the already-justified and already-sanctified self. And this response, this becoming, ought not to be judged according to ossified and outmoded standards. Who is to say how God shapes God's children? Yet, to switch the view once more, it is not the case that the self is totally open-ended, adrift on a swelling sea of chaotic possibilities. Far from it. The only thing that the human cannot *not* be is saved. *This* is the significance of Christ's life, death, and resurrection. The one thing that we cannot change, try as we may, is the fact that God loves us steadfastly, jealously, and perfectly.

---

ler's pioneering work, *Gender Trouble: Feminism and the Subversion of Identity* (New York: Routledge, 1990). A representative series of claims, pertinent to my concluding paragraph: "*[W]oman* itself is a term in process, a becoming, a constructing that cannot rightfully be said to originate or end. As an ongoing discursive practice, it is open to intervention and resignification. . . . [Sex is n]o longer believable as an interior 'truth' of dispositions and identity [but] a performatively enacted signification [that] can occasion the parodic prolif- eration and subversive play of gendered meanings" (p. 33). For an interesting consideration of Butler's work from a theological perspective, see also Sarah Coakley, "The Eschatological Body: Gender, Transformation and God," in *Powers and Submissions: Spirituality, Philosophy and Gender* (Malden, MA: Blackwell, 2002), pp. 153-67.

APPENDICES: Examples of Barth on Scripture

On 1 Samuel 25: David and Abigail

IV/2, pp. 424-32

This, then, in a first form and aspect, was the man whom God reconciled and seized and exalted to Himself in the man Jesus. Seen and measured by that One, he is this slothful man; the man who from the standpoint of his own action, or inaction, lets himself fall in this way, and is so stupid, such a fool. God has taken this man to Himself — not in ignorance but with a full awareness of this sin. What God willed and accomplished in the existence of that One was the healing of the sickness from which we all realise that we suffer in the light of that One; the instruction of the fools that we must all confess ourselves to be. His light shines in the darkness. And if it is true that the darkness has not comprehended it, it is even more true, and a better translation of Jn. 1:5, that the darkness has not overcome it.

The fool or simpleton in his godlessness and the resultant imprudence and insecurity gives us a very concrete picture, as he is portrayed especially in Proverbs and Ecclesiastes, of the folly which stands in such marked contrast to the divine and practical wisdom of which these two books speak and which is personified in the wise man, the man of prudence and understanding, the man who fears God. We may recall at this point some of the basic traits in the character of the fool. He is the man who trusts in his own understanding (Prov. 28:26). He does not think it necessary to take advice but thinks that his own way is right (12:15). He thus gives himself heedlessly to that which is wrong (14:16). Folly is joy to him (15:21). He wears it like a crown (14:24). He proclaims it (12:23). The awful thing about him is that the speech in which he shows himself to be a fool continually emphasises the fact. His own lips "will swallow up himself. The beginning of the words of his mouth is foolishness: and the end of his talk is mischievous madness" (Eccl. 10:12f.). He might pass for a wise man if only he would be silent, and for a man of understanding if only he would keep his lips shut (Prov. 17:28). But he does not do so, and this means that he has a mouth which is "near destruction" (10:14), for it covers violence (10:11). Foolishness pours out from it (15:2). We need to beware of a fool, because he is always meddling (20:3). His lips bring contention and his mouth provokes blows (18:6). "If a wise man contendeth with a foolish man, whether he rage or laugh, there is no rest" (29:9). "A companion of fools shall be broken" (13:20). "Let a bear robbed of her whelps meet a man, rather than a fool in his folly" (17:12). There is also an infectious quality in folly. The fool passes on folly as the wise man bequeaths wisdom (14:18). "A stone is heavy, and the sand weighty; but a fool's wrath is heavier than them both" (27:3). It is even worse when he is clever. As "the legs of the lame are not equal" — or "as a thorn goeth up into the hand of a drunkard, so is a parable in the mouth of fools" (26:7, 9). Even his prayer is an abomination (28:9). Can we do nothing for him? Can he not improve himself? No, "as a dog returneth to his vomit, so a fool iterateth his folly" (26:11). "Though thou shouldest bray a fool in a mortar among wheat with a pestle, yet will not his foolishness depart from him" (27:22). For his heart is corrupt (15:7). He will die in his lack of understanding (10:21). He will always be a fool, for he cannot and will not receive admonition (12:1).

Who is this fool of the wisdom literature? There can be no doubt that its authors have in mind specific individuals or groups. They are thinking of certain signs of decadence in the society of later Judaism. The reference is to concrete situations. Not all those whom they addressed were guilty of all the individual follies indicated — disobedience to parents, sexual and economic dissipation, drunkenness, blatant hardness of heart, bloodthirstiness, raillery, etc. We also misunderstand these proverbs if we expound them with reference to a recognisable group, an unpleasant stratum or party, that of "fools," which can be differentiated from the opposing group or stratum or party of the wise, and accused and condemned. The sign of decadence to which the term "fool" has reference is basically a characteristic of the whole life of Israel in its later stages. It applies virtually and even actually to all its members. And in the last resort it is a characteristic of the life of all men. "Therefore the Lord will cut off from Israel head and tail, branch and rush, in one day . . . for everyone is an hypocrite and an evildoer, and every mouth speaketh folly," is what we are told concerning Northern Israel in Is. 9:14, 17; and in a condemnation of idolatry in Jer. 10:8, 14 the same is said concerning the Gentiles: "But they are altogether brutish and foolish: the stock is a doctrine of vanities. . . . Every man is brutish in his knowledge." It is also to be noted how in Rom. 3:10f. Paul quotes from the context of the saying in Ps. 14:1 about the man who denies God: "They are corrupt, they have done abominable works, there is none that doeth good. The Lord looked down from heaven upon the children of men, to see if there were any that did understand, and seek God. They are all gone aside, they are all together become filthy: there is none that doeth good, no, not one" (Ps. 14:1-3, cf. Ps. 53:2f.). This is why even the righteous man (not the godless) has to confess (Ps. 69:5): "O God, thou knowest my foolishness," and (Ps. 73:22): "So foolish was I, and ignorant: I was as a beast before thee" — although he can then continue: "Nevertheless I am continually with thee: thou hast holden me by the right hand." Folly even extends to the heart of the child (Prov. 22:15), and the rod of affliction which is to drive it from him has much wider and deeper reference than to corporal punishment and other pedagogic measures. In Eccl. 9:3 we read that "the heart of the sons of men is full of evil, and madness is in their heart while they live, and after that they go to the dead." If this is the case, the folly envisaged in these writings does not refer — for all the concreteness of its manifestations — only to specific individuals as opposed to others who are superior and unaffected. It is not just the affair of a group. It is a determination under which the wise and clever who understand and seek after God, while they are certainly distinguished from the fools and simpletons who do not understand and do not seek after God, are also united with them, because the latter are at the very place from which they themselves have come and continually come, from which they have constantly to break away, at which they would spend their whole lives were it not given to them — and this is what makes them wise — by the omnipotent Word of God, which liberates them for knowledge, to break away from it, to turn their back on their folly; so that they too have need always to be recalled, and to recall themselves, by these proverbs. Folly is something which concerns Israel — for when was Israel not addressed by the prophets as a foolish people in its relationship to God? It is also something which concerns the nations who come under the light of the history of Israel, i.e., of the God who rules Israel. It is the concern of every man as he is revealed in the divine judgment. This picture of the fool is the mirror of the merited rejection held out to all men — a rejection from which there is no escape except by the gracious election of God, by the mighty Word of God which calls and chides. Thus the unfolding of this picture involves the call to decision as it has been heard, and must be continually heard, by the wise man, and as he loves to hear it. Who is the wise man but the fool of yesterday who will also be the fool of to-day and to-morrow without a fresh issue of this summons and fresh obedience? And who is the fool but the man who is summoned by the Word of God to be the wise man of to-day and to-morrow? Even the fool who is incorrigible as such is man before God — or, rather, man in the history in which God is about to fulfil and realise His covenant with him, the covenant which he himself has broken but God has kept. The picture of the fool shows with pitiless clarity where it is that man comes from, who and what he is there where he does not seek but is found by God, and who and what he would remain if he were not found by God. No wise man will obviously see fools except as they are seen in the wisdom literature. None will fail to take with absolute seriousness their godlessness and their consequent imprudence and insecurity. On the other hand, it is not a wise man, but only a fool, who will not remember that God is also the God of the fool, and only as such the God of the wise; who will therefore only contrast himself with the fool, and not admit his solidarity with him, and speak about him and to him in this solidarity. The picture of the fool in the Book of Proverbs is not an invitation to this unwise wisdom. The Book of Ecclesiastes can and must also be regarded as a warning against this misunderstanding of Proverbs. Particular attention must be paid in this respect to the remarkable passage in Eccl. 7:16-18: "Be not righteous over much; neither make thyself over wise: why shouldest thou destroy thyself? Be not over much wicked, neither be thou foolish: why shouldest thou die before thy time? It is good that thou shouldest take hold of this; yea, also from this withdraw not thine hand: for he that feareth God shall come forth of them all." But even in the Book of Proverbs itself we have to take note of the surprising words of Agur the son of Jakeh (30:2f.): "Surely I am more brutish than any man, and have not the understanding of a man. I neither learned wisdom, nor have the knowledge of the holy. Who hath ascended up into heaven, or descended? who hath gathered the wind in his fists? who hath bound the waters in his garment? who hath established all the ends of the earth? what is his name, and what is his son's name, if thou canst tell?" There can be no doubt that it is a wise man who puts these questions. But there can also be no doubt that it is one who is wise in the fact that in and with these questions concerning God he ranges himself with the fool, acknowledging himself to be a fool. Is he wise all the same, and able and called to teach the fool wisdom? This is undoubtedly the case, for in vv. 5f. he is given and gives himself the answer: "Every word of God is pure: he is a shield unto them that put their trust in him. Add thou not unto his words, lest he reprove thee, and thou be found a liar."

It is of a piece with this — with the required modesty with which alone the wise man, if he is to be truly wise, can look upon (and not therefore look down upon) the fool — that in Mt. 5:22 the address μωρέ, thou fool, is forbidden on the severest penalties as a term of reproach directly and personally flung by one man at another. It is, indeed, the most terrible form of what Jesus describes as "murder" in exposition of the Old Testament commandment. It does, of course, occur several times in the New Testament in the context of teaching or prophecy. For example, we find it in Lk. 11:40 in the condemnation of the Pharisaic view of cleansing: ἄφρονες, "did not he that made that which is without make that which is within also?"; in Mt. 23:17 in the attack on the pharisaic practice as regards oaths: μωροὶ καὶ τυφλοί, "for whether is greater, the gift, or the altar that sanctifieth the gift?"; in Mt. 25:2f., where in the parable five of the virgins are called μωραί; in 1 Cor. 15:36: ἄφρων, "that which thou sowest is not quickened, except it die"; and in Lk. 12:20, to the rich man who planned to build greater barns: ἄφρων, "this night thy soul shall be required of thee: then whose shall those things be, which thou hast provided?" It is to be noted that this is not said to him by a man, but by God. It is also to be noted that in all these passages the primary condemnation is not of the individual but of specific ways of thinking and acting. It is the former which is forbidden in Mt. 5:22 as a qualified form of murder, as an absolute breach of communication with one's brother. In this respect there is again brought out the whole basic seriousness of the concept "fool." For all its lavish and drastic appearance in the Old Testament it is always used in the third person, never in the second. It is impossible not to speak of the fool. There are innumerable representatives of folly — its poor slaves, but also its priests and bold prophets and protagonists. And therefore there are innumerable fools. Yet no one has either place or right to see and treat another as such. It may well be that he confronts me as such in a terribly concrete way, so that I seem almost to get the touch and smell of the fool. But he does not confront me in such a way that I can really recognise him concretely as such. To say "fool" of another man is to curse him, and as such to murder him, to invade the divine prerogative as a qualified murderer, to act in ignorance of God, and therefore to show oneself a fool. The curse is one which recoils on the man who utters it. For it is only those who are themselves godless and stupid that will feel free to apply this murderous term of opprobrium and condemnation to their companions in stupidity.

There is, however, one notable example in the Old Testament (1 Sam. 25) of a man who is as his name is (v. 25) — Nabal, a fool. This man, sharply contrasted with his wife Abigail as the representative of wisdom and David as the exponent of the divine action and promise in and with Israel, plays in the form of folly a very important — if, as is only fitting, subsidiary — role. It will be worth our while briefly to consider the story. It certainly provides us with a "study in desert customs" (R. Kittel), but it is hardly for this reason that it has found a place in the collection of dynastic records of which the two Books of Samuel form the starting-point. Even the contracting of David's second or third marriage (with Abigail), which is the culmination of the story, is hardly a sufficient justification for so detailed an account of what precedes. It is evident that in the depiction of the strange happenings which took place between these three characters our attention is drawn to something of material significance. And the emphasis given to them, especially to Nabal and Abigail, shows unmistakeably that what we have here is an encounter of David, the bearer of the promise κατ᾽ ἐξοχήν, with two contrasting types, the expressly foolish and the expressly wise, and his rejection by the former who is called Nabal, and acknowledgment and humble acceptance by the latter, Abigail.

The event takes place in Carmel, south-east of Hebron, which is the abode of the prosperous Nabal, the owner of 3000 sheep and 1000 goats, who is just about to keep the feast of shearing (v. 2). The story belongs to the records of David's experiences and activities when, although he is already elected and called and anointed to be the future king, he is forced into exile by the attacks of Saul. David and his 600 men are in the western part of the wilderness of Judah on the borders of Carmel, where the shepherds of Nabal have taken his sheep to pasture. David hears of the sheep-shearing, and sends ten of his men to Nabal. They are to greet him as a brother, saying: "Peace be both to thee, and peace be to thine house, and peace be unto all that thou hast" (v. 6). The message which they are to give is that no injury has been done to the shepherds (as they themselves can and do testify, v. 15) by the roving band into whose sphere of influence they have come, nor have the flocks themselves suffered the loss that might have been expected (v. 7). On the contrary, David and his men have protected the flocks and shepherds against alien robbers. Far from constituting a threat, they have been "a wall unto them both by night and day" (v. 16). David is not reminding Nabal of the positive achievement, but of the integrity and loyalty which he and his men have proved. And he requests only the customary hospitality at festivals of this kind when he asks Nabal to be generous to his emissaries and to give them "whatsoever cometh to thine hand" for David and his servants. He even describes himself as "thy son David" (v. 8).

It is at this juncture, however, that Nabal lives up to his name and shows himself to be "churlish and evil," a true son of Caleb (v. 3), "this man of Belial," as he is later called by his own wife (v. 25) — and so much so "that a man cannot speak to him" (v. 17). "Who is David? and who is the son of Jesse? there be many servants now a days that break away every man from his master. Shall I then take my bread, and my water, and my flesh that I have killed for my shearers, and give it unto men, whom I know not whence they be?" What is the folly of this foolish speech? Is it that it is the speech of an unusually self-opinionated and standoffish and intolerably priggish bourgeois? This is one aspect of it. He seems to be completely lacking in any feeling for a neighbour in need, or even in ordinary civility in his dealings with his fellows. He is a quite impossible neighbour. But there is more to it than this if we are not simply to read the story in moralistic terms. Nabal was addressed "in the name of David" (v. 9). The different reaction of Abigail as soon as she heard the name of David shows where the decisive folly of the speech is to be found. Note the beginning and end of his words. It is not just a bedouin sheikh but the elect of Yahweh that he refuses to recognise, and thinks that he can scorn and despise, accusing him of being a runaway servant and so inhospitably refusing him food and drink. How could he possibly miss the threefold *shalom* with which David greeted him? But he did miss it. It was really an encounter with his own and Israel's salvation that he neglected and so rudely rejected. It was Yahweh's own presence and action in the person of this man that he despised, refusing his services, and insisting so snobbishly upon his own right of possession and therefore control. He had to do with Yahweh Himself, and he acted as one who was completely ignorant of Him. That is why he was so impossible.

David, of course, was a man like others, who normally give a rough answer to churlishness, replying with anger and vengeance to foolish words and actions, and in this way, i.e., in the name of avenging righteousness, with folly to folly. When he received news of Nabal's reception he took 400 of his 600 men, and when they had girded on their swords they set out westward towards Carmel — a thunder-cloud which according to the practice of the times threatened complete extermination to Nabal and all his house (v. 12). We can see later (vv. 21f., 34) how David looked at the matter: "Surely in vain have I kept all this fellow hath in the wilderness, so that nothing was missed of all that pertained unto him: and he hath requited me evil for good. So and more also do God unto David, if I leave any men of all that pertain to him by the morning light."

It is at this point that Abigail takes a hand. According to v. 3 she is a woman "of good understanding, and of a beautiful countenance." One of Nabal's servants has come (v. 14) and told her what has taken place (according to v. 25 in her absence): "Now therefore know and consider what thou wilt do; for evil is determined against our master, and against all his household" (v. 17). But her wisdom has as little need of lengthy deliberation as the folly of her husband. What is it that she knows and he does not know? That this is not the way to treat people? Yes, she knows this too. But this is not the decisive point. She hears the name of David and knows with whom they have to do (with the same immediacy as her husband does not know). She takes in the situation at a glance and acts accordingly (vv. 18f.). "Whatsoever cometh to thine hand" is what David had asked of Nabal. But she now takes two hundred loaves, and two bottles of wine, and five sheep ready dressed, and five measures of parched corn, and an hundred clusters of raisins, and two hundred cakes of figs, and loads them on asses. Some of the servants are to go on before, and she herself follows — eastward towards David. And she does all this without even consulting her husband. When the elect of God draws near, and with him the judgment, wisdom does not dispute with folly, but ignores it and does that which is commanded.

There then follows her encounter with David and his band. According to v. 20 it takes place in the fold of a valley, and is a surprise meeting for both parties, Abigail coming down from the one side and David from the other. "And when Abigail saw David, she hasted, and lighted off the ass, and fell before David on her face, and bowed herself to the ground" (v. 23) — the full prostration of worship like that of Abraham before God (Gen. 17:3) and Joshua before the angel (Josh. 5:14) and before the ark (7:6). A sign of anxiety? No, but of something very different — an unconditional respect. Abigail has no anxiety. She knows very well what she wants and what she has to represent with a very definite superiority. What she now does is the demonstration of the fact that in this situation she knows with whom she has to do in the rather threatening person of this man. This is the core and guiding light of the long speech which is now put on her lips (vv. 24-31). This is the reason for her attitude and for the gifts that she has brought to David. It is also the basis of the requests that she makes. It is on this account that she must and will make good the evil of Nabal, and prevent the evil that David himself is on the point of committing. It is in this respect that she shows herself to be of a good understanding. The point is that the name David means something to her. She knows and solemnly declares who he is and will be. Since the wordless anointing of David by Samuel in 1 Sam. 16:1-13 — and it is not for nothing that the death of Samuel is reported at the beginning of this chapter — it has not been reported that anyone has said anything to this effect either of or to David: "Yahweh shall do to my lord all the good that he hath spoken concerning thee, and appoint thee ruler over Israel" (v. 30); and even more emphatically: "For the Lord will certainly make my lord a sure house, because my lord fighteth the battles of the Lord, and evil hath not been found in thee all thy days. Yet a man is risen to pursue thee, and to seek thy soul: but the soul of my lord shall be bound in the bundle of life with the Lord thy God; and the souls of thine enemies, them shall he sling out, as out of the middle of a sling" (vv. 28b-29). Everything else depends upon, and has its meaning and power in, the fact that Abigail knows and has to say this of David, and therefore of the will and promise, the secret of the covenant, of the God of Israel.

It is this knowledge which commits and constrains her fearlessly and whole-heartedly to take up the cause of Nabal with David. As the one who does not know in this decisive respect, Nabal and all that he says and does in consequence can only be found wanting in this situation. This will be proved later in what is for him a terrible sense. In the first instance, it means that he does not even come into consideration in the discussion and bargaining with David: "Let not my lord, I pray thee, regard this man of Belial, even Nabal: for as his name is, so is he; Nabal is his name, and folly is with him" (v. 25a). Abigail can only ask David to listen to her and not to him: "Let thine handmaid, I pray thee, speak in thine audience, and hear the words of thine handmaid" (v. 24). But this means that she accepts responsibility for what Nabal has said and done; that she takes his place in relation to David. She knows and says that she had no part in the event: "But I thine handmaid saw not the young men of my lord, whom thou didst send" (v. 25b). And yet: "Upon me, my lord, upon me let this iniquity be" (v. 24a). The first practical meaning of her prostration is that she gives herself into David's hands for good or evil if only he will hear her, and hear her in the place of Nabal.

What is it that she has to say to him? In the first instance, she has to act: to make good the mistake that Nabal has made; to fulfil the request that he had rejected; to unload the asses and present the bread and wine and sheep and corn and raisins and figs to David. "And now this present which thine handmaid hath brought unto my lord, let it be even given unto the young men that follow my lord" (v. 27). And then: "Forgive the trespass of thine handmaid" (v. 28a). Why should David forgive? Because she has made good the mistake and given the present? No, but because David — there now follow the words of promise in vv. 28b-29 — is already the anointed and future king of Israel. It is as the one who knows him as such that Abigail has interposed herself between him and Nabal. And it is as the one who knows this, and in view of what she knows, that she asks for forgiveness. And the granting of this request carries with it the sparing of Nabal and his house from impending destruction. Even to her personally there will not now occur (as we learn from v. 34) the worst evil that could come on any woman in Israel, the loss of her sons. But she is not concerned about this danger, as had been the servant who first told her what had happened and what it would necessarily entail. What moves Abigail is not that vengeance should be averted from Nabal and his house and indirectly herself, but that it should not be committed by David. In her intervention she is particularly unconcerned as to the fate of Nabal. Indeed, she counts on it as something which is as good as done that he will come to a bad end: "Let thine enemies, and they that seek evil to my lord, be as Nabal" (v. 26b). What she wills to prevent when she throws herself down before David, and accepts the guilt of Nabal, and asks that it should be forgiven, is that David should be the instrument of Nabal's destruction, and therefore incur guilt himself.

Does she only will to prevent this? The remarkable thing in her speech to David is that she regards it as something which objectively is prevented already. With such superiority does she confront the wrathful David (before whom she prostrates herself), so little does she fear him or doubt the success of her intervention, that from the very first she speaks in terms of an accomplished fact: "Now therefore, my lord, as the Lord liveth, and as thy soul liveth, seeing the Lord hath withholden thee from coming to shed blood, and from avenging thyself with thine own hand . . ." (v. 26a). We find the same daring anticipation in the words of promise in relation to David's future as the one whom Yahweh has raised up and protected to be a prince over Israel. When God has done this (and it is assumed that He will), "this shall be no grief unto thee, nor offence of heart unto my lord, either that thou hast shed blood causeless, or that my lord hath avenged himself" (v. 31). This is the wisdom of Abigail in her relationship with David, who in the act of vengeance which he purposes stands in the only too human danger of making himself a fool. She knows that as the one he is and will be he may not and cannot and therefore will not actually do what he plans to do. The elect of Yahweh may not and cannot and will not avenge himself, making himself guilty of the blood of Nabal and many others who were innocent, and thus violating the prerogative of Yahweh, which none can ever escape. She towers above David with this knowledge as she makes this pronouncement.

And what of David? The practical consequence is as follows: "So David received of her hand that which she had brought him, and said unto her, Go up in peace to thine house; see, I have hearkened to thy voice, and have accepted thy person" (and intervention, v. 35). But the reason why he forgives, and therefore foregoes his intended revenge, is not because he has received the present or changed his mind as to what Nabal deserves. He still fully acknowledges his purpose: "For in very deed, as the Lord God of Israel liveth, which hath kept me back from hurting thee, except thou hadst hasted and come to meet me, surely there had not been left a man unto Nabal by the morning light" (v. 34). The ground of his forgiveness is exactly the same as that of Abigail's request for forgiveness. And in his words as in hers it is one which has to be taken into consideration and therefore discussed, but one which is already realised and operative, excluding from the very outset the execution of his purpose. The beginning of his answer is decisive: "Blessed be the Lord God of Israel, which sent thee this day to meet me: and blessed be thy advice, and blessed be thou, which hast kept me this day from coming to shed blood, and from avenging myself with mine own hand" (vv. 32f.). The request of Abigail did not need to be fulfilled. It had been fulfilled already — even before it was made. It simply reminded David of the accomplished fact that he could not and would not do what he intended to do. For, indicated by the voice of Abigail, it is Yahweh the God of Israel who withstands him as an absolutely effective obstacle on the way which he has planned to follow, arresting and turning him back again. And in face of this obstacle David can only break out into praise of God and of the understanding Abigail. As the one he is on the basis of the election of Yahweh, and as the one he will be in the power of the calling of Yahweh, he is not in a position to execute his purpose. As the Lord liveth — Yahweh and he himself would have to be other than they are if he were to be in a position to execute it. The wisdom of Abigail consists in the fact that she knows Yahweh and therefore knows David. When David hears the voice of this wisdom, no particular decision is needed. The matter is decided already. He is restrained from doing what he had intended to do.

The story has two endings. The first is a sombre one. Nabal has escaped the wrath of David. But he runs none the less to his destruction. The death overtakes him to which he has fallen a victim in his own corruption.

The second is brighter. It speaks of the marriage of David and Abigail as the result of their encounter and remarkable agreement.

Nabal is removed. When Abigail returns from her enterprise to Carmel she finds this rash and foolish fellow engaged in a fresh act of madness: "He held a feast in his house like the feast of a king; and Nabal's heart was merry within him, for he was very drunken: wherefore she told him nothing, less or more, until the morning light" (v. 36). But he has to learn what danger he has incurred, under what threat he has actually stood, and above all how — while he himself feasted and amused himself so regally, and therefore so little deserved it — he was saved from destruction in the power of the redemptive will of Yahweh as it is focused on David and known and proclaimed by Abigail. Therefore "in the morning, when the wine was gone out of Nabal, . . . his wife told him these things" (v. 37a). But it is not the fact that he has been saved that makes an impression on this fool and causes him to think, although this might have been an excellent opportunity to learn to know the one whom hitherto he had not known. Even now that he is sober he is still the fool he was in and before his carousal. And it is the account of that from which he has been saved, and therefore of that by which (like the rider on Lake Constance) he was threatened, that suddenly comes home to him and obviously affects him like a stroke — his subsequent fear being all the greater than his previous sense of security. "His heart died within him, and he became as a stone. And it came to pass about ten days after, that the Lord smote Nabal, that he died" (vv. 37b-38). The message of salvation itself, not being recognised by him, turns to his own judgment and death. He can and does only disappear from the scene. And on learning of Nabal's end, and in the light of it, David can only praise Yahweh, that He has acted as his avenger, and that He has kept David himself from evil (v. 39a).

But the death of Nabal means that Abigail is now a widow. She does not remain so long. She becomes the wife of David. At first sight this is rather surprising, for there are no hints of any romantic developments in the earlier part of the story. The dealings between herself and David had been strictly matter of fact, and it would be wrong to allow artistic imagination to impart to them a different and preparatory character in the light of the outcome. There is, in fact, no trace of sentimentality even in the portrayal of the conclusion itself. It must be understood in the sober context of the main part of the narrative. "And David sent, and communed with Abigail, to take her to him to wife" (v. 39b). The proposal was made by the servants of David (v. 40) and it was accepted by Abigail with the same unquestioning resolution as had marked all her previous speech and action, and the same unconditional subjection as that which she had known when she had fearlessly and critically instructed this great and fearsome leader, and told him the truth concerning Yahweh and himself. She does not compromise herself, but simply carries through to the end the role allotted to her in her wisdom, when we read that "she arose, and bowed herself on her face to the earth, and said (as though addressing David himself and not merely his servants), Behold, let thine handmaid be a servant to wash the feet of the servants of my lord. And Abigail hasted, and arose, and rode upon an ass, with five damsels of hers that went after her; and she went after the messengers of David, and became his wife" (vv. 41-42). We really ought not to be surprised by this development, for as by an inner necessity the main narrative hastens towards the death of Nabal and the new life of Abigail in union with David. The meaning is not to be sought in any special importance of Abigail in the future history of David. There is only one other mention of her, together with David's other wives, in 2 Sam. 3:3, where we read that she was the mother of Chileab, who in the parallel in 1 Chron. 3:1 is called Daniel. Michal and later Bathsheba play a much more imposing role in the tradition. But we are forced to say of Abigail that of all the wives of David, or even of the Old Testament as a whole, she is outstanding as the only one to whom there is ascribed the function described in 1 Sam. 25: that of the woman of good understanding who recognises and honours the Lord's anointed, and therefore the Lord's will for Israel, at a time when he is so severely assailed and so deeply concealed, and when her foolish husband is so blind and deaf and stupid in face of him; but who also represents and declares to the elect himself the will and purpose of Yahweh and the logic of his election and calling, keeping him from putting his trust in his own arm and sword and therefore himself becoming a fool. In this function she belongs to David even before she does so in fact. She belongs to him as the wisdom which takes the place of folly and speaks for it, and without which he could not be the one he is as the elect of Yahweh, or be the king of Israel, as he will be in virtue of his calling. Ordained to be his help-meet (Gen. 2:18f.) in this function, she belongs indispensably to him. This is what David actualises and confirms with his swift proposal — once the existence of the fool and the work of his folly have been removed — and which she herself also actualises and confirms with her swift and unquestioning acceptance. David would not be David without Abigail and without recognising Abigail; just as Abigail would not be the wise Abigail without David and without recognising David. Therefore he has to take her to wife and she has to become his wife, so that they are one flesh. To no other marriage of David, or indeed of the Old Testament, does the biblical account give the distinctive mark of this inner necessity in the context of the history of salvation.

On the Gospel of John:
The Prophetic Work of Christ

IV/3, pp. 231-37

We may sum up the conclusions thus far reached as follows. At its beginning, the history of the prophecy of Jesus Christ is one which (1) in and with its own history, (2) which speaks for itself and (3) is distinctive in relation to all other events, (4) does not merely belong to the past in its singularity, but is divinely present (5) within the world, (6) inaugurated by God in His sovereign freedom and (7) unequivocally revealing His grace. We must not overlook any of these characteristics if we are to understand correctly the commencement and therefore the continuation of the prophetic work of Jesus Christ, of the dawning of His light, and the declaration of His Word as the Word of the covenant. We are not suggesting, of course, that any of these characteristics in isolation can set us on the way to true understanding but rather that all of them are essential in the unity in which they mutually condition and supplement each other. No word or name or concept must be used to denote this unity apart from the one name of Jesus Christ. None of them, therefore, can point to any other reality than that of Jesus Christ Himself. But if the reference to Him is to go beyond the mere naming of His name, which in the last resort is alone adequate and comprehensive, it is hard to see how in this context any of the characteristics mentioned can be left out in substance, however we might enumerate or define them in detail.

As they have been here adduced and cursorily described, I have tacitly taken them from the total witness of Holy Scripture, with constant reference both to its Old Testament form and also to the way in which the work of the prophecy of Jesus Christ begins in its secondary form in Christian knowledge as it is to be understood according to the guidance of the New Testament. Whether the proposals and descriptions attempted really fit the facts and are accurate and satisfactory can be decided and judged only in relation to the relevant witness of Scripture in the same totality. But I do not think that on this basis we shall quickly come to conclusions on this matter which differ essentially or decisively from those advanced.

In view of the importance of the question, however, it is perhaps not wholly superfluous that we should check at least one element in the biblical witness which particularly demands our attention, namely, the Gospel of John. By means of this we can show in outline that the seven characteristics adduced were not selected and presented at random, but in the light of the source by which Christian theology must always orientate itself and be authoritatively instructed in what it must venture to say and not to say. It is especially relevant that we should consider the verdict of this Gospel in the present context because the terms Word, light, revelation, speech and witness denote the specific angle from which the history of Jesus Christ is seen and recounted in this Gospel. Epigrammatically, we might almost say that the Gospel of John is the Gospel of the Gospel itself, i.e., of the prophetic work of Jesus Christ. Our present concern, however, is with what we learn from it concerning the beginning or initiation of this work.

1. It is crystal clear that everything here begins with the entry, speech and action of Jesus Himself among men. "I am" is both the presupposition and the epitome of what He has to impart and of what the Evangelist has accordingly to say to the community and the world. I am the way, the resurrection, the life, the door, the bread, the vine, the Shepherd, and also the truth, the light, the Word. Accordingly the Baptist, with whom the author seems in some sense to identify himself under the name John, has no witness to bear except to the fact — and he points away from himself in a way which is exemplary for all true witnesses — that "this (οὗτος) is he." And it would be difficult to contest that the same οὗτος is not already announced in the Prologue: "The same was in the beginning with God" (1:2), i.e., the Word which was made flesh (1:14) and to whose presence the Baptist later points (1:15, 30, 34). From the very moment when John sees Him "coming unto him," His history absorbs that of the Baptist. He is the Son of Joseph of Nazareth (1:45), and concrete features are occasionally mentioned to make it clear that He is a real man. Yet He is an absolutely dominating and almost more than life-size figure beside whom the disciples, the hostile "Jews," the people, Nicodemus, the Samaritan woman and finally Pilate, with all their speeches, questions, answers and attitudes, seem to have only the function of giving Him occasion to express and present Himself. In everything that takes place and is said and done it is a matter of His person

and the work accomplished in His existence. For all others, for the world and His disciples, it is a matter of what He is for them and among them, of His mission and coming and going and abiding and coming again; and on their side of their positive or negative attitude to Him, of their being as His friends or enemies. To have faith, and in faith eternal life, means quite distinctly to believe in Him; and not to have faith (and therefore to be condemned) means not to believe in Him. Eternal life (17:3) is to know the one true God, and with Him Jesus Christ whom He has sent.

2. His work, the sum of the work laid upon Him by the Father who sent Him, and accomplished or still to be accomplished by Him as the One who has been sent, consists in His being the light and Witness and Revealer of the glory which He has not usurped and which is not in this sense His own, but which has been given in all its fulness by the One who sent Him and which is therefore His own (1:14). As soon as He appears in the Fourth Gospel He is this Revealer. The Baptist has only to see Him and at once — not on the basis of spontaneous knowledge (1:31, 33), but on the basis of the immediate revelation of Him who sent Him — he describes Him as "the Lamb of God, which taketh away the sin of the world." And it is with the recognition that He is the Messiah "of whom Moses in the law, and the prophets did write" (1:45), "the Son of God . . . the King of Israel" (1:49), i.e., with the knowledge later expressed by Peter at Caesarea Philippi, that those who are to be His disciples come to Him and on this basis are called to follow Him. Here, then, His prophetic work is already being done even before He commences His teaching and miracles. In the beginning of all beginnings with God (1:1), namely, in the disposition of God which precedes history, and as Himself God, He not only spoke but was the very Word by which all things were made and without which nothing was made that was made. In Him was life. He was the light of life which lightens man. He was the power of the saving work of God to speak for itself as it is accomplished. As He was this light, He now is, and He thus shines in the darkness and cannot be overcome by it. The Baptist, too, can be called a "burning and a shining light" (λύχνος, 5:35), yet He is not that light (φῶς), but can only be called its witness, the witness of this incomparable Witness. He Himself was this Word and light. He did not have to become a Witness and Revealer. He was so from the very first. With His present "I am" He reaches back even behind the time of Abraham (8:58). He shares the glory of the Father before the world was (17:5). He is loved by the Father before the foundation of the world (17:24). And it is thus that He raises His voice, the voice which the dead shall hear and live (5:25). He

really does raise it. The beginning does not make the continuation super-fluous, nor His history as such empty and meaningless. The Gospel of John recounts the history of works, of revealing words and acts, of genuine encounters and decisions. But it recounts them with the orientation and dynamic proper to this history from the very outset, i.e., in the light of its basis in God Himself and then in the first beginning in time, of the unity in which the being and action of Jesus as such are also His word, or rather the Word of Him that sent Him. Far from this weakening the history of the prophecy of Jesus Christ, it is the very thing which gives it its clear and distinctive light and thus enables it to be told as illuminating history.

3. It is inevitable that in John's Gospel the prophetic work of Jesus should be differentiated and marked off quite unmistakeably from all other prophecies, revelations, witnesses, voices, words and lights. The acknowledgment of the Baptist is plain: "He bare witness unto the truth" (5:33). "But I have greater witness than that of John" (5:36). Indeed, the witness of John himself points consistently in this direction: "After me cometh a man which is preferred before me: for he was before me" (1:30). "He that cometh from above is above all: he that is of the earth is earthly, and speaketh of the earth" (3:31). In this respect the Baptist has his own place, and his own task and authorisation within these limits. "I am not the Christ, but am sent before him. He that hath the bride is the bridegroom; but the friend of the bridegroom, which standeth and heareth him, rejoiceth greatly because of the bridegroom's voice: this my joy therefore is fulfilled. He must increase, but I must decrease" (3:28f.). Again, there is a plain acknowledgment of the Old Testament, which also precedes and points to the prophetic work of Jesus Christ. "Search the scriptures; for in them ye think ye have eternal life: and they are they which testify of me" (5:39). "Your father Abraham rejoiced to see my day: and he saw it, and was glad" (8:56). "Do not think that I will accuse you to the Father: there is one that accuseth you, even Moses, in whom ye trust. For had ye believed Moses, ye would have believed me: for he wrote of me. But if ye believe not his writings, how shall ye believe my words?" (5:45f.). It is in this positive presentation of the place and function of other genuine witnesses that the basic particularity of that of Jesus emerges. "No man hath seen God at any time; the only begotten Son, which is in the bosom of the Father, he hath declared him" (1:18 cf. 6:46). Hence He is the Way, the Truth and the Life, and no man comes to the Father except by Him (14:6). Hence the disciples, having believed on Him and known Him, cannot go to any other, for He and He alone has the words of eternal life (6:68). Hence they cannot con-

fuse His voice with any other. As He calls them by name and leads them out, they hear Him and "follow him: for they know his voice. And a stranger will they not follow, but will flee from him: for they know not the voice of strangers" (10:3f.).

4. In recounting this history, the Fourth Gospel does not narrate a past history, but one which is present in its unique content. To be sure, it speaks not only of His coming and existence, but also quite emphatically of His going, of His exaltation from the earth, of His return to the Father. To be sure, His presence among His own and in the world seems to be limited in a way which seriously threatens His whole work by the irruption of His suffering and death as they are ever more plainly intimated after the great uproar of the seventh chapter. Yet it would be quite inadequate to describe as "parting words" the content of the three chapters (14–16) which stand supremely under this shadow of the cross. Already in 6:56f. we read: "He that eateth my flesh, and drinketh my blood, dwelleth in me, and I in him. As the living Father hath sent me, and I live by the Father: so he that eateth me, shall live by me," and this twofold living in and with one another, which obviously cannot be broken by any parting, is the tenor of the later passages too. The One who to-day is "the resurrection and the life" (11:25), will also be this to-morrow. The One who can promise to those who believe in Him that they will live though they die, will also Himself live though He dies. And it is not just in spite of His departure but because of it — for it is the completion of His life — that He will be definitively present to His own and to the world, and they to Him, and also and precisely on the far side of this departure. "Now is the Son of man glorified, and God is glorified in him," is the boldest possible anticipation of 13:31 immediately after the unmasking of the purpose of Judas and therefore at the commencement of the story of the passion. This glorifying is indestructible by its very nature. In the light of it we cannot be too faithful to the positive content of the parting discourses. "Let not your heart be troubled: ye believe in God, believe also in me" (14:1). "For all things that I have heard of my Father I have made known unto you" (15:15). "Now ye are clean through the word which I have spoken unto you" (15:3). "I will not leave you comfortless: I will come to you" (14:18). "A little while, and ye shall not see me: and again, a little while, and ye shall see me" (16:16). "But I will see you again, and your heart shall rejoice, and your joy no man taketh from you" (16:22). "He that loveth me shall be loved of my Father, and I will love him, and will manifest myself to him" (14:21). "Whatsoever ye shall ask in my name, that will I do" (14:13f., 15:7, 16:23, 26). The Holy Spirit, sent by the

Father and Himself, will be the "Comforter" who will make all this true to them, who will continually glorify Him afresh, who will teach them all things as He takes of His and shows it to them, who will lead them into all truth, but who will also convince the world of the sin of their unbelief, of the meaning of His death (cf. 12:31) and of the judgment already executed on its prince (14:26, 15:26f., 16:7-14). Hence: "In the world ye shall have tribulation, but be of good cheer; I have overcome the world" (16:33). For after He has lived His life to the final point of self-offering, He does not live any less, but really lives and is really present to His own and to the world. This is how His history continually becomes a new reality to His own and to the world.

5. All this can and must be the case because it is the history which here below, on earth and among men, is inaugurated from above, from heaven and by God. The man who speaks in it is not alone (8:16, 16:32). He does not speak of Himself (5:30, 12:49, 14:10). He has not come to do His own will (6:38), nor for His own glory (8:50), like those who speak of themselves (7:18). Again, He does not bear witness of or to Himself, for otherwise He would not be a true Witness (5:30, 8:14). Yet He does not need human witness or honour (5:31). As the Son of the Father, He speaks what He has heard of Him (8:26, 40), what He has been commissioned by Him to speak (12:49), and as He has been taught by Him (8:28). He gives His own the words which He has received from the Father (17:8). His meat is to do His will and to finish His work (4:34). Hence He does not do His own works, but those of the Father who sends Him (9:4). It is the indwelling Father who does them (14:10). He Himself does them only in His name (10:25). Only as He does them in this way do they bear witness (5:36), the Father thus witnessing to Him and for Him (5:37, 8:18). As the One who glorifies the Father, He Himself is glorified by Him (12:23, 13:31, 17:1f.). This twofold glorification, however, takes place as He is in the Father and the Father in Him (10:38, 14:10, 17:21), as He and the Father are one (10:30), so that to see Him is to see the Father (14:9) and to honour Him is to honour the Father (5:23). It is in this fellowship of action and being with God that the man Jesus is the Revealer, the Light, the Witness of the truth. To believe in Him is thus to know that what He says and does is said and done in this fellowship.

6. It is at this point that the mystery of the divine freedom must be considered. The fellowship of action and being with God in which the man Jesus is the Revealer rests, of course, as regards its basis and possibility, on the divine disposition which precedes all history and indeed the creation of the world, and which is the theme of the Prologue and of later passages

which either refer to this or are in harmony with it. But since the inner divine disposition as such is grounded in the freedom of God and not in a compulsion to which He is subject, so is its historical actualisation, the temporal event of the incarnation of the Word. This is the absolutely sovereign act of God which in John's Gospel is continually described as the Father's sending of the Son or the Son's being sent by the Father. It cannot be taken for granted that this self-revealing work of God among men not only can take place on the basis of that divine disposition, but that it actually does take place, that the concrete fellowship of God and man there decreed and sealed in the height of the divine counsel is in fact enacted and manifested here in this one person. That the Word itself was once and once-for-all as we are, that it tabernacled among us, that its glory was perceptible to and perceived by us (1:14) — this is the unexpected and therefore absolutely majestic declaration, transforming our whole situation, of a Messenger from another sphere imparting and bringing what we neither have nor can have, namely, eternal life. As we read in the clear-cut saying in 3:16, God gave His Son "that whosoever believeth in him should not perish, but have everlasting life." Like the life itself, the revelation in the world which makes faith possible is a free gift of God, grounded only in the fact that He loved the world which was and is quite unworthy of such love. But it is again a free gift of God, according to the emphatic declaration of the Fourth Gospel, when His Messenger is heard and obeyed. "No man can come to me, except the Father which hath sent me draw him. . . . Every man therefore that hath heard and hath learned of the Father, cometh unto me" (6:44f.). Hence the disciples whom He finds and who find Him are called those who are given Him out of the world. "Thine they were, and thou gavest them me" (17:6). They are born, "not of blood, nor of the will of the flesh, nor of the will of man, but of God" (1:13). Those who do not believe are not thereby excused. Nowhere in the New Testament are such sharp and stern sentences passed on unbelievers who despise and reject the gift of faith as in the Fourth Gospel. And yet according to the same Gospel those who may believe can never doubt for a moment that they owe to the divine freedom both the objective presupposition and the subjective fulfilment of this action and therefore their whole existence in this circle, so that they can receive and honour not only the Son but also their faith in Him only as a free and quite unmerited gift made over to the world and to them.

7. What does Jesus reveal according to the Fourth Gospel? What is the positive thing which He makes known, which He causes to shine as the

light of the world, as He reveals Himself and His own glory (1:14, 2:11)? We look back for a moment to our fifth point, and must first reply that He reveals Himself as the One who as the Son of God exists in this fellowship of action and being with the Father, by whom the Father's work is done, and who for His part wills to do and does this work. His glory consists in the fact that He glorifies the Father and in so doing (showing Himself to be sent by Him) is Himself glorified by Him. It consists in the fact that the Father is in Him and He in the Father, that He and the Father are one. But the expression "fellowship of action and being" is too weak to describe what Jesus reveals as this glory of His. The Gospel characterises what takes place in this fellowship with greater force and content when it speaks of the love of the Son for the Father and of the Father for the Son. Their fellowship, unity and indwelling are thus described as their action and being in free and mutual affirmation and surrender, the Son loving the Father and being loved by Him, and *vice versa*. This love is the content of the Word or declaration of Jesus, the positive thing which He makes known to the world. In the perfection of its movement it is the light which in His person shines in the darkness. Is this, then, the revelation of the inner divine mystery? It is this, too, and it is because it is the revelation of perfect love in God Himself that even in its conflict with darkness it has and maintains its positive character, its superiority and invincibility. But the revelation of this mystery can and does take place only because it does not remain this inner divine mystery, but discloses itself within the reality distinct from God, the Word being made flesh, the Son who loves and is loved by the Father becoming identical with the man Jesus, so that Jesus is the One who is in the Father and the Father in Him, who glorifies the Father and is glorified by Him, who does the work of God and by whom this work is thus done. He, the man Jesus, the son of Joseph of Nazareth, can and does reveal love in God because He Himself exists in its perfect movement. In His human person therefore — and this outbreaking of the divine mystery is the point and true content of His revelation — the world is brought into this movement as the world which loves God and is loved by Him. What took place (3:16) in the sending and giving of His only begotten Son, who loved and was loved by Him, was that God did not love Him alone but also loved the world, and that He was not loved by Him alone but also by the world. It is as this man loving and loved by the Father, sent by Him into the world (10:36, 17:18), coming out from Him and coming into the world (16:28), that He speaks in and to the world (8:26, 17:13) and is the light of the world. The world does not know Him, nor the light which shines in Him, nor His sending, nor His intervention for it, nor what it is therefore in Him (1:10, 17:25). But this does not alter the fact of what He is for it nor the fact that in His person it is drawn into the movement of the love of God as the world which is loved by God and loves Him in return. In spite of its ignorance He Himself is the pledge that it is this world. And with Him, as His disciples, those who believe in Him, the community of His followers, are a similar pledge. As they follow the drawing of the Father to the Son (6:44), the mutual love and fellowship and union, the reciprocal affirmation and surrender of the Father and the Son, are also in them. As they believe in Jesus, there is realised in them that which He achieves by His intervention as the One sent by God. Believing in Him, they have eternal life. Believing in the light, they are "the children of light" (12:36). For their own sake? Certainly for their own sake, yet primarily and decisively that they should shine in the world with what is realised in them by faith in Jesus, that they should love one another (13:34, 15:12, 17), that others should believe in Him through their word (17:20), that the world should believe "that thou hast sent me" (17:21). From the body of those who believe in Him there are to flow rivers of living water (7:38). It is, therefore, the love which is in God Himself, which goes forth and breaks into the world in the existence of the man Jesus, and which is first actualised in those who believe in Him that they should be its witnesses — it is this love which the Jesus of the Fourth Gospel reveals as He manifests His glory. He reveals the self-affirmation of God as His affirmation of the world. He reveals Himself as the One in whom this affirmation of the world takes place, as the Saviour of the world (4:42), the Bread of God which gives life to the world (6:33, 51), the fulness of life, so that what He gives and what is received from Him is absolutely, unequivocally and exclusively grace, "grace and truth" (1:14, 17), "grace for grace" (1:16), inexhaustible, victorious grace which can be followed only by more grace. "Whosoever drinketh of the water that I shall give him shall never thirst; but the water that I shall give him shall be in him a well of water springing up into everlasting life" (4:14). Τετέλεσται: "It is finished, the goal is reached," is the last saying of the Johannine Jesus (19:30). In Him, therefore, there is no negative alternative foreseen by the Father who sends Him and the One sent by Him. This can arise only contrary to all plan and purpose as No is said to the unconditional divine Yes pronounced in His sending, as the hour of the clock which stands already at completion is wilfully pushed back, as the world already saved by Him acts as though it were not, as though it were not nourished by Him. This impossible No must be negated by the divine Yes, by the Yes of Jesus. It recoils upon those who are guilty of it. "He that believeth not is condemned already" (3:18). "He that rejecteth me, and receiveth not my words, hath one that judgeth him: the word that I have spoken, the same shall judge him in the last day" (12:48). "He . . . shall not see life; but the wrath of God abideth on him" (3:36). "This is the condemnation, that light is come into the world, and men loved darkness rather than light, because their deeds were evil" (3:19). To this extent the sending of Jesus becomes in fact a sending for the omnipotent execution of true and righteous judgment (5:22, 27, 30, 8:16), making a distinction in which the blind are shown to see and the seeing to be blind (9:39). It is to be noted, however, that it only becomes this in its conflict with darkness and in its relation to those who ignore and reject. It is so unavoidably as it must negate their negation. It is so in its *opus alienum*. But it is not so in itself, in its *opus proprium* which cannot be altered by any darkness, by any human opposition, nor by its own opposing of this opposition. "I judge no man" (8:15). "God sent not his Son into the world to condemn the world; but that the world through him might be saved" (3:17). And therefore "he that heareth my word, and believeth on him that sent me, hath everlasting life, and shall not come into condemnation; but is passed from death unto life" (5:24, 3:18). He has judgment, condemnation and death behind him, and not as an alternative ahead. For in the revelation of the glory of Jesus, in the love of the Father for the Son and the Son for the Father, in the light of love which shines in the darkness, there is no alternative, since this light is absolutely, unequivocally and exclusively the positive light of life.

On the Barmen Declaration:
How Scripture Continually Saves the Church

II/1, pp. 172-78

We will conclude with a short historical commentary on the first article of the *Theological Declaration* of the Synod of Barmen on May 31st, 1934. The text is as follows:

> *"I am the way, the truth, and the life: no man cometh unto the Father, but by me" (Jn. 14:6).*
>
> *"Verily, verily, I say unto you, He that entereth not by the door into the sheepfold, but climbeth up some other way, the same is a thief and a robber. . . . I am the door: by me if any man enter in, he shall be saved" (Jn. 10:1, 9).*
>
> *Jesus Christ, as He is attested to us in Holy Scripture, is the one Word of God, whom we have to hear and whom we have to trust and obey in life and in death.*
>
> *We condemn the false doctrine that the Church can and must recognise as God's revelation other events and powers, forms and truths, apart from and alongside this one Word of God.*

This text is important and apposite because it represents the first confessional document in which the Evangelical Church has tackled the problem of natural theology. The theology as well as the confessional writings of the age of the Reformation left the question open, and it has actually become acute only in recent centuries because natural theology has threatened to turn from a latent into an increasingly manifest standard and content of Church proclamation and theology. The question became a burning one at the moment when the Evangelical Church in Germany was unambiguously and consistently confronted by a definite and new form of natural theology, namely, by the demand to recognise in the political events of the year 1933, and especially in the form of the God-sent Adolf Hitler, a source of specific new revelation of God, which, demanding obedience and trust, took its place beside the revelation attested in Holy Scripture, claiming that it should be acknowledged by Christian proclamation and theology as equally binding and obligatory. When this demand was made, and a certain audience was given to it, there began, as is well known, the so-called German Church conflict. It has since become clear that behind this first demand stood quite another. According to the dynamic of the political movement, what was already intended, although only obscurely outlined, in 1933 was the proclamation of this new revelation as the only revelation, and therefore the transformation of the Christian Church into the temple of the German nature- and history-myth.

The same had already been the case in the developments of the preceding centuries. There can be no doubt that not merely a part but the whole had been intended and claimed when it had been demanded that side by side with its attestation in Jesus Christ and therefore in Holy Scripture the Church should also recognise and proclaim God's revelation in reason, in conscience, in the emotions, in history, in nature, and in culture and its achievements and developments. The history of the proclamation and theology of these centuries is simply a history of the wearisome conflict of the Church with the fact that the "also" demanded and to some extent acknowledged by it really meant an "only." The conflict was bound to be wearisome and even hopeless because, on the inclined plane on which this "also" gravitated into "only," it could not supply any inner check apart from the apprehension, inconsistency and inertia of all interested parties. Actually in these centuries too the Church was — as always miraculously — saved because the Bible remained in face of the "also" of invading natural theology and its secret "only." For it threw its own "only" into the scales, and in this way — not without the co-operation of that human apprehension, inconsistency and inertia — did at least maintain the point that for their part God's revelation in Jesus Christ and faith and obedience to Him are "also" not actually to be reduced to silence and oblivion. Thus things were not carried as far as the logic of the matter really demands. The logic of the matter demands that, even if we only lend our little finger to natural theology, there necessarily follows the denial of the revelation of God in Jesus Christ. A natural theology which does not strive to be the only master is not a natural theology. And to give it place at all is to put oneself, even if unwittingly, on the way which leads to this sole sovereignty. But during the developments of these centuries this whole state of affairs was almost entirely hidden, particularly from the eyes of those who wanted in good faith to defend the validity and value of the biblical revelation. It is noteworthy that it was conservative movements within the Church, like those inspired by Abraham Kuyper and Adolf Stöcker, which acted most naively. But the naivete reigned at every point. The concept of revelation and that of reason, history or humanity were usually linked by the copulative particle "and," and the most superficial provisos were regarded as sufficient protection against all the possible dangers of such combinations. Happy little hyphens were used between, say, the words "modern" and "positive," or "religious" and "social," or "German" and "Evangelical," as if the meaning then became self-evident. The fact was overlooked that all this pointed to the presence of a trojan horse within which the superior enemy was already drawn into the city. For in the long run the fundamentally peaceful acknowledgment of the combination came to be accepted as the true orthodoxy, as the basis of theology (especially of Church governments). The resistance occasionally offered to it necessarily came under suspicion as fanatical one-sidedness and exaggeration.

This was how matters stood when the Church was confronted with the myth of the new totalitarian state of 1933 — a myth at first lightly masked, but unmasked soon enough. It need not be said that at first the Church stood entirely defenceless before this matter and simply had to succumb to it for the time being. Once again, as so often for two hundred years — or so it seemed — the representative of a new trend and movement of the human spirit knocked at the door of the Church. Its petition was very understandable in the light of every precedent. It asked simply that its ideas and ideals should be allowed into the Church like those of all earlier times and phases. Its argument was that they constituted a more timely form, a new historical hinterland, a point of contact given by God Himself, *rebus sic stantibus,* for the proclamation of the Gospel, which in itself, of course, would remain unaltered. Exactly the same thing had happened at the beginning of the 18th century with the reviving humanism of the Stoa; or a century later with Idealism; or, in its train, with Romanticism; and then with the positivism of the bourgeois society and scholarship of the 19th century; and the nationalism of the same period; and a little later socialism: they had all wanted to have their say in the Church. And in face of these clear precedents there could be no basic reason for silencing this new nationalism of race. Whether it was as worthy as its predecessors to be heard and to have its say in the Church is a matter on which there might be different opinions outside Germany. A neg-

ative answer would normally be given where the phenomenon of race nationalism is unknown or known only from a distance, and a different political and philosophical position causes it to be regarded with repugnance.
But we must not fail to realise that inside Germany an affirmative answer
could be given with what is basically just the same right. If it was admissible
and right and perhaps even orthodox to combine the knowability of God in
Jesus Christ with His knowability in nature, reason and history, the proclamation of the Gospel with all kinds of other proclamations — and this had
been the case, not only in Germany, but in the Church in all lands for a long
time — it is hard to see why the German Church should not be allowed to
make its own particular use of the procedure. And the fact that it did so
with customary German thoroughness is not really a ground of reproach.
What the "German Christians" wanted and did was obviously along a line
which had for long enough been acknowledged and trodden by the Church
of the whole world: the line of the Enlightenment and Pietism, of
Schleiermacher, Richard Rothe and Ritschl. And there were so many parallels to it in England and America, in Holland and Switzerland, in Denmark
and the Scandinavian countries, that no one outside really had the right to
cast a stone at Germany because the new combination of Christian and natural theology effected there involved the combination with a race nationalism which happened to be rather uncongenial to the rest of the world, and
because this combination was now carried through with a thoroughness
which was so astonishing to other nations. Now that so many other combinations had been allowed to pass uncontradicted, and had even been affec-
tionately nurtured, it was about two hundred years too late to make any
well-founded objection, and in Germany there were at first good reasons to
make a particularly forceful stand for this new combination. It had the
merit of recommending itself especially to German Lutheranism as, so to
say, its distinctive and perhaps definitive solution of the question of the relationship of Christian and natural theology and proclamation. It could
seem like the powerful river in which the different separate streams of the
older and oldest history of the German Church and religion might possibly
unite. It seemed to promise the exponents of culture and fellowship the unexpected fulfilment of their deepest wishes. It seemed to raise like a tidal
wave the ship of the Church which many people felt had run aground, and
at last, at long last to be trying to bear it back again to the high seas of the
real life of the nation and therefore into the sphere of reality. Humanly
speaking, it was inevitable that in 1933 the German Evangelical Church
should accede to the demand made of it, to the new "also," and the "only"

which lay behind it, with exactly the same abandon as it had done to so many other demands, and as the Church in other lands — wittingly or unwittingly — had continually done to so many other demands. The only question was whether the Bible, which was not at first to be suppressed, and the usual apprehension, inconsistency and inertia of all concerned, would not this time too act as a counter-weight and prevent matters being carried to extremes.

It was, therefore, an astonishing fact — and this is the significance of the first article of the Barmen *Declaration* — that within Germany there arose an opposition to the new combination which was aimed not only at this particular combination, but basically at the long-accustomed process of combination, at the "and" which had become orthodox in Germany and in the whole world, at the little hyphen as such and therefore at no more and no less than the condominion of natural theology in the Church. For when in Barmen Jesus Christ as attested to us in Holy Scripture was designated as the one Word of God whom we have to trust and to obey in life and in death; when the doctrine of a source of Church proclamation different from this one Word of God was repudiated as false doctrine; and when, in the concluding article of the whole *Declaration,* the acknowledgment of this truth and the repudiation of this error were declared to be the indispensable theological foundation of the German Evangelical Church — an assertion was made (far above the heads of the poor "German Christians" and far beyond the whole momentary position of the Church in Germany) which, if it was taken seriously, contained in itself a purifying of the Church not only from the concretely new point at issue, but from all natural theology. The German Christians were contradicted by the contradiction of the whole development at whose end they stood. The protest — this was expressed with blunt words at Barmen by Hans Asmussen, who had to explain the whole proposal — was "against the same phenomenon which for more than two hundred years had slowly prepared the devastation of the Church." The protest was without doubt directed against Schleiermacher and Ritschl. The protest was directed against the basic tendencies of the whole 18th and 19th centuries and therefore against the hallowed traditions of all other Churches as well. And it must be noticed that this protest was formulated in a contemporary application of the confession of the Reformation yet without the possibility of appealing to any express formula in that confession. In the unity of faith with the fathers something was expressed which they had not yet expressed in that way. The venture had to be made, even at the risk of the suspicion and later the actual charge of innovation in the Church. It was under the sign of this protest that the German Church conflict continued from this point. All its individual and practical problems were and still are directly and indirectly connected with the first article of Barmen. The Church was the "confessional" Church precisely in the measure that it took this decision seriously in all its aspects. The conclusions of the Synod of Dahlem in November 1934 clarified its position in relation to Church law. But this clarification was dependent upon the dogmatic clarification of Barmen and could be carried through only in conjunction with it. The accumulated errors and vacillations in the Confessional Church are connected with the fact that the insight expressed at Barmen — Jesus Christ is the one Word of God whom we have to trust and to obey — did not at first correspond to the flesh and blood reality of the Church but contradicted it, and had still to be repeated, attained and practised in a wearisome struggle. Where this did not happen, no other attitude could be reached in practice than that of continual partial retreats and compromises. Where it did happen, it carried with it automatically the will and the power to resist. The German Confessional Church has either the power of the ecumenical gift and task which it received and accepted at Barmen, or it has no power. It either fights for the purification of which the Evangelical Church has long been in need and is everywhere in need, or in reality it does not fight at all. Had it been concerned simply with the German error of 1933, or with certain fatal consequent manifestations of this error, its conflict would have had no less but also no more meaning than the different reactions within the great modern disorder which had never been entirely lacking earlier and are not entirely lacking elsewhere. It would then not have been a real and serious conflict. It is a real and serious conflict so far as it is concerned with the matter as a whole; and not merely because what is at issue is obviously the opponent natural theology in its newest form, but because it is this time a question of the Church itself in its repudiation of natural theology as a whole, because it is a question of its own fundamental purification. But the very thing which (in what is best described as a cry of need and of joy) is expressed in the first article of the Barmen *Declaration* is that this is at issue. The fact that in 1934 the basic opposition could be made which is laid down in this article, and that, in spite of all uncertainty and reverses, this opposition could since prove and maintain itself as the nerve of the whole attitude of the Confessional Church in a position of the severest tribulation, is something which, however things may develop, we can already describe as one of the most notable events in modern Church history.

It was not the new political totalitarianism, nor was it the methods of beleaguerment which precipitated this event. And it is naive in the extreme to find in "Calvinism" or the activity of this or that professor of theology the effectual power of salvation (or corruption) in this affair. The fact is that, when nothing else was left for the Church, the one Word of God who is called Jesus Christ remained. The fact is that it could not let itself fall into the abyss, as was demanded, but that it could take and had to take a new stand. The fact is that this time the logic of the case worked irresistibly on the other side and therefore this time it was arrested in the Church. And all this has to be appraised spiritually or it cannot be appraised at all. What might have been expected was that, having so often blunted the temptation in its earlier, finer forms, the Church would now be tired and its eyes blurred and it would be inwardly exhausted, so that it would succumb all the more easily and this time for good to the assault of the blatant temptation. But the fact is that this did not happen. The Word of God still remained, in spite of everything, in the same Church in which it had been so often denied and betrayed. Men could still be so terrified by the spectre of the terrible form of the new god and his messiah as not to give way to it. They could still come to the position of knowing that there is another possibility than that of crashing into the abyss. In spite of every weakness they could still reach after this other possibility, reading the Bible again, confessing again its clear assertions, and therefore uttering the cry of need and of joy from Barmen. And they could at once stand and hold their position on this ground after all other grounds had crumbled under their feet. That this could be the case certainly has its spiritual-historical, theological and political presuppositions and determinations. But all the same it was impossible, and in the end a miracle, in the eyes of those who saw it at close quarters. And so the first article of Barmen was not merely a pretty little discovery of the theologians. The position in the spring of 1933 was not one in which a fortune could be made in Germany with little theological discoveries. Basically it was quite simply a public statement of the very miracle that against all expectation had once again happened to the Church. When it had lost all its counsellors and helpers, in the one Word of God, who is called Jesus Christ, it still had God for its comfort. Things being as they were, to whom else could it give its trust and obedience; to what other source of its proclamation could it and should it cling? *Rebus sic stantibus,* any other source could only be myth and therefore the end of all things and certainly the end of the Church. But from this very end the Church now saw itself pulled back and guarded by the Word of God in contemporaneous self-attestation. What option had it but to confess this Word of God alone? If we want really to understand the genesis of Barmen, we shall be obliged to look finally neither to the Confessional Church as such nor to its opponents. For there is not much to be seen here. The Confessional Church was, so to speak, only the witness of a situation in which simultaneously there took place a remarkable revelation, as there had not been for a long time, of the beast out of the abyss, and a fresh confirmation of the one old revelation of God in Jesus Christ. It was only a witness of this event. Indeed, it was often a most inconspicuous and inconvenient witness. But it was a witness. It was obliged to notice what was going to be seen on this occasion — that Satan had fallen from heaven like lightning and that the Lord is mighty over all gods. What it noticed on this occasion was the fact of the unique validity of Jesus Christ as the Word of God spoken to us for life and death. The repudiation of natural theology was only the self-evident reverse side of this notice. It has no independent significance. It affirms only that there is no other help — that is, in temptation — when it is a question of the being or not being of the Church. What helps, when every other helper fails, is only the miracle, power and comfort of the one Word of God. The Confessional Church began to live at the hand of this notice and at its hand it lives to this day. And it is this notice which it has to exhibit to other Churches as the testimony which it has received and which is now laid upon it as a commission. It will be lost if it forgets this testimony, or no longer understands it, or no longer takes it seriously; the power against which it stands is too great for it to meet it otherwise than with the weapon of this testimony. But it will also be lost if it does not understand and keep to the fact that this testimony is not entrusted to it simply for its own use, but at the same time as a message for the worldwide Church. And it may well be decisive for other Churches in the world, for their existence as the one, ecumenical Church of Jesus Christ, whether they on their side are able to hear and willing to accept the message of the Confessional Church in Germany.

For the understanding of what the first article of Barmen has to say in detail, it is perhaps advisable not to pass over the preceding verses from Jn. 14 and Jn. 10, but to understand everything from them as a starting-point. The emphasis of everything said previously lies in the fact that Jesus Christ has said something, and, what is more, has said it about Himself: I myself am the way, the truth, and the life. I myself am the door. The Church lives by the fact that it hears the voice of this "I" and lays hold of the promise which, according to this voice, is contained in this "I" alone; that therefore it chooses the way, knows the truth, lives the life, goes through the door, which is Jesus Christ Himself alone. Moreover, it is not on its own authority, or in the execution of its own security programme, but on the basis of the necessity in which Jesus Christ Himself has said that no man comes to the Father but by Him, and that any by-passing of Him means theft and robbery, that the Church makes its exclusive claim, negating every other way or truth or life or door apart from Him. The negation has no independent significance. It depends entirely on the affirmation. It can make itself known only as the affirmation makes itself known. But in and with the affirmation it does and must make itself known. For this reason the positive assertion has precedence even in what follows, and for this reason the resulting critical assertion can be understood only as its converse and unambiguous elucidation. The Church lives by the fact that it hears the Word of God to which it can give entire trust and entire obedience and that in life and in death — that is, in the certainty that it will be sustained in this trust and obedience for time and eternity. Precisely because it is allowed and invited to entire trust and obedience, it knows that the Word said to it is the one Word of God by which it is bound but in which it is also free, alongside whose Gospel there is no alien law and alongside whose Law there is no alien gospel, alongside or behind or above which we do not have to honour and fear any other power as way, truth, life or door. And this one Word is not first to be found, but has already given itself to be found: in Him who has the power and the right to call Himself the way, the truth, the life and the door because He is these things. This one Word means Jesus Christ from eternity to eternity. In this form it is attested in the Holy Scriptures of the Old and New Testaments. In this form it has founded the Church; and upholds and renews and rules, and continually saves the Church. In this form it is comfort and direction in life and in death. In this form and not in any other! It is of the "not in any other" that the concluding critical article speaks. We may notice that it does not deny the existence of other events and powers, forms and truths alongside the one Word of God, and that therefore throughout it does not deny the possibility of a natural theology as such. On the contrary, it presupposes that there are such things. But it does deny and designate as false doctrine the assertion that all these things can be the source of Church proclamation, a second source alongside and apart from the one Word of God. It excludes natural theology from Church proclamation. Its intention is not to destroy it in itself and as such, but to affirm that, when it comes to saying whom we have to trust and obey in life and in death, it can have no sense and existence alongside and apart from the Word of God. Whatever else they may be and mean, the entities to which natural theology is accustomed to relate itself cannot come into consideration as God's revelation, as the norm and content of the message delivered in the name of God. When the Church proclaims God's revelation, it does not speak on the basis of a view of the reality of the world and of man, however deep and believing; it does not give an exegesis of these events and powers, forms and truths, but bound to its commission, and made free by the promise received with it, it reads and explains the Word which is called Jesus Christ and therefore the book which bears witness to Him. It is, and remains, grateful for the knowledge of God in which He has given Himself to us by giving us His Son.

Contributors

Robert McAfee Brown (1920-2001) taught theology and religion at Union Theological Seminary (NYC), Stanford University, and the Pacific School of Religion. He was the author of twenty-nine books, including *The Spirit of Protestantism* (New York: Oxford University Press, 1961) and *Theology in a New Key: Responding to Liberation Themes* (Philadelphia: Westminster Press, 1978).

Hans W. Frei (1922-1988) was Professor of Religious Studies at Yale University. Among his writings are *The Eclipse of Biblical Narrative* (New Haven: Yale University Press, 1974), *Types of Christian Theology* (New Haven: Yale University Press, 1992), and *Theology and Narrative: Selected Essays* (Oxford: Oxford University Press, 1993).

Kathryn Greene-McCreight is Associate Priest, St. John's Episcopal Church, New Haven, CT. She is the author of *Feminist Reconstructions of Christian Doctrine* (Oxford: Oxford University Press, 2000) and *Ad Litteram: How Augustine, Calvin, and Barth Read the Plain Sense of Genesis 1–3* (New York: Peter Lang, 1999).

A. Katherine Grieb is Professor of New Testament at Virginia Theological Seminary. She has written *The Story of Romans: A Narrative Defense of God's Righteousness* (Louisville: Westminster/John Knox, 2002). She is presently completing a book on Hebrews and another on the Sermon on the Mount.

George Hunsinger is McCord Professor of Systematic Theology at Princeton Theological Seminary. In 2010 he was awarded the Karl Barth Prize by the Union of Evangelical Churches in Germany. Among his books are *How to Read Karl Barth: The Shape of His Theology* (New York: Oxford University Press, 1993); *Disruptive Grace: Studies in the Theology of Karl Barth* (Grand Rapids: Eerdmans, 2000); and *Evangelical, Catholic, and Reformed: Essays on Barth and Other Themes* (Grand Rapids: Eerdmans, forthcoming).

Paul Dafydd Jones is Associate Professor of Religious Studies at the University of Virginia. He is the author of *The Humanity of Christ: Christology in Karl Barth's* Church Dogmatics (London: T. & T. Clark, 2008). He is currently writing a book on Protestant views of the atonement.

Paul D. Molnar is Professor of Systematic Theology, Department of Theology and Religious Studies, St. John's University, New York. His publications include: *Karl Barth and the Theology of the Lord's Supper: A Systematic Investigation* (New York: Peter Lang, 1996); *Divine Freedom and the Doctrine of the Immanent Trinity: In Dialogue with Karl Barth and Contemporary Theology* (Edinburgh: T. & T. Clark/Continuum, 2002); *Incarnation and Resurrection: Toward a Contemporary Understanding* (Grand Rapids: Eerdmans, 2007); and *Thomas F. Torrance: Theologian of the Trinity* (Farnham, UK: Ashgate, 2009).

Katherine Sonderegger is Professor of Theology at Virginia Theological Seminary. She is the author of *That Jesus Christ Was Born a Jew: Karl Barth's "Doctrine of Israel"* (University Park, PA: Penn State Press, 1992). Her forthcoming work, *Systematic Theology,* is under contract with Westminster/John Knox Press.

John Webster is Professor of Systematic Theology, University of Aberdeen. He served as editor of *The Cambridge Companion to Karl Barth* (Cambridge: Cambridge University Press, 2003). Among his other books are *Barth's Ethics of Reconciliation* (Cambridge: Cambridge University Press, 1995) and *Holy Scripture: A Dogmatic Sketch* (Cambridge: Cambridge University Press, 2003).

world of opinion